D1068173

An Annotated Bibliography
of the
British Army
1660-1914

Garland Reference Library of Social Science (Vol. 14)

An Annotated Bibliography
of the
British Army
1660—1914

A.P.C. Bruce

Garland Publishing, Inc., New York & London

1975

Copyright © 1975

by Garland Publishing, Inc.

All Rights Reserved

Library of Congress Cataloging in Publication Data

Bruce, Anthony Peter Charles.
   An annotated bibliography of the British Army, 1660-
1914.

   (Garland reference library of social science ; v. 14)
   Includes index.
   1. Great Britain. Army--Bibliography. I. Title.
Z6725.G7B78 [UA649]   016.3553'0941   75-23072
ISBN 0-8240-9988-5

Printed in the United States of America

Contents

CONTENTS

Introduction

The consistent, if not growing, scholarly and popular interest of recent years in the history of the British army, as measured by the number of books and articles annually published, has not produced a corresponding number of scholarly bibliographical studies of the subject. Indeed in the last one hundred years only three full length bibliographical works devoted specifically to the history of the army have been compiled. Firstly, in 1893, a bibliography by M.J.D. Cockle of the works on the cavalry in English and French was published in Calcutta. Though only partially annotated it is still of much value, and was the first bibliography of substance on any aspect of the post-Restoration army. Secondly, A.S. White, a former War Office Librarian, produced in 1965 *A bibliography of regimental histories of the British army* which while making a major contribution to the subject was not annotated, and did not, rather surprisingly, include any significant listing of material from periodicals, or personal reminiscences, which would have greatly added to its value. Finally, Robin Higham edited a collection of essays, published in 1972 as *A guide to the sources of British military history,* of which only four were directly concerned with the army during the period, 1660-1914. The value of this collection was somewhat undermined by a considerable number of factual and typographical errors, by the fact that the contributions of the various authors appear to have been written in isolation without effective co-ordination by the editor, and because very little attention had been paid either to unpublished sources or to articles in the main specialist periodicals.

The foregoing criticisms and comments indicate both the main areas of neglect in the subject and the broad scope of the present work, which is an attempt to provide a general survey of full length published studies of the British army between

INTRODUCTION

1660-1914. In addition, much emphasis has been placed on providing a balanced and representative selection of unpublished personal papers and of articles in serials and the publications of learned societies.

These objectives indicate the main criteria for resolving perhaps the most difficult problem in a work of this kind: the selection of the items for inclusion in it. The criteria are briefly: the listing of all the major scholarly works on the army; wherever appropriate, the inclusion of studies produced at different periods so that the state of knowledge existing at various times may be determined and differing interpretations of the same subject may be appreciated; the coverage of all the main aspects of the subject, notwithstanding the fact that in some cases the material available on it may not be fully adequate, in either quality or quantity; and finally, to indicate, as far as possible, the sources of further information on particular, more specialized, subjects.

The arrangement of the bibliography has been dictated by these criteria, by the desire to avoid repetition and by ease of use. The broad subject areas listed in the table of contents are supplemented by the more detailed subject matter entries in the index. For this reason, cross references in the text (which are indicated by round brackets, and the number of the particular item) are only used in a limited number of essential cases. All authors, and editors, are included in the index, as are the titles of anonymous works for which no suitable subject matter reference could be determined.

The material is basically arranged alphabetically although there are a number of obvious deviations from this rule: for example, the chronological order of content in the case of studies of military campaigns, and those works on tactics, discipline and drill which are arranged according to the date of publication of the first edition.

Certain measures have been adopted to ensure that this bibliography is not unnecessarily long. Publishers are not listed, nor normally is the place of publication, which is London unless otherwise stated. No references are made to sizes of works, but the full title of items is given, unless

INTRODUCTION

otherwise indicated in the text. Usually the date of publication is that of the first edition and further editions are not normally specified unless the inclusion of extra material makes it necessary. Military titles are shortened according to standard practice, and a full list of abbreviations is given below.

Abbreviations

A.H.R.	—*American Historical Review.*
A.Q.	—*Army Quarterly*
add.	—additions, additional
Add. MSS.	—additional manuscripts, British Museum
anon.	—anonymous
app.	—appendix
assoc.	—association
B.M.	—British Museum
bibliog.	—bibliography, bibliographical
Bost.	—Boston, Mass.
bull.	—bulletin
C.O.	—Colonial Office
Camb.	—Cambridge
chap.	—chapter
comp.	—compiler
coll.	—collection
Conn.	—Connecticut
C.R.O.	—county record office
D.N.B.	—*Dictionary of National Biography*
doc.	—document
E.H.R.	—*English Historical Review*
ed.	—editor, edited.
Edin.	—Edinburgh
edn.	—edition
H.J.	—*Historical Journal.*
H.M.C.	—Historical Manuscripts Commission
J.B.S.	—*Journal of British Studies*
J.M.H.	—*Journal of Modern History*
J.R.U.S.I.	—*Journal of the Royal United Service Institution*
J.S.A.H.R.	—*Journal of the Society for Army Historical Research.*

ABBREVIATIONS

jour.	—journal
mag.	—magazine
Mass.	—Massachusetts
MS., MSS.	—manuscript, manuscripts.
n.d.	—no date
N.L.S.	—National Library of Scotland
N.L.W.	—National Library of Wales
n.p.	—no place
n.s.	—new series
N.Y.	—New York
no.	—number
Oxf.	—Oxford
P.R.O.	—Public Record Office
pt.	—part
quart.	—quarterly
R.A.	—Royal Artillery
repr.	—reprinted
R.O.	—record office
R.U.S.I.	—**Royal United Service Institution**
S.A.H.R.	—Society for Army Historical Research
S.H.R.	—*Scottish Historical Review*
Soc.	—society
Suppl.	—supplement
Trans.	—transactions
U.S.M.	—*United Service Magazine*
Vol.	—volume
V.S.	—*Victorian Studies*
Wash.	—Washington

PART I   BIBLIOGRAPHIES, GUIDES AND INDEXES.

1.   BIBLIOGRAPHY OF BIBLIOGRAPHY

     No bibliography of British military bibliography exists
as such. The following list consists of those works containing
relevant material, although in most cases, this is rarely
presented in more than one or two pages.

   1. BESTERMAN, THEODORE. A world bibliography of
      bibliographies.   Geneva, 5 vols. 1965-66. In
      general, the most complete work of its kind.
      Several pages are devoted to a list of bibliographies,
      and catalogues of various armies.

   2. BIBLIOGRAPHIC INDEX: A CUMULATIVE BIBLIOGRAPHY
      OF BIBLIOGRAPHIES. N.Y. 1938+. Issued quarterly,
      and cumulates into annual and multi-annual volumes.
      It is a subject index only, and includes bibliographies
      published separately as books and pamphlets, and
      those published as parts of books, pamphlets and
      periodical articles. Many of the issues contain items
      of interest.

   3. COLLISON, R.L.   Bibliographies subject and national.
      A guide to their contents arrangements and use. 1968.
      A useful survey of the major sources.

   4. COURTNEY, W.P.   A register of national bibliography:
      with a selection of the chief bibliographical books
      and articles printed in other countries. 3 vols. 1905-12.
      Some interesting entries relating to the army.

   5. INTERNATIONAL BIBLIOGRAPHY OF HISTORICAL SCIENCES.
      Paris. 1926+. Published annually.

   6. LIST OF BIBLIOGRAPHICAL WORKS in the reading room
      of the British Museum. 1889.

   7. WALFORD, A.J.   Guide to reference material. 3 vols.
      1966-70. Published by the Library Association, this
      guide contains a short list of military bibliographies,
      and a longer one of basic reference works. Perhaps the
      most useful modern work.

   8. WINCHELL, C.M.   Guide to reference books. Chicago.
      1967. See also First and Second supplements, 1965-66
      and 1967-68, published in 1968 and 1970.

2.   CATALOGUES AND BIBLIOGRAPHIES RELATING TO THE
        BRITISH ARMY

Relevant material may also occasionally be found in
the 'Notes' published in each issue of the J.S.A.H.R. (548).
See also the material listed under section 3 'Library
Catalogues and Guides', some of which give useful
bibliographical information.

9. THE AMERICAN REVOLUTION.   A selected reading list.
   Wash. 1968. A short guide produced by the Library of
   Congress, with several items on military aspects of
   the conflict.

10. ANNUAL BULLETIN OF HISTORICAL LITERATURE, 1911+.
   1912+. A select annotated bibliography, published
   by the Historical Association. Not a very useful
   quick reference work, as the layout is poor and
   individual items are not normally easily identifiable.

11. BALDRY, W.Y. 'Early articles of war'. J.S.A.H.R.
   Vol.IV no. 18 October, 1925,   166-7. Location of
   copies of articles of war, 1385-1799.

12. BELLOT, H.H., et.al.,   eds. Writings on British
   history, 1901-1933. 5 vols. 1968. A valuable series.
   Continued by Milne, listed below (40).

13. BEVAN, MARGARET. Dr. James Barry (1795?-1865)
   Inspector-General of Military hospitals. A
   bibliography. Johannesburg. 1966. On the British
   army doctor, believed to have been a woman by some
   authorities.

14. BRITISH NATIONAL BIBLIOGRAPHY, 1950+. 1951+.   The
   British Museum's union catalogue.

15. BULLOCH, J.M. 'Literature concerning the Royal
   Scots (Royal Regiment)'. J.S.A.H.R. Vol. XII no. 46,
   Summer 1933, 69-72. A short annotated guide.

16. ----------. 'Rambling remarks on regimental history'
   Ibid. Vol. II no. 7, January 1923, 38-43. Details of
   unpublished sources, including those outside national
   collections, for regimental history, are given.

17. CATALOGUE OF BRITISH REGIMENTAL HISTORIES, with notes
   of their service in South Africa. Johannesburg. 1953.
   Published by the city's Public Library.

18. COCKLE, M.J.D. Bibliography of English military books
   up to 1642 and of contemporary foreign works. 1900.
   Useful for background material for the later period.

19. ----------. Catalogue of books relating to the military history of India. Simla. 1901. Cockle was the first scholarly bibliographer of British military history. Many of the items are annotated.

20. CRAIG, HARDIN. A bibliography of encyclopaedias and dictionaries dealing with military, naval and maritime affairs, 1577-1965. Houston, Texas. 1965. rev. edn. A comprehensive guide, with many entries relating to the British army. Dictionaries published as appendices to books are also included. The bibliography is not annotated.

21. DAVIES, GODFREY AND KEELER, M.F. Bibliography of British history. Stuart period, 1603-1714. 1970 rev. edn. A fine work, with a useful section on military history and biography.

22. EDWARDS, FRANCIS. Military catalogue. Books, pamphlets, etc. on military history and biography. 1907-8. A commercial catalogue of a long established London military bookseller and publisher, with many items of interest.

23. ELLIOT, G.H. Cavalry literature: a bibliographic record of works on the history, organization, tactics, and administration of cavalry. Calcutta. 1893. Still of much value, listing French, as well as English, studies.

24. ELTON, G.R. modern historians on British history, 1485-1945. A critical bibliography, 1945-1969. 1970. A brief guide to modern historical writings, with a few military references.

25. FIRTH, SIR C.H. 'Bibliography of the military writings of Sir Charles Firth.' J.S.A.H.R. Vol. III no. 31, January 1929, 53-6. Of some value, although his period of scholarly interest was mainly before 1660.

26. FREWER, L.B. Bibliography of historical writings published in Great Britain and the empire, 1940-1945. Oxf. 1947. A comprehensive survey listed by subject, which includes articles in a wide range of journals.

27. GOOCH, B.D. 'The Crimean War in selected documents and secondary works since 1940.' V.S. Vol. I no. 3., March 1958, 271-9. A perceptive analysis of the main studies of the war published in recent years, and the material they were based upon.

28. GROSE, C.L. A select bibliography of British history, 1660-1760. Chicago. 1939. Repr. N.Y. 1966. A standard bibliography for general history, but not very valuable for the army.

29. HALKETT, S. and LAING,J. Dictionary of anonymous and pseudonymous English literature. New edn. by J. Kennedy, W.A. Smith, and A.F. Johnson. 7 Vols. 1926-34.   The standard reference work on the subject.

30. HIGHAM, ROBIN, ED. A guide to the sources of British military history. London. 1972. Not a systematic or reliable guide. Perhaps the most useful essay is that by A.V. Tucker on the nineteenth century army.

31. KELLAWAY, WILLIAM. Bibliography of historical works issued in the United Kingdom, 1957+. 1962+. 3 volumes so far published, covering the period down to 1970.

32. LANCASTER, J.C. Bibliography of historical works issued in the United Kingdom, 1946-1956. 1957. Continued by the work listed immediately above. For a useful section on military history, see pp. 48-61.

33. LEFROY, GENERAL SIR J.H. 'Catalogue of works on artillery and gunnery'. Minutes of Proceedings of the R.A. Institution. Vol. II, 1871, 3-12. Covers the period from earliest times to the end of the eighteenth century.

34. LESLIE J.H. 'A bibliography of flags'. J.S.A.H.R. Vol. I no. 6, December 1922, 242-3. A short list of works on regimental colours.

35. ----------. 'Militia regiments of Great Britain. A calendar of their records and histories' Ibid. Vol. XII no. 45, Spring 1933, 45-9; no. 46, Summer 1933, 96-99. Largely superseded by (63), but originally a pioneering work.

36. ----------. and SMITH, DAVID. A bibliography of works by officers, non commissioned officers and men who have ever served in the Royal, Bengal, Madras or Bombay artillery. Leicester. 1909. A comparable work for the entire army would be a valuable research aid.

37. MATTHEWS, WILLIAM. British autobiographies: an annotated bibliography of British autobiographies published or written before 1951. Hamden, Conn. 1968.

38. ------- British diaries: an annotated bibliography
of British diaries written between 1442 and 1942.
1950. There are a few military references in these
two standard bibliographies compiled by Matthews. A
second revised edition of the bibliography of diaries
is planned.

39. MAURICE, SIR JOHN FREDERICK. War. Reproduced with
amendments from the article in the last edition of the
"Encyclopaedia Britannica" to which is added an essay
on military literature and a list of books with brief
comments. 1891. There is a bibliographical section
on pp. 93-114. appended to Maurice's celebrated essay.

40. MILNE, A.T. Writings on British history, 1934-1945.
8 Vols. 1937-60. Particularly useful for identifying
biographical items, with many references to articles
in a wide range of periodicals. A carefully produced
definitive work of its kind.

41. MORGAN, W.T. A bibliography of British history, 1700-15,
with special reference to the reign of Queen Anne.
Bloomington, Ind. 5 Vols. 1939-42. Valuable for its
extensive lists of contemporary pamphlets and books,
although ms. sources, and later works are not ignored.
It is the definitive work.

42. MOYSE-BARTLETT, LIEUT. COL. H. 'Military historiography,
1850-1860'. J.S.A.H.R. Vol. XLV no. 184, winter 1967,
199-213. A valuable and detailed account of the greatly
increased volume of military literature which was
published during this period, largely because of the
wide interest generated in the army by the Crimean War.

43. MULLER, C.F.J., JAARSVELD, F.A. van, and WIJK, THEO van.
A select bibliography of South African history. A guide
for historical research. Pretoria 1966. See for the
sections on the Boer War, pp. 65-70.

44. MUNRO, D.J. Writings on British history, 1946-1948.
1973. A long delayed continuation of the earlier volumes
in the series, by A.T. Milne listed above, produced to the
same high standards.

45. NATIONAL BOOK LEAGUE. The British soldier: an exhibition
of books, manuscripts and prints covering the last 250
years, by G.A. Shepperd. 1956. A useful list of the
more important standard works, with some critical comments.

46. OMAN, SIR C.W.C. Wellington's army, 1809-1814. 1912.
See Appendix III 'Bibliography of British diaries,
journals and memoirs'. The most comprehensive list
available, though now in need of revision. There is
also a chapter on the literature of the Peninsula war.

47. PAINE, J. 'A bibliography of British military music.'
J.R.U.S.I. Vol. LXXIII no. 490, May 1928, 334-341.
An interesting list of works on a relatively neglected
subject.

48. ----------. 'A bibliography of regimental colours'.
A.Q. Vol. LXVII. no. 1, October 1953, 123-8.

49. ----------. 'Light brigade survivors' reminiscences'
J.S.A.H.R. Vol. XLVIII no. 193, spring 1970, 4-7.
A comprehensive list of the published reminiscences of
those who charged with the light brigade at the battle
of Balaclava on 25 October 1854, and survived.

50. ----------. 'The literature of a line regiment'. Ibid.
Vol. XIII no. 50, summer 1934, 107-113. Works on the
1st battalion, East Surrey regiment (31st Foot), and
a list of reminiscences by officers and men who served
in it.

51. ----------. 'The literature of the Gordon Highlanders'
Ibid. Vol XL no. 164, December 1962, 187-195. Includes
similar types of material to that in his article on the
31st Foot.

52. ----------. 'The records of the Victoria Cross'. J.R.U.S.I.
Vol. LXXVII no. 507, August 1932, 602-6. A list of
mainly popular works on the highest military award in
Britain.

53. PARGELLIS, STANLEY AND MEDLEY, D.J. eds. Bibliography
of   British history. The eighteenth century,
1714-1789. Oxf. 1951. A valuable work which is now in
need of revision.

54. PEDDIE, R.A. Subject index of books published before
1880. 4 Vols. 1930-48. A standard guide.

55. POHLER, JOHANN. Bibliotheca historico-militaris.
Systematische uebersicht der erscheinungen aller sprachen
auf dem gebiete der geschichte der kriege und
kreigswissenschaft seit erfindung der buchdruckerkunst
bis zum schluss des jahres 1880. Leipzig. 4 Vols.
1887-99. An extensive general military bibliography,
with much relevant material, particularly relating to
the campaigns of the army on the continent.

56. READE, CONYERS. A bibliography of British history
Tudor period, 1485-1603. Oxf. 1959. Some of the general
material referred to is relevant for later periods.

57. SHORT-TITLE CATALOGUE of books printed in England,
    Scotland, Ireland, Wales, and British America, and
    of English books printed in other countries, 1641-
    1700. By D.G. Wing. N.Y. 1945-51. The standard
    guide to the published works of the period.

58. SILVERTHORNE, L.C. and GASKIN, W.D. The British
    Foot Guards. A bibliography. N.Y. 1960. A short
    guide which includes many personal reminiscences of
    officers and men of the Guards, as well as the standard
    histories, with a few critical observations.

59. SPAULDING, THOMAS M. and KARPINSKI, LOUIS C. Early
    military books in the University of Michigan libraries.
    Ann Arbor. 1941.

60. SWEETMAN, JOHN. 'Uncorroborated evidence: one problem
    about the Crimean war'. J.S.A.H.R. Vol. XLIX. no. 200,
    Winter 1971, 194-8. A brief discussion of some of the
    main sources.

61. WHITE, A.S. 'The army list'. Ibid. Vol. XXV. no. 103,
    autumn 1947, 118-27. An important contribution to
    knowledge on this subject. The standard reference guide.

62. ---------. 'A bibliography of volunteering'. Ibid.
    Vol. XXIII no. 93 spring, 1945,   2-29; 'Supplement'.
    Ibid. Vol. XXIV no. 98, summer 1946, 83-7. Incorporated
    into his bibliography listed immediately below.

63. ---------. A bibliography of regimental histories of
    the British army. 1965. A list of almost all the
    full length studies, but few references to articles
    or personal reminiscences. Nonetheless, this is a
    standard reference work, unlikely to be superseded.

3.   LIBRARY CATALOGUES AND GUIDES.

    In the absence so far of a published catalogue of books
held by the National Army Museum, a valuable source of reference
there is the unpublished card catalogue in the reading room.
Some periodical articles, including those in regimental
journals, are noted in this index.

64. BARWICK, G.B. ed. The ASLIB directory, a guide to
    sources of special information in Great Britain and
    Ireland. 1928. A general guide to specialist
    libraries.

65. CLARK, G. KITSON, and ELTON, G.R. Guide to research facilities in history in the universities of Great Britain and Ireland. Camb. 1963. Notes some of the resources to be found at major libraries.

66. BRITISH MUSEUM, DEPARTMENT OF PRINTED BOOKS. Catalogue of printed books. 95 Vols. 1881-1900. Suppl. 15 Vols. 1900-5.

67. ———— ————. General catalogue of printed books. 263 Vols. 1931-66. Revised edition of the above. For accessions since that date, the unpublished indexes in the reading room of the British Museum should be consulted.

68. ———— ————. Index - catalogue of Indian offical publications in the library, British Museum. 1900. See pp. 36-43 for publications relating to the army in India.

69. ———— ————. Subject index of modern works added to the British Museum library. 1881+. Indexes for the period since 1961 have not yet been published, but are available in the reading room at the museum on microfilm.

70. GRENADIER GUARDS, ORDERLY ROOM. Catalogue of manuscripts, books, etc., contained in the regimental orderly room of the Grenadier Guards, 1908. 1908.

71. INDIA OFFICE. A guide to the India Office Library. 1967.

72. MINISTRY OF DEFENCE LIBRARIES. Accessions to the Ministry of Defence Libraries. 1964+. Published monthly.

73. PATENT OFFICE. The subject list of works on military and naval arts in the library of the Patent Office.1907. Includes some items not found in the War Office Library catalogues, listed below in this section.

74. ROYAL UNITED SERVICE INSTITUTION. Catalogue of the library of the Royal United Service Institution. 1865. Rev. edns. published in 1890, and 1908. See also List of accessions to the library, 1908-1914. 6 pts.

75. SHEPPARD, E,W. 'The Prince Consort's Library, Aldershot'. A.Q. Vol. LXXXI no. 1, October 1960, 52-3. A short article on the first military library in England, which was opened in October, 1860, and which is still functioning.

76. WAR OFFICE. Classified catalogue of books ... in the library of the War Department. 1864.

77. --- ------ Catalogue of the War Office library. 3 pts. 1906-12. Supplement to Pts. I-II. 1916. Annual supplement to Pt. III. 1912-1940. This catalogue serves as, perhaps, the best guide to British military literature published prior to its compilation, and consists of both author and subject indexes. There is useful background material in F.J. Hudleston, 'The War Office Library' A.Q. Vol. 1 no. 2, January 1920, 366-75.

4. MANUSCRIPT COLLECTIONS

The main manuscript collections are at the Public Records Office, and the British Museum, although there are smaller collections in other institutions. The largest single collection relating to the British army is that held at the National Army Museum and a catalogue of the manuscripts held there is being prepared for publication. In the meantime, for detailed references, the card indexes in the reading room of the museum may be referred to. Information about the collections there may also be found in the annual reports of the National Army Museum, and in some of the standard reference guides listed below.

78. LIST OF ACCESSIONS TO REPOSITORIES. 1958+. Published by the National Register of Archives, it lists all accessions from the beginning of 1957. Before 1957, this information can be found in the Bull. of the Institute of Historical Research. (532)

79. BULLETIN OF THE NATIONAL REGISTER OF ARCHIVES. 1948+. Information about manuscript collections. Many catalogues, mostly unpublished, of collections of manuscripts are held at the offices of the N.R.A. in London. A four volume unpublished personal index, also produced by the N.R.A., based on these catalogues, identifies references to particular individuals, and is a very valuable aid to research. A supplement containing recent additions has been produced, and further lists with new material will be issued.

80. ARCHIVES. 1949+. The journal of the British Records Association, which contains information on many collections.

81. CRICK, B.R. and ALMAN, M.A. A guide to manuscripts
    relating to America in Great Britain and Ireland.
    1961.   Useful as a general guide to British archives,
    as well as for its stated purpose.

82. A GUIDE TO THE PAPERS OF BRITISH CABINET MINISTERS,
    1900-1951. By C. Hazlehurst and C. Woodland. 1974.
    An indispensable and exhaustive reference work
    published by the Royal Historical Society. Frequent
    revisions are planned.

83. HISTORICAL MANUSCRIPTS COMMISSION. The Prime Ministers'
    papers 1801-1902. 1968. A useful short guide to the
    main collections of prime ministers' papers, and of
    their principal correspondents.

84. RECORD REPOSITORIES IN GREAT BRITAIN. 1964. A list
    of the names and addresses of record offices.

(a)   Official collection of records.

85. PUBLIC RECORD OFFICE. Guide to the contents of the
    Public Record Office. 3 Vols. 1963-69. See Vol. II,
    'State papers and departmental records', and Vol. III,
    'Documents transferred to the Public Record Office
    1960-1966'.   This guide supersedes the earlier hand-
    book by M.S. Giuseppi, Guide to the manuscripts
    preserved in the Public Record Office. 2 Vols.
    1923-24.

86. ----- ----- ----- List of War Office records
    preserved in the Public Record Office. 1908. The
    main but incomplete published list of military records.

87. ----- ----- ----- An alphabetical guide to War Office
    and other military records preserved in the Public
    Record Office. 1931. A selective guide which should
    be used with care. There is, additionally, a useful
    regimental index.

88. ----- ----- ----- List of War Office records. Vol. I.
    N.Y. 1968. This is a continuation of the list produced
    in 1908, and is based on the typewritten and ms. indexes
    at the P.R.O. A further volume is in preparation.

89. ----- ----- ----- List of Cabinet papers, 1880-1914.
    1964. Titles of individual papers are given, and many
    are of interest for the history of the army.

90. ----- ----- ----- Records of the Colonial and
    Dominions Offices. 1964.

91. ----- ----- ----- List of papers of the Committee
    of Imperial Defence, to 1914. 1964. The title and
    length of each paper is given.

92. ----- ----- ----- Guide to the materials for American
    history to 1783 in the Public Record Offices of Great
    Britain. By C.M. Andrews. 2 Vols. Wash. 1912-14.

93. PUBLIC RECORD OFFICE, IRELAND. Guides to the records
    in the Public Record Office, Ireland. By H. Wood. 1920.

94. PUBLIC RECORD OFFICE, NORTHERN IRELAND. Reports of the
    Deputy Keeper of the Public records. 1924+.

95. ----- ----- ----- Guide to the war records 1482-1945.
    1966.

96. SCOTTISH RECORD OFFICE. A guide to the public records
    of Scotland deposited in H.M. Register House, Edinburgh.
    Edin. 1905. The main guide, in need of revision.

97. ----- ----- ----- 'Accessions of public records to the
    Register House since 1905'. S.H.R. Vol. 26, 1947,
    26-46. A useful updating of the guide listed immediately
    above.

(b)   Other collections in Great Britain

98. BRITISH MUSEUM. The catalogues of the manuscript
    collections. 1951. rev. edn. 1962. A guide to the
    several published and unpublished indexes, which are not
    listed separately here, with one exception.

99. ----- ----- --- Class catalogues of manuscripts
    (military) Vol. 50. An unpublished catalogue in the
    students' room in the Department of Manuscripts. By
    no means a comprehensive guide to the resources of the
    British Museum for this subject.

100. ----- ----- --- 'Notes on class catalogue, no. 50
    (military) in the Department of Manuscripts, British
    Museum'. By Major E.W.H. Fyers. J.S.A.H.R. Vol. IV
    no. 15, January 1925, 38-48. Extracts some of the more
    important individual items from the subject catalogue
    listed immediately above.

101. CAMBRIDGE UNIVERSITY LIBRARY. A handlist of the
    Cholmondeley (Houghton) Mss. Sir Robert Walpole's
    archives. Camb. 1953.

102. JOHN RYLANDS LIBRARY. 'Handlist of the collection
of English manuscripts in the John Rylands Library
1928'. By M. Tyson. John Rylands Lib. Bull.
Vol. XIII, 1929, 152-219; see, Ibid. Vol. XIX, for
additions to 1935.

103. ----- ----- ----- 'The military papers of Col.
Samuel Bagshawe, 1713-1762'. By James Hayes. Ibid.
Vol. XXXIX no. 2, 1957, 356-89. A collection of
major importance which sheds a good deal of light on
the day to day life of a regiment in the eighteenth
century. Extensive parts of the papers deserve to be
published.

104. NATIONAL ARMY MUSEUM. 'Lake's Mahratta war campaigns.
Report on the Call journals, 1803 to 1805, now in the
Royal United Service Institution'. By T.H. McGuffie.
J.S.A.H.R. Vol. XXIX no. 118, summer 1951, 55-62.
Diary of events by George Call, 27th Light Dragoons
now in the N.A.M.

105. ----- ----- ----- 'The military papers of Field
Marshal Sir George Nugent, Bt.'. By T.H. McGuffie.
J.R.U.S.I. Vol. XCIX no. 573, February 1949, 101-7.
Largely official papers relating to service between
1792 and 1815, mainly useful for his tenure as commander-
in-chief in Jamaica.

106. NATIONAL LIBRARY OF IRELAND. 'Index to the mss. of
military interest in the National Library of Ireland'.
D. Linehan. comp. Irish Sword, Vol. II, 1954-6,
33-9. A useful short summary of the available records.

107. ----- ----- ----- 'The Kilmainham papers'. By Sir
Henry McAnally. J.S.A.H.R. Vol. XVI no. 61, spring
1937, 3-23. Notes on the correspondence and papers
of the commanders of the forces in Ireland from 1780
to 1894, preserved in the National Library of Ireland.

108. NATIONAL LIBRARY OF SCOTLAND. Catalogue of mss.
acquired since 1925. Edin. 3 Vols. 1938-68.

109. ----- ----- ----- 'Military manuscripts in the
National Library of Scotland'. By M.R. Dobie,
J.S.A.H.R. Vol. XXVII, autumn 1949, 118-20. A note
of the more important material available which includes
papers relating to Field Marshal Wade, Col. John
Drinkwater, and General Sir George Brown, as well as
the collection listed immediately below. There are
various papers and documents relating to all the major
campaigns of the army.

110. ----- ----- -----   'The papers of General the Rt.
Hon. Sir George Murray' by M.R. Dobie. *Ibid*. Vol. X
no. 39, January 1931, 34-9. A collection of major
importance, particularly for the Peninsula war.

111. NATIONAL LIBRARY OF WALES. Handlist of manuscripts
in the National Library of Wales. Aberystwyth.
3 Vols. 1943-61.

(c)   Collections in foreign archives

112. NATIONAL UNION CATALOGUE of manuscript collections
1959+. A register of mss. in American repositories.

113. HAMER, P.M. Guide to archives and manuscripts in
the United States. New Haven. Conn. 1961. The best
general guide.

114. HUNTINGTON LIBRARY AND ART GALLERY. 'Huntington
library collections'. By G.W. Sherburn. *et.al.*
Huntington Lib. Bull. no. 1. May 1931, 33-106. There
are several manuscript collections relevant to the
history of the army including papers of James
Abercrombie, earl of Loudoun, Sir George Yonge, and
the 1st duke of Chandos.

115. ----- ----- ----- 'The letters and accounts of James
Brydges, 1705-1713'. By E.L. Harvey. *Huntington Lib.*
Bull. no. 2, November 1933, 123-47. Describes the
papers of the duke of Chandos as paymaster-general
of the forces abroad, 1705-1713.

116. ----- ----- ----- 'The Loudoun Scottish papers in the
Huntington Library'. By T.I. Rae. *S.H.R.* Vol. XLIX
no. 148, October 1970, 227-31. Short account of the
papers relating to Scotland, in the large Loudoun
collection which includes material on the Jacobite
rebellions of 1715 and 1745.

117. PUBLIC ARCHIVES OF CANADA. A guide to the documents
in the manuscript room at the Public Archives of
Canada. Ottawa. 1914. The Public Archives of Canada
contain the records accumulated by the British army
in Canada, and is now known as the 'C series'.

118. WILLIAM L. CLEMENTS LIBRARY. Guide to the manuscript
collections in the William L. Clements Library.
Howard H. Peckham, comp. Ann Arbor.1942.

119. ----- ----- ----- Guide to the mss. collections in
the William L. Clements Library. W.S. Ewing. comp.
Ann Arbor. 1953. The main guide to the records.

120. ----- ----- ----- The headquarters papers of the
British army in North America during the war of the
American revolution. A brief description of Sir
Henry Clinton's papers in the William L. Clements
library. By R.G. Adams. Ann Arbor. 1926.

121. ----- ----- ----- The papers of Lord George Germain.
A brief description of the Stopford-Sackville papers
now in the William L. Clements library. By R.G.
Adams. Ann Arbor. 1928.

5.   GUIDES TO PARLIAMENTARY RECORDS

Most of the indexes to the printed papers presented to
Parliament should be used with caution, as they are often,
particularly for the earlier period, select guides, and not
always very accurate. The accounts and papers published in
the journals of Parliament should not be overlooked,
particularly during the eighteenth century.

122. BOND, M. A guide to the records of parliament. 1971.
For manuscript (and printed) records of the army, see
particularly pp. 138-9, 150, 153, 210, and 242. The
standard published guide.

123. CATALOGUE OF PAPERS printed by order of the House of
Commons from the year 1731 to 1800. 1870. repr. 1954.
A catalogue of the incomplete collection of papers
assembled by Speaker Abbott at the beginning of the
nineteenth century.

124. FORD, P. and G. A breviate of parliamentary papers,
1900-1916. The foundation of the welfare state. Oxf.
1957. Entries are annotated.

125. ------ A guide to parliamentary papers. Where they
are: how to find them: how to use them. Oxf. 1955.
A useful simple introduction to the subject.

126. ------ eds. Hansard's catalogue and breviate of
parliamentary papers, 1696-1834. Oxf. 1953. Consists
of an introduction to, and facsimile reprint of, the
1834 edition, which was entitled, Catalogue of
Parliamentary reports, and a breviate of their contents,
arranged...according to the subjects, 1696-1834. 1834.

127. ------ Select list of British parliamentary papers,
1833-1899. Shannon. 1969 rev. edn.

128. GENERAL ALPHABETICAL INDEX to the bills, reports,
estimates, accounts, and papers printed by order
of the House of Commons and to the papers presented
by command 1852-1899. 1909. The usefulness of this
index is rather undermined   by the omission, in
error, of the command numbers.

129. GENERAL INDEX to the accounts and papers, reports
of commissioners, estimates etc., printed by order
of the House of Commons and presented by command,
1801-1852. 1853.

130. GENERAL INDEX to the bills printed by order of the
House of Commons, 1801-1852. 1853.

131. GENERAL INDEX to the bills, reports and papers printed
by order of the House of Commons and to the reports
and papers presented by command 1900-1948 -9. 1960.

132. GENERAL INDEX to the bills, reports, estimates, accounts
and papers printed by order of the House of Commons
and to the papers presented by command, 1852-1909.
6 Vols. 1870-1912.

133. GENERAL INDEX to the reports of select committees
printed by order of the House of Commons, 1801-1852.
1853.

134. LAMBERT, SHEILA ed. List of House of Commons sessional
papers 1701-1750. List and Index Society Special series.
Vol. I. 1968. A comprehensive work, which largely
supercedes (126) for the period. A similar index is
urgently needed for the period 1750-1800.

135. LEES-SMITH, H.B. A guide to parliamentary and official
papers. 1924.

136. MENHENNET, DAVID. The journal of the House of Commons.
A bibliographical and historical guide. 1971. A full
guide.

137. OLLE, J.G. An introduction to British government
publications. 1973. 2nd. rev. edn. Useful list of indexes,
with some critical comments.

138. O'NEILL, T.P. British parliamentary papers: a mono-
graph on blue books. Shannon 1968.

139. PARSONS, K.A.C. A checklist of British parliamentary
papers, 1801-1950. Camb. 1958. The best work of its
type.

140. WOODS, J.A. A bibliography of parliamentary
debates of Great Britain. 1956. A comprehensive
survey, with critical commentary, of a rather
complex subject.

6.   BIBLIOGRAPHIES OF AND GUIDES TO PERIODICAL AND
      SOCIETY PUBLICATIONS

141. BOEHM, E. and ADOLPHUS, L. eds. Historical periodicals:
an annotated world list of historical and related serial
publications. Santa Barbara, Calif. 1961.

142. BRITISH HUMANITIES INDEX. 1962+.Annual. The most useful
index for the history of the army. It is a continuation
of The subject index to periodicals listed below in
this section.

143. BRITISH UNION CATALOGUE OF PERIODICALS. A record of
periodicals of the world from the seventeenth century
to the present day in British libraries. By J.D. Stewart
M.E. Hammond, and E. Saenger. 4 Vols. 1955-8. See
particularly under heading 'Great Britain: army'.

144. HARLAND-OXLEY, W.E. 'Regimental magazines'. Notes
and Queries. Vol. X (Eighth series), 12 September 1896,
214-5. A short list.

145. HOUGHTON, W.E. ed. The Wellesley index to Victorian
periodicals 1824-1900. 2 Vols. Toronto. 1966-72. Extensive
and comprehensive lists of individual articles from all
the main Victorian periodicals and some less well known.

146. MATHESON, C. A catalogue of Scottish historical and
kindred clubs and societies... 1908-1927. 1928.

147. MULLINS, E.C.L. A guide to the historical and
archaeological publications of societies in England and
Wales, 1901-1933. 1968. Articles from J.R.U.S.I. are
indexed here. Surprisingly very little relevant material
from other learned societies was apparently published
during this period.

148. ————————. Texts and calendars: an analytical guide
to serial publications. 1968.

149. READERS GUIDE TO PERIODICAL LITERATURE. N.Y.
1882+. Known as Poole's Index.

150. SERVICE PERIODICALS OF THE WORLD. 1889.

151. THE SUBJECT INDEX TO PERIODICALS ..... 1915-16. -
1961. 1919-62. A very useful index produced by the
Library Assoc.

152. TERRY, C.S. A catalogue of the publications of
Scottish historical and kindred clubs ... 1780-1908.
1909.

153. TOASE, MARY. ed. Guide to current British periodicals.
1962. Military periodicals listed, pp. 33-37. Contains
a useful list of current regimental magazines, which
often contain articles of historical interest.

154. UNITED STATES AIR UNIVERSITY. Union list of foreign
military periodicals. Ed. by P.H. Spence and H.J.
Hopewell. Maxwell, Alabama. 1957.

7.   INDEXES TO THESES AND DISSERTATIONS

See also the 'Theses Supplement' to Bull. Institute of
Historical Research (532) published February 1933+. Information on theses in progress is included.

155. INDEX TO THESES ACCEPTED FOR HIGHER DEGREES in the
Universities of Great Britain and Ireland. 1950+. This
annual publication is the standard guide, indexed by
author and subject, and listed by the latter.

156. COMPREHENSIVE DISSERTATION INDEX 1861-1972. Ann Arbor. 1973
See especially Vol.28. entitled 'History'.

PART II.   GENERAL WORKS

8.   HISTORIES AND MISCELLANEOUS WORKS ON THE ARMY

     Other works containing historical accounts of the army
are listed elsewhere; see especially sections 13 and 14.

(a)   General.

  157. ADYE, SIR JOHN MILLER. The British army, past and
       present. 1887. A magazine article republished in
       pamphlet form.

  158. ANDERSON, SIR W.H. Outline of the development of the
       British army up to the commencement of the Great war,
       1914 etc. 1920. A useful pamphlet.

  159. ATKINSON, JOHN. ABC of the army: an illustrated guide
       to military knowledge for those who seek a general
       acquaintance with elementary matters pertaining to the
       British army. 1910. A popular guide of little scholarly
       value.

  160. BANKS, MARJORIE. The blessed trade. 1971. A popular
       guide to some of the main characteristics of British
       army organization, mainly during the period before the
       Restoration.

  161. BARNES, R.M. The soldiers of London. 1964. A study
       of the regiments and soldiers associated with London,
       arranged as a reference work rather than a continuous
       narative, with an emphasis on military uniforms.

  162. BARNETT, CORELLI. Britain and her army 1509-1970. A
       military, political and social survey. 1970. Generally
       regarded as the best modern one-volume survey of the army
       history, although it does not appear to be based on a
       wide range of sources. Neither the themes nor conclusion
       of this study seem to be very profound or original.

  163. THE BRITISH ARMY. By a Lieut. Colonel in the British
       army. 1899. Believed to have been written by Lieut. Col.
       J.M. Grierson, R.A. Based on, inter alia, published
       official orders, there is a historical introduction,
       followed by a discussion of the component parts of the
       army, and the conditions of service of officers and men.

  164. BUSH, E.W. Salute the soldier: an anthology of quotation
       poems and prose. 1966. An interesting collection, not
       confined to Great Britain.

165. CLODE, CHARLES MATTHEW. The military forces of the crown: their administration and government. 2 vols. 1869. A widely known Whig interpretation of the history of the army by a mid-nineteenth century War Office solicitor. Contains numerous key documents, some of which are not now easily available, and was the most detailed account of the subject which had appeared up to that time. A similar work, incorporating the results of modern research, would be a useful addition to the literature.

166. CONNOLLY, T.W.J. The romance of the ranks or anecdotes, episodes and social incidents of military life. 1859. Mainly relates to the first half of the nineteenth century.

167. DANIEL, WILLIAM HENRY. The military forces of the crown. Their organization and equipment. Ed. by T. Miller Maguire. 1901.

168. DE FONBLANQUE, EDWARD B. Treatise on the administration and organization of the British army, with especial reference to administration and supply. 1858. A detailed examination by a commissariat officer, and army reformer, who was associated with Sir Charles Trevelyan's campaign to secure fundamental changes in military organization.

169. DILLON, HON. H.A. A commentary on the military establishments of the British empire. 1811. A useful picture of the organization of the army and some of its defects during the period of the Peninsula war. Proposals for reforms are included.

170. DUPIN, F.P.C., BARON. View of the history and actual state of the military force of Great Britain. 2 vols. 1822. The English translation of a work originally published in France, which gives a rare insight into French views of the British army as well as providing a general history of the organization. See also, 'A French view of the post-Waterloo British army'. By A.E. Sullivan. A.Q. vol. LXXXV no. 2, January 1963, 188-97.

171. EDWARDS, T.J. Military customs. Aldershot. 1961. Rev. edn. A detailed guide to some of the traditions of the army.

172. FARRER, J.A. Military manners and customs. 1885. An interesting guide.

173. FORTESCUE, HON. SIR J.W. History of the British army. 13 Vols. 1899-1930. The classic history with a strong emphasis on the campaigns of the army. Although the bulk of the work is on the Napoleonic period, the period covered is from earliest times to 1870. May be criticized for its slight treatment of army administration, for the author's political prejudices which tend often to affect his assessment of historical situations, and for the fact that few of his sources are identified. See also, 'Fortescue's history of the army' by A.E. Sullivan. A.Q. Vol. LXX no. 1, April 1955, 53-9.

174. ------ The empire and the army. 1928. The story of the British soldier from medieval times to 1914.

175. ------ Military history. Lectures delivered at Trinity College, Cambridge. Camb. 1914. The role of the army in the eighteenth and nineteenth centuries was the theme of these lectures.

176. GILBY, THOMAS. ed. Britain at arms: a scrapbook from Queen Anne to the present day. 1954. A useful anthology.

177. GOODENOUGH, W.H. and DALTON, J.C. The army book for the British empire: a record of the development and present composition of the military forces and their duties in peace and war. 1893. An official publication which gives a very detailed account of military organization in the late nineteenth century.

178. GORDON, LAWRENCE, L. Military origins. Ed. by J.B.R. Nicholson. 1971. Examines, in a popular style, the origins and subsequent history of some of the major elements of English military organization.

179. GRIFFITHS, A.G.F. The English army: its past history, present condition, and future prospects. 1878. Mainly an account of the organization of the army.

180. GROSE, FRANCIS. Military antiquities respecting a history of the English army from the conquest to the present time. 2 Vols. 1786-8. Although the bulk of this book is concerned with the period before 1660, there is some material down to the eighteenth century particularly in the second edition published 1812. One of the first works of its kind, although much of the content is of antiquarian interest.

181. HARRIS, P.V. The British army up to date. 1944.
Like many of the other general histories, better for
campaigns and the histories of regiments than the
administration and organization of the army.

182. HAY. IAN. The King's service. An informal history
of the British infantry soldier. 1938. A short
popular study covering a wider area than its title
implies.

183. HUTCHINSON, LIEUT. COL. G.S. The British army,
1945.

184. KING, C.C. The story of the British army.1897.
Popular.

185. LING, PETER. Gentlemen at arms. Portraits of soldiers
in fact and fiction, in peace and at war. An
anthology of prose and poetry. 1969.

186. MARSHALL, HENRY. Historical details relative to
the military force of Great Britain, from the earliest
periods to the present time 1066-1839. n.d. A short
work consisting of a list of the main events connected
with the history of the army.

187. MYATT, FREDERICK. The soldier's trade: British
military developments, 1660-1914. 1974. A useful work
on the evolution of weapons, drill, tactics and
organization from the creation of the standing army.

188. PASLEY, SIR CHARLES WILLIAM. Essay on the military
policy and institutions of the British empire. Pt. I.
1810. No further parts were published. The first part
is a valuable account by a noted military writer.

189. PHILIPPART, JOHN. Observations on the military systems
of the British empire. 1813.

190. SAMUEL, E. An historical account of the British army,
and of the law military, as declared by the ancient and
modern statutes, and articles of war for its government:
with a free commentary on the Mutiny Act, and the rules
of articles of war; illustrated by various decisions of
courts martial. 1816.

191. SCOTT, SIR SIBALD. The British army: its origin, progress
and equipment. 3 Vols. 1868-80. Covers the period down
to 1688. Although in many ways superseded by later
research it remains a valuable source of information.

192. SHEPPARD, E.W. A short history of the British army. 1950. A very clear concise account of the campaigns of the army, but there is little on the development of military organization.

193. ――――――――. Red coat. An anthology of the British soldier during the last three hundred years. 1952. Serves as a useful guide to some of the literature on the army. Full references to the extracts quoted are given.

194. STOCQUELER, J.H. A familiar history of the British army, from the restoration in 1660 to the present time, including a description of the Volunteer movement and the progress of the volunteer organization.1871. Mainly the history of campaigns, and not really of much value now.

195. ――――――――. The British soldier: An anecdotal history of the British army from its earliest foundation to the present time. 1857.

196. TALBOT-BOOTH. E.C. The British army: its history, customs, traditions and uniforms. 1940.

197. THOMSON, H.B. The military forces and institutions of Great Britain and Ireland: their constitution, administration, and government, military and civil. 1855. One of the more comprehensive early guides.

198. TRENCHARD, T. A short history of standing armies in England. 1689. An important contribution to the standing army debate written from a Whig viewpoint.

199. WALTERS, JOHN. Aldershot review. 1970. Popular history of Aldershot as a military centre.

200. WHEELER, OWEN. The story of our army. 1902.

201. WILSON, GENERAL SIR ROBERT T. An enquiry into the present state of the military force of the British empire, with a view to its reorganization addressed to the Rt. Hon. William Pitt. 1804. A critical review of the army by a remarkable soldier, which yields some interesting information.

202. WOLSELEY, GARNETT JOSEPH, VISCOUNT. 'The standing army of Great Britain'. In The armies of today. A description of the armies of the leading nations at the present time. N.Y. 1893.

203. YOUNG, PETER. The British army. (1642-1970). 1967. A
short popular survey based on secondary sources, it is
of little interest for the specialist.

204. ————————. and LAWFORD, J.P. eds. History of the British
army. 1970. A collection of simple introductory essays,
with numerous illustrations which give it its main
value.

(b)   Particular periods.

Items are listed here in approximate chronological order
of content.

205. WALTON, COL. CLIFFORD. History of the British standing
army. A.D. 1660-1700. 1894. A very thorough and long
work, based on primary sources, chiefly on army organization. There are appendices of key documents and
letters drawn from a variety of collections.

206. HARVEY, C. CLELAND. 'Military papers of the time of
Charles the second'. S.H.R. Vol. XII no. 46, January
1915, 145-56. Includes establishments of the Foot
Guards, 1662 and documents relating to the militia
in Scotland. Valuable because of the dearth of extant
records relating to the army at this time.

207. DAVIES, GODFREY. 'The army and the restoration of 1660'.
J.S.A.H.R. Vol. XXXII no. 129, spring 1954, 26-9. A
discussion of the role of the army in, and its reaction
to, the restoration of the monarchy.

208. COTTESLOE, LORD. 'The earliest 'establishment' - 1661 -
of the British standing army'. Ibid. Vol. IX. no. 37,
July 1930, 147-161; no. 38, October 1930, 214-242.
Extracts from a ms. volume entitled 'An establishment for
the new raised forces begun the 26 January 1660. The
first known forerunner of the volumes known as army
establishment books, of which there are several examples
in the P.R.O. the earliest dating from 1685.

209. ATKINSON, C.T. 'Two hundred a fifty years ago: James
II and his army' Ibid. Vol. XIV. no. 53, spring 1935,
1-11. Mainly on the new regiments raised at this time.

210. DAVIES, GODFREY. 'Letters on the administration of
James II's army'. Ibid. Vol. XXIX. no. 118, Summer 1951,
69-84. Letters of William Blathwayt while Secretary at
War, preserved at the Public Record Office.

211. ──────. 'The reduction of the army after the peace
of Ryswick, 1697'. Ibid. Vol. XXVIII. no. 113, spring
1950, 15-28. A scholarly account of the effects of the
controversial decision to disband the army.

212. MILLER, E.A. 'Some arguments used by English
pamphleteers, 1697-1700 concerning a standing army'.
J.M.H. Vol. XVIII no. 4., December 1946, 306-313.
A useful summary of the controversy.

213. BARKER, SIR ERNEST. Development of public services in
Western Europe, 1660-1930. Oxf. 1944. See the short
section entitled 'The English army in the eighteenth and
nineteenth centuries'.

214. WILLIAMS, D. ELWYN. 'Military studies of the 1700-1850
period'. A.Q. Vol. LIV no. 1. April 1947, 76-81; no.2,
July 1947, 222-31. A brief guide to organization and
tactics.

215. SCOULLER, MAJOR R.E. The armies of Queen Anne. Oxf.
1967. The standard history, based on extensive use
of primary sources. A similar analytical work is
urgently needed for the remainder of the eighteenth
century.

216. ATKINSON, C.T. 'The army under the early Hannoverians.
More gleanings from W.O. IV and other sources in the
Public Records Office'. J.S.A.H.R. Vol. XXI no. 83,
autumn 1942, 138-47. Extracts from, inter alia, the
Secretary at War's out-letter books, (W.O. 4) at the
P.R.O.

217. HAYES, JAMES. 'The royal house of Hannover and the
British army 1714-60'. Bull. John Rylands Library Vol.
40 no. 2. 1958, 328-57. The attempts of the Hannoverians to reform the army in general and the officer
corps in particular.

218. FORTESCUE, HON. SIR J.W. 'The army'. In Johnson's
England. An account of the life and manners of his age.
Ed. by A.S. Turberville. Oxf. 1967. Vol. I, 66-87.

219. VIVIAN, FRANCES ST. C. 'John Andre as a young officer,
the army in the eighteenth century and a young man's
impressions on first joining his regiment in the 1770s'.
J.S.A.H.R. Vol. XL no. 161, March 1962, 24-32; no. 162,
June 1962, 61-77.

220. OBSERVATIONS ON THE PREVAILING ABUSES in the British
army, arising from the corruption of civil government.
1775. Useful information on the army at the time of
publication is contained in this highly critical work.

221. FORTESCUE, HON. SIR J.W. The British army, 1783-1802.
Four lectures delivered at the Staff College and Cavalry
School. 1905. One of his most useful works, not
encumbered with excessive detail.

222. McGUFFIE, T.H. Life in the British army, 1793-1820 in
relation to social conditions. University of London.
Unpublished M.A. thesis. 1940. Conditions of service
of officers and men during the Napoleonic wars and after.

223. GLOVER, RICHARD. Peninsula preparation: the reform of
the British army 1795-1809. Camb. 1963. The standard
account based on a wide range of MSS, and contemporary
published, material.

224. FORTESCUE, HON. SIR J.W. 'The army in the year of
Trafalgar'. U.S.M. Vol. XXXII. (N.S.), October, 1905,
73-93.

225. HALEVY, ELIE. A history of the English people in the
nineteenth century. Trans. by E.I. Watkin and D.A. Barker. 5 Vols. 1924-34. The first volume contains a fine
survey of the army in 1815 with a useful explanation
of its position in English society.

226. BLANCO, RICHARD L. 'Reform and Wellington's post-Waterloo
army, 1815-1854'. Military Affairs. Vol. 29, fall 1965,
123-31.

227. JONES, P.D. The British army in the age of reform, 1830-
1854. Duke University. Unpublished Ph. D. thesis. 1968.

228. DE WATTEVILLE, H.G. 'A hundred years of the British
army I Personnel and administration'. J.R.U.S.I. Vol.
LXXVI. no. 502, May 1931, 285-99. 'II Weapons and
Equipment'. by M.L. Wilkinson Ibid. 300-10.

229. WOLSELEY, GARNET JOSEPH, VISCOUNT. 'The army'. In
The reign of Queen Victoria, a survey of fifty years of
progress. Ed. by T.H. Ward. 1887. Vol. I, 155-225. An
account of the reform and campaigns of the army.

230. FORTESCUE, HON. SIR J.W. 'The army'. In Early
Victorian England 1830-1865. Ed. by G.M. Young. Oxf.
1934. Vol. I, 345-75.

231. MOYSE-BARTLETT, LIEUT. COL. H. 'British army in 1850'.
J.S.A.H.R. Vol. LII no. 212, Winter 1974, 221-37. The
organization and personnel of the army in 1850.

232. BLAKE, ROBERT. 'Great Britain. The Crimea to the First
World War'. In Soldiers and governments. Nine studies
in civil military relations. Ed. by M.E. Howard. 1957,
27-50. An introductory historical survey, without any
serious analysis of, or explanation for, the political
role of the army, during the nineteenth century.

233. WILSON, H.S. The army and public opinion from 1854 to
the end of 1873. University of Oxford. Unpublished
B. Litt. thesis. 1955. A detailed examination of the
role of public opinion in a period of army reform.

234. BOND, BRIAN. 'Prelude to the Cardwell reforms, 1856-1868'.
J.R.U.S.I. Vol. CVI, 1961, 229-36. The changing
circumstances of the post Crimean army are examined.

235. ALLEN, F.S. The British army 1860-1900: a study of the
Cardwell manpower reforms. Harvard University.
Unpublished Ph. D. thesis. 1960.

236. HANHAM, H.J. 'Religion and nationality in the mid
Victorian army'. In War and society. Historical essays
in honour and memory of J.R. Western, 1928-1971. 1973,
159-81. Religion, and changing popular attitudes to the
soldier.

237. WHEATON, J. The effect and the impact of the administrative reform movement upon the army in the mid-Victorian
period. Manchester University. Unpublished Ph. D.
thesis.1968.

238. HOOPER, G. 'The army' In Questions for a reformed
parliament, 1867, 219-32. A critique of the army, and
proposals for reform.

239. TREVELYAN, SIR CHARLES EDWARD. The British army in
1868. 1868. An examination of the army by one of the
leading campaigners for army reform in general and the
abolition of the purchase system in particular. On
this latter subject see also his pamphlet, The Purchase
system in the British Army. 1867.

240. BIDDULPH, GENERAL SIR ROBERT. Lord Cardwell at the
War Office, 1868-74. 1904. The only full length account
of the reforms introduced during Gladstone's first
administration based on Cardwell's private papers.
Sir Robert Biddulph was Cardwell's private secretary,
and his account is rather uncritical.

241. BOND, BRIAN. 'Edward Cardwell's army reforms 1868-1874'.
A.Q. Vol. LXXXIV no. 1, April 1962, 108-17.

242. ESSON, D.M.R. 'Cardwell and the military reformation'
     Ibid. Vol. CII no. 4. July 1972, 496-508. A resume of
     Cardwell's reforms in a historical context, and includes
     some of those less widely known.

243. WHIGHAM, SIR ROBERT. 'The Cardwell reforms - a retrospect'
     Ibid. Vol. VII. no. 1, October 1923, 15-22. A summary
     of the introduction of the Cardwell system.

244. BOND, BRIAN. The introduction and operation of short
     service and localisation in the British army, 1868-1892.
     University of London. Unpublished M.A. thesis. 1962.
     A detailed examination of one of the major Cardwell reforms.

245. TUCKER, A.V. 'Army and society in England 1870-1900: a
     reassessment of the Cardwell reforms'. J.B.S. Vol. II,
     May 1963, 110-41. Provides much convincing evidence
     to support his view that the Cardwell reforms were not
     a turning point in the history of the army.

246. BOND, BRIAN. 'The effect of the Cardwell reforms on
     army organization 1878-1904'. J.R.U.S.I. Vol. CV, 1960,
     515-24.

247. —————. 'The late Victorian army' History Today. Vol.
     XI. 1961, 616-24. A valuable summary.

248. DUNLOP, J.K. The development of the British army 1899-
     1914: from the eve of the South African war to the eve
     of the Great War, with special reference to the territor-
     ial force. 1938. Focuses on the changes implemented
     following the assessment of the causes of the army's
     performance in the Boer war.

249. FALLS, CYRIL. 'The army'. In Edwardian England 1901-
     1914. Ed. by Simon Nowell Smith. Oxf. 1964, 509-44. A
     valuable summary of the period of reform and preparation
     between the Boer War and World War I.

250. SATRE, L.J. The Unionists and army reform: the abortive
     proposals of St. John Brodrick. University of South
     Carolina. Unpublished Ph. D. thesis, 1968.

251. TUCKER, A.V. 'Army reform in the Unionist Government,
     1903-05' H.J. Vol. IX. 1966, 90-100. A review of the
     far reaching changes introduced while H,0. Arnold Forster
     was Secretary for war.

252. BARNES, R.M. The British army of 1914: its history,
     uniforms and contemporary continental armies. 1968. A
     further original survey on the pattern of his earlier
     books listed below.

253. RYAN, A.P. Mutiny at the Curragh. 1956. A well
     written summary.

254. FERGUSSON, SIR JAMES. The Curragh incident. 1964.

9.   OFFICIAL RECORDS AND PAPERS

     This section is concerned with the official records of
the British army preserved at the Public Record Office. These
records are unfortunately by no means comprehensive and many
important documents which originated from the War Office and
Horse Guards or other official organizations, now exist only
in private collections, if indeed they are still extant.

     The indexes, published and unpublished, to these
documents and papers vary greatly in detail and usefulness, and
many records are identified by little more than their department of origin, and the period of time they cover. Thus, for
example, in the numerous series of letter-books it is necessary
to refer to the indexes in individual volumes, prepared as the
records were created, to gain any detailed information as to
the contents.

     Personal papers preserved at the Public Record Office
which have been acquired by gift, deposit or purchase, are not
listed here but are noted in the biographical sections under
the names of the individuals to whom they refer.

(a)   Manuscript

     The material is listed here in order of the reference
numbers although some minor classes of documents have been
omitted. For a complete classification by subject, see the
P.R.O. Guide, listed above (85).

          War Office

255. IN-LETTERS. 1732-1868. 1,138 Vols. W.O.I. Bound
     volumes of letters, despatches, and papers, addressed to
     the secretary at war, and for the later period, the
     secretary of state for war.

256. INDEXES OF CORRESPONDENCE 1759-1858. 107 Vols. W.O.2.
     Notes of letters sent by the secretary at war, some of
     which are not now extant.

257. COMMANDER-IN-CHIEF OUT-LETTERS. 1765-1868. 617 Vols.
     W.O.3. Public, and some private, correspondence of the
     commander-in-chief and the adjutant-general.

258. SECRETARY AT WAR: OUT LETTERS 1684-1861. 1,053 Vols. W.O.4. A most useful collection, particularly for the early period, although, of course, the great mass of letters are of a routine nature.

259. MARCHING ORDERS 1683-1852. 122 Vols. W.O.5.

260. SECRETARY OF STATE FOR WAR: OUT-LETTERS 1793-1859. 214 Vols. W.O.6.

261. DEPARTMENTAL OUT-LETTERS 1715-1862. 130 Vols. W.O.7. Includes the letter books of the Board of General Officers, the Chaplin-General, the Medical Department, and the Muster Master General.

262. IRELAND: OUT-LETTERS 1709-1823. 12 Vols. W.O.8. Includes the entry books of the Muster Master General of Ireland.

263. ACCOUNTS. 1679-1865. 48 Vols. W.O.9. Miscellaneous collection of accounts and documents relating to the Militia, Yeomanry and other reserve forces.

264. MUSTER BOOKS AND PAY LISTS - ARTILLERY 1708-1878. 2,876 Vols. W.O.10. Useful for tracing a soldier"s service when he was not eventually discharged to a pension, and his discharge papers are not therefore to be found in the class entitled 'Soldiers' documents', W.O. 97, listed below.

265. --------------------------. ENGINEERS 1816-1878. 432 Vols. W.O.11. Similar type of records to the artillery.

266. --------------------------. GENERAL. 1732-1878. 13,305 Vols. W.O.12. Covers the Guards, Cavalry and Infantry.

267. --------------------------. MILITIA AND VOLUNTEERS. 1780-1878. 4,675 Vols. W.O.13.

268. --------------------------. SCUTARI DEPOT 1854-1856. 130 Vols. W.O.14. Muster rolls of soldiers in the Crimean War.

269. --------------------------. FOREIGN LEGION 1854-1856. 102 Vols. W.O.15.

270. --------------------------. NEW SERIES 1878-1898. 3,049 Vols. W.O.16. A continuation of W.O.12, listed above, for a further twenty years.

271. REGIMENTAL MONTHLY RETURNS 1759-1865. 2,812 Vols.
W.O.17. These show the distribution of each regiment
and its effective strength. Also included are general
particulars of the health of the regiment and various
miscellaneous information.

272. ORDNANCE OFFICE Vouchers for agents' disbursements,
Artillery. 213 Vols. W.O.18. Original warrants issued
by the Board of Ordnance to its agents for payments.

273. ROYAL GARRISON REGIMENT 1901-1906. 9 Vols. W.O.19.
Records and returns in the early years of the twentieth
century.

274. PENSION RETURNS 1842-1883. 300 Vols. W.O.22. Periodic
returns of pensions paid or payable.

275. PENSIONS-CHELSEA REGISTERS 1805-1895. 123 Vols. W.O.
23. Various registers of pensioners.

276. ESTABLISHMENTS 1661-1846. 892 Vols. W.O. 24. Royal
sign-manual warrants authorising the establishments of
regiments: the numbers of each rank, pay and cost of
provisions.

277. VARIOUS PENSIONS REGISTERS 1660-1938. 3,992 Vols. W.O. 25.

278. MISCELLANY BOOKS 1670-1817. 42 Vols. W.O. 26. Valuable
collection of royal warrants, not arranged always in
strict chronological order.

279. INSPECTION RETURNS 1750-1912. 507 Vols. W.O.27. Consists
mainly of completed inspection forms which gave a general
report on the condition of each regiment and other basic
factual information.

280. HEADQUARTERS RECORDS 1746-1901. 346 Vols. W.O.28. Those
of several major campaigns are preserved in this class.

281. MISCELLANEOUS DOCUMENTS AND PAPERS 1684-1903. 132 Vols.
W.O. 30. Includes reports and papers on clothing,
internal security, various army reforms, the reorganization of the Royal Artillery, 1858 to 1871, etc.

282. MEMORANDA PAPERS, COMMANDER IN CHIEF 1793-1870. 1,565
bundles. W.O.31. Documents relating to individual
applications for appointments, promotions and retirement.
Useful material for the study of the social origins of
the officer corps.

283. REGISTERED PAPERS, GENERAL SERIES 1855-1925. 1,764 boxes.
W.O. 32. A selection of papers relating to all aspects
of War Office business. There is a subject index.

284. REPORTS AND MISCELLANEOUS PAPERS 1853-1896. 56 Vols.
W.O.33. Printed papers, many formerly confidential, on
a wide range of important subjects.

285. IRELAND 1775-1922. 205 Vols. W.O. 35. Records of the
army in Ireland.

286. AMERICAN REBELLION: ENTRY BOOKS 1773-1783, 1798-1799.
4 Vols. W.O. 36. Includes a series of orders issued
by the British army in America.

287. SELECTED UNNUMBERED PAPERS 1753-1815. 32 bundles. W.O.
40. In-letters and reports addressed to the Secretary
at War on such subjects as allowances, America, barracks,
billeting, chaplains, Chelsea hospital, recruiting, and
Yeomanry. Indexed.

288. SELECTED 'ACCOUNTS' PAPERS 1810-1822. 98 Vols. W.O. 41.
In-letters relating to accounts.

289. SELECTED 'VERY OLD SERIES' AND 'OLD SERIES' PAPERS
1809-1857. 107 bundles. W.O. 43. Miscellaneous correspondence and papers of varying importance.

290. ORDNANCE OFFICE IN-LETTERS 1682-1873. 732 Vols. W.O. 44.
Mainly of nineteenth century dates.

291. --------------- REFERENCE BOOKS 1783-1870. 298 Vols.
W.O. 45. Indexes of in-letters of the Board of Ordnance
and of the Master General.

292. --------------- OUT-LETTERS 1660-1811. 169 Vols W.O. 46.
Entry books of out-letters from a number of sections of
the Ordnance.

293. --------------- MINUTES 1644-1856. 2,897 Vols. W.O. 47.
Minutes of the Board of Ordnance.

294. --------------- LEDGERS 1660-1847. 357 Vols. W.O. 48.
Contains the items of expenditure on which the summarized
accounts of the Treasurers and paymasters of the
Ordnance in the declared accounts of the Audit Office
were based.

295. --------------- VARIOUS ACCOUNTS 1592-1858. 293 Vols.
W.O. 49. Accounts and background papers on a variety
of subjects.

296. ――――――――― BILL BOOK SERIES I-IV 1677-1822.
1,650 Vols. W.O. 50,51,52 and 53. Detailed items of
expenditure: these supplement the ledgers, W.O. 48,
listed above.

297. ―――――――― REGISTERS 1594-1871. 947 Vols. W.O.
54. Includes lists of officers, pay, and papers
relating to appointments.

298. ―――――――― MISCELLANEA 1568-1923. 3,038 Vols. W.O.
55. Miscellaneous books,papers and correspondence.

There is also a miscellaneous collection of official
records of the Board of Ordnance, consisting of account,
delivery, receipt, and contract,books, and of warrants,
correspondence and papers, the majority relating to the
reign of Charles II, although the period covered is 1627-1745.
20 Vols. See P.R.O. 30/37.

299. COMMISSARIAT DEPARTMENT IN-LETTERS 1806-1817. 58 bundles.
W.O. 57.

300. ――――――――――― OUT-LETTERS 1793-1888. 178 Vols.
W.O. 58.

301. ――――――――――― MINUTES 1816-1854. 76 Vols.
W.O. 59.

302. ――――――――――― ACCOUNTS 1774-1858. 112 Vols.
W.O. 60.

303. ――――――――――― REGISTERS 1791-1889. 135 Vols.
W.O. 61. Includes lists of appointments, establishments
and pay.

304. ――――――――――― MISCELLANEA 1798-1859. 50 Vols.
W.O. 62. Various documents, accounts and letter-books
kept by commissariat officers at various stations.

305. ――――――――――― IRELAND 1797-1852. 161 Vols.
W.O. 63. Letter books and accounts.

306. ARMY LISTS: MANUSCRIPT 1702-1823. 13 Vols. W.O. 64.

307. ――――――――. PRINTED: ANNUAL 1754-1879. W.O. 65. There
are manuscript additions and corrections.

308. ――――――――. PRINTED: QUARTERLY 1879-1900. 86 Vols.
W.O. 66.

309. DEPOT DESCRIPTION BOOKS 1768-1908. 34 Vols. W.O. 67.
Descriptions and information about individual soldiers.

310. MILITIA RECORDS 1759-1925. 564 Vols. W.O. 68. Records
of militia regiments, including statistical information,
order books, and correspondence.

311. ARTILLERY RECORDS OF SERVICE 1765-1906. 314 Vols. W.O.
69. Records of ncos and men, similar to those in W.O.
67, listed above.

312. VOLUNTEER AND TERRITORIAL RECORDS 1860-1912. 21 Vols.
W.O. 70.

313. COURTS MARTIAL PROCEEDINGS 1668-1850. 342 Vols. W.O.
71. Records and minutes.

314. ---------------------------. LETTERS AND DOCUMENTS 1696-
1850. 103 bundles. W.O. 72. In-letters, with enclosures,
relating to courts martial.

315. MONTHLY RETURNS: DISTRIBUTION OF THE ARMY 1859-1938. 141
Vols. W.O. 73. Distribution of the army both by divisions
and stations, and by regiments.

316. ARMY PURCHASE COMMISSION PAPERS 1871-1908. 194 Vols.
W.O. 74. Correspondence relating to the work of the
Commission established under the act of 1871 ending the
purchase system, to determine the financial compensation
payable to officers.

317. RECORDS OF OFFICERS' SERVICES. 1771-1919. 378 Vols. W.O.
76. Supplements the returns in W.O. 25 listed above.

318. MAPS AND PLANS 1627-1946. 4,991 pieces. W.O. 78.

319. OFFICE OF JUDGE ADVOCATE GENERAL-LETTER BOOKS 1715-1900.
133 Vols. W.O. 81.

320. ----------------------- OFFICE DAY BOOKS 1817-1899. 24
Vols. W.O. 82. Daily registers of letters received and
notes of their contents.

321. ----------------------- MINUTE BOOKS 1871-1900. 10 Vols.
W.O. 83. Lists of the decisions of the Judge Advocate
General.

322. ----------------------- CHARGE BOOKS 1857-1882. 4 Vols.
W.O. 84. Entry books of out letters relating to the
preparation of charges for trial by courts martial.

323. GENERAL COURTS MARTIAL 1666–1829. 5 Vols. W.O. 89.
For the periods 1666 to 1697 and 1758 to 1760 these
records are entry books giving the proceedings in
full, but for 1812–1829 they are only registers
giving the charges, the name, rank, and regiment of each
prisoner, place of trial, nature of the charge and
sentence. For similar registers see W.O. 86, 87, 88,
and 90. Other documents relating to General Courts-
martial may be found in W.O. 91, 92, 93.

324. MILITIA ATTESTATION PAPERS 1806–1915. 1,522 boxes.
W.O. 96. These were forms filled in at the time of
recruitment and, in most cases, were annotated to the
date of discharge to form a complete record of service.

325. SOLDIERS' DOCUMENTS 1760–1900. 4,231 boxes. W.O. 97.
The main series of service documents of soldiers.

326. VICTORIA CROSS 1856–1864. 2 boxes. W.O. 98. Contains
documents, and correspondence about individual cases.
See also W.O. 100, 101, 102, and 104 for papers
concerning other medals and awards, including the classes
on campaign medals, and long service awards.

327. ROYAL MILITARY COLLEGE, SANDHURST 1798–1866. 34 boxes.
W.O. 99. Correspondence, accounts, papers, and the
minutes of the governing body.

328. DIRECTORATE OF MILITARY OPERATIONS AND INTELLIGENCE:
PAPERS 1837, 1870–1925. 65 boxes. W.O. 106.

329. QUARTERMASTER GENERAL: PAPERS 1763–1914. 12 boxes. W.O.
107. Papers relating to trooping programmes and to
various, mainly colonial, expeditions.

330. BOER WAR PAPERS 1899–1905. 83 Vols. W.O. 108. Mainly
correspondence of the commander in chief of the army in
South Africa.

331. FINANCE DEPARTMENT: PRECEDENTS 1878–1919. 9 Vols. W.O.
113. Collection of precedents relating to the pay and
conditions of officers and other ranks.

332. OUT-PENSIONS RECORDS, ROYAL HOSPITAL CHELSEA ADMISSION
BOOKS 1715–1882. 154 Vols. W.O. 116. Registers of the
award of out pensions to soldiers discharged from the
army or militia on account of disability. For other
out-pensions, Royal Hospital Chelsea, see W.O. 22, 23
and 97 above, and W.O. 117, 120, 121, 122, and 131. For
out-pensions, Royal Hospital Kilmainham, see W.O. 118 and
119.

333. ARMY CIRCULARS, MEMORANDA AND ORDERS 1856-1907. 49
Vols. W.O. 123. Bound printed copies of orders issued
by the War Office and Commander-in-Chief.

334. SCHOOL OF MUSKETRY, HYTHE 1853-1928. 15 Vols. W.O. 140.
Records of experiments and trials at the school.

Other departments of state with collections of relevant
material preserved at the Public Record Office include:-

State Paper Office

The publication of printed calendars of state papers
has made reference to some of the originals listed here
unnecessary. (See Section (b)).

335. STATE PAPERS DOMESTIC, CHARLES II. 1660-1685. 450 Vols.
S.P. 29, S.P. 30.

336. --------------------, JAMES II. 1685-1688. 5 Vols. S.P.
31.

337. --------------------, WILLIAM AND MARY. 1689-1702. 17
Vols; 4 cases. S.P. 32, S.P. 33.

338. --------------------, ANNE 1702-1714. 38 Vols. S.P. 34.

339. --------------------, GEORGE I 1714-1727. 78 bundles.
S.P. 35.

340. --------------------, GEORGE II. 1727-1760. 163 bundles.
S.P. 36.

341. --------------------, GEORGE III 1760-1782. 27 bundles.
S.P. 37.

342. --------------------, MILITARY 1640-1782. 48 bundles. S.P
41. Letters from the Secretary at War, the officers of
the Ordnance, and others to the Secretaries of State,
and other papers relating to military affairs between
1702 and 1782. References to documents in this class are
given in the printed calendars, listed below.

343. --------------------. ENTRY BOOKS 1661-1828. S.P. 44.
418 Vols. Contains notes or full copies of letters sent
out from the offices of the Secretaries of State, of
warrants, petitions and other matters. One section
consists of military correspondence, commissions and
warrants from 1679 to 1782.

344. STATE PAPERS, FOREIGN, GERMANY (STATES) 1577-1784.
197 Vols. S.P. 81. See for financial claims arising
out of military operations during the war of the
Austrian succession, and during the seven years' war.
Material on German troops in the British service.

345. --------------------- MILITARY EXPEDITIONS 1695-1763.
48 Vols. S.P. 87.

Colonial Office

The records of this department have been arranged, as
far as possible topographically, and reference may be made
to the documents relating to a particular colony for
information about its military affairs. Only classes containing collections of papers relating to the colonies
generally are referred to below. For a fuller account see
the list noted above (90).

346. SUPPLEMENTARY CORRESPONDENCE 1759-1929. 156 Vols.
C.O. 537. Includes material on military affairs in
various colonies.

347. ORIGINAL CORRESPONDENCE 1689-1940. 1,812 Vols. C.O.
323. This class consists of general colonial
correspondence. Between 1801 and 1854, when the
departments of War and Colonies were under the same
Secretary of State, much of the correspondence was
the concern of both departments.

Exchequer and Audit Department

348. DECLARED ACCOUNTS 1536 - 1828. 2,541 rolls. A.O.1. Many
papers of military interest, including the declared
accounts of paymasters general in America.

349. ACCOUNTS, VARIOUS 1539-1886. 1,430 rolls. A.O.3. Gives
detailed information concerning many military accounts
and expenditure.

350. ESTABLISHMENTS AND REGISTERS 1604-1867. 40 Vols. A.O.11.
Includes papers relating to British officers in
Portuguese service, 1809 to 1814, and Commissariat
establishments in the Peninsula, 1810 to 1813.

351. MISCELLANEA 1568-1910. 196 Vols. A.O.16. Includes
documents relating to the army 1568-1826, and the
commissariat, 1793-1857.

352. ABSORBED DEPARTMENTS 1580-1867. A.0.17. Includes the records of the Comptroller of Army Accounts, 1705-1835.

Home Office

353. DEPARTMENTAL CORRESPONDENCE AND PAPERS - WAR AND COLONIAL OFFICE 1794-1840. 5 bundles. H.O. 30. Original in-letters from the Secretary for War and the Colonies and an entry book (1815-1836) of out letters.

354. CORRESPONDENCE RELATING TO DISTURBANCES 1812-1855. 59 bundles. H.O.40. Includes military reports on civil disorders. See also H.O. 41 1816-1898 (33 Vols) for entries of out-letters on the same subject.

355. GEORGE III CORRESPONDENCE 1782-1820. 218 Vols. H.0.42. Continuation of series in State Paper Office listed above (341).

356. GEORGE IV, AND LATER, CORRESPONDENCE 1820-1861. 55 bundles H.O. 44.

357. ENTRY BOOKS 1782-1898. 206 Vols. H.0.43. Entries of the domestic out-letters.

358. MILITARY CORRESPONDENCE 1782-1840. 462 Vols. H.0.50. Original correspondence from the Commander in Chief, the Secretary at War and other military departments relating to internal defence, with lists of commissions, etc in the Militia and Volunteers.

359. MILITARY ENTRY BOOKS 1758-1855. 194 Vols. H.0.51. Entries of commissions, appointments, warrants, out-letters etc relating to the Militia, Volunteers, Yeomanry and Ordnance.

360. ENTRY BOOKS VARIOUS - FEES, SERIES I 1782-1880. 22 Vols. H.0.88. Includes entries of fees paid for military commissions.

361. ------------------- PRECEDENTS. VICTORIA 1 Vol. H.O. 96. Contains a few examples of army commissions.

362. IRELAND - CORRESPONDENCE 1782-1851. 263 Vols. H.O. 100. Correspondence and papers on military affairs included.

363. ------- GENERAL LETTER BOOKS 1782-1871. 24 Vols. H.O. 122. Includes out-letters relating to military affairs.

364. ------- MISCELLANEOUS ENTRY BOOKS 1768-1877. 32 Vols. H.O. 123. Entry books of military commissions.

Paymaster General's Office

Papers of the Paymaster general, and of his predecessor (before 1835) for the army: the paymaster general of the forces.

365. ARMY ESTABLISHMENT-LETTERS 1784-1867. 115 Vols. P.M.G.1. Indexed.

366. ------------------ LEDGERS 1757-1840. 227 Vols. P.M.G.2.

367. ARMY SERVICES - ESTIMATES 1756-1766, 1807-1820. P.M.G.60. 3 Vols.

See also, P.M.G. 3 to P.M.G. 14, P.M.G. 33 to P.M.G. 36, for material on pensions and half-pay.

Treasury

368. TREASURY BOARD PAPERS 1557-1920. 12,625 Vols. T.I.

369. OUT LETTERS VARIOUS 1763-1885. 113 Vols. T.28. Included are letters to the Secretary for War, 1796-1856, and to the war departments, 1849-1856. 3 Vols.

370. OUT LETTERS-WAR DEPARTMENTS 1855-1920. 63 Vols. T.24.

371. DEPARTMENTAL ACCOUNTS 1558-1881. 825 Vols. T.38. Includes miscellaneous accounts, estimates of wars, 1685-1795.

372. VARIOUS. 1547-1874. 401 Vols. T.64. Includes a section on the army, 1685-1485: reports of the Controllers of army accounts, miscellaneous reports and lists.

(b) Printed

373. CALENDAR OF STATE PAPERS, DOMESTIC, CHARLES II 1660-1685. 28 Vols. 1860-1947.

374. --------------------------------. JAMES II 1685-1689. 3 Vols. 1960-72.

375. --------------------------------. WILLIAM III. 1689-1702. 11 Vols. 1896-1937.

376. --------------------------------. ANNE. 1702-1704. 2 Vols. 1916-25. In progress.

377. --------------------------------. HOME OFFICE PAPERS GEORGE III. 1760-1775. 4 Vols. 1878-99.

378. CALENDAR OF STATE PAPERS, COLONIAL 1513-1738. 44 Vols.
1860-1969. Mainly consists of the records for America
and the West Indies, which have reached the year 1738.

379. CALENDAR OF TREASURY PAPERS. 1557-1728. 6 Vols. 1868-89.

380. CALENDAR OF TREASURY BOOKS 1660-1718. 32 Vols. 1904-58.

381. CALENDAR OF TREASURY BOOKS AND PAPERS. 1729-1745 5 Vols.
1898-1903.

382. CALENDAR OF STATE PAPERS RELATING TO IRELAND CHARLES II
1660-1670. 4 Vols. 1905-11. From 1670 the State Papers
relating to Ireland are included in the Calendar of state
papers, domestic, the various volumes of which are listed
above in this section.

10.   PARLIAMENTARY PAPERS

Below is a select list of parliamentary papers consisting
mainly of the reports of some of the more important royal
commissions and select committees. Also listed are some
departmental committees established by the Secretary of State
for war, although the numerous more specialized parliamentary
accounts and papers, mainly consisting of factual statements,
are not noted here. The papers are listed in chronological
order of publication. The date of publication is followed by
the command, volume and page numbers. No separate reference
is made here to other records of Parliament and apart from
such obvious items as Hansard's editions of parliamentary
debates, and the Journals of the House, reference should be
made to the guides and bibliographies listed above. See also
(744).

383. REPORT FROM THE SELECT COMMITTEE appointed to consider
the state of his majesty's land forces and marines. 1746.
1st Series. Vol. II. p.73. An important source for
the eighteenth century army, particular useful for
regimental financial arrangements and the clothing
system.

384. REPORT FROM THE SELECT COMMITTEE, to whom it was referred
to consider and examine the accounts of extraordinary
services incurred and paid, and not provided for by
Parliament, which have been laid before the House of
Commons in the year 1776, 1777, and 1778. 1778. Provides
much information on provision contracts and the
victualling system.

385. REPORTS FROM THE COMMISSIONERS OF ACCOUNTS 1780–1787. 15 reports printed in the Commons Journal, Vols. 38–42. Useful for the administration of the army.

386. REPORTS OF THE COMMISSIONERS OF MILITARY INQUIRY into the management of the military department, and into the means of preventing abuses therein. 1806–1816. 19 reports and general index. A major source of information on the administration of the army, and its efficacy.

387. MINUTES OF EVIDENCE taken before the committee of the whole house appointed to investigate the conduct of H.R.H. the duke of York the Commander in Chief, with regard to promotions, exchanges, and appointments to commissions in the army and staff of the army, and in raising levies for the army. 1809 (20) Vol. II. 1. The enquiry resulted in the resignation of the duke of York.

388. MINUTES OF EVIDENCE taken before the committee of the whole house appointed to consider the policy and conduct of the late expedition to the Scheldt. 1810 (12). Vol. VIII. 1.

389. REPORT FROM THE SELECT COMMITTEE appointed to inquire into the establishment of the garrisons, of pay and emoluments of general and staff officers, and into the emolument of naval officers holding the appointments of vice and rear-admirals of the United Kingdom, or of generals and colonels of marines, and whether any or what reduction or alteration can be made in them without detriment to the public service. 1833. (650) Vol. VII. 1. The pay and promotion of the army examined in the light of demands for reduction in military expenditure.

390. REPORT FROM THE SELECT COMMITTEE appointed to inquire into the military establishment and expenditures of the British empire in the colonies. 1834 (570) Vol. VII. 1. Second report from the same committee: 1835. (473) Vol. VI. 1.

391. REPORT OF THE COMMISSIONERS for inquiry into the system of military punishments in the army. 1836 (59) Vol.XXII. 1. Useful evidence contained in this report which generally upheld the status quo.

392. REPORT FROM COMMISSIONERS appointed to inquire into
the practicability and expediency of consolidating the
different departments connected with the civil administration of the army. 1837. (78) Vol. XXXIV. Part I, 1.
Under the chairmanship of Earl Grey (then Lord Howick)
it recommended the centralization of the civil
administration of the army. Much information is provided
on that subject.

393. REPORT OF COMMISSIONERS for inquiry into naval and
military promotion and retirement. 1840 (235) Vol. XXII.
1. This commission was largely constituted to attempt to
devise some means of alleviating the stagnation of
promotion in the services because of the long period of
peace

394. FIRST REPORT FROM THE SELECT COMMITTEE on army and
ordnance expenditure. 1849 (277) Vol. IX. 1. This report,
and the second,(1849 (499) Vol. IX. 5) deal with the
ordnance. Subsequent reports, in 1850 (622) Vol. X.1.
and 1851 (564) Vol. VII.735 are concerned with the army.
Useful information on the central organization of the
army, and finance.

395. REPORT ON THE DISCIPLINE and management of military
prisons. 1849. (1110) Vol. XXVI. 303; 1850. (1241) Vol.
XXIX. 35; 1851 (1411) Vol. XXVIII 333; 1852 (1522) Vol.
XXIV. 449.

396. REPORT OF THE COMMISSIONERS appointed to inquire into
the several modes of promotion and retirement in the
army. 1854 (1802) Vol. XIX. 833.

397. REPORTS OF THE SELECT COMMITTEE on the army before
Sebastapol. First report 1854-5 (86) Vol IX Pt. I.
1. Second report, Ibid (156) Vol. IX Pt. I. 7. Third
report Ibid. (218) Vol. IX Pt. II. 1. Fourth report
Ibid. (247) Vol. IX Pt. III. 1. Fifth report, Ibid.
(318) Vol. IX Pt. III. 365 Index Ibid. (318) Vol. IX
Pt. III 431. The inquiry was established as a result of
public concern and radical agitation over the breakdown
of the army in the Crimea. Known as the Roebuck
committee it sat in almost continuous session for four
months in 1855, and produced a report highly critical
of the administration of Lord Aberdeen.

398. REPORT OF THE SELECT COMMITTEE on the Royal Military
College, Sandhurst. 1854-55. (317) Vol. XII. 311. A
major source for the history of Sandhurst from the end
of the Napoleonic wars.

399. **REPORT FROM AN OFFICIAL COMMITTEE** on barrack accommodation for the army. 1854-5 (405) Vol. XXXII. 37.

400. REPORT FROM THE SELECT COMMITTEE appointed on the medical department of the army. 1856 (331) Vol. XIII. 359.

401. REPORT OF THE COMMISSION OF INQUIRY into the supplies of the British army in the Crimea. 1856 (2007) Vol. XX 1.

402. REPORT OF THE BOARD OF GENERAL OFFICERS appointed to inquire into the statements contained in the reports of Sir John McNeill and Col. Tulloch, and evidence taken by them relative thereto, animadverting upon the conduct of certain officers on the general staff and others in the army. 1856 (2119) Vol. XXI. 1. See also Sir Alexander Murray Tulloch, The Crimean commission and the Chelsea board: being a review of the proceedings and report of the board. 1857.

403. REPORT ADDRESSED TO THE SECRETARY OF STATE FOR WAR on foreign military education.1856 (406) Vol. XL. 455. A survey of officer education in the major European states.

404. REPORTS OF COMMISSIONERS appointed by the Secretary of State for War on re-organizing the system for training officers for the Scientific Corps; with an account of foreign and other military education. 1857 (sess. 1) (52) Vol. VI. 1. 555.

405. REPORT OF COMMISSIONERS appointed to inquire into the system of purchase and sale of commissions in the army. 1857 (sess.2) (2267) Vol. XVIII. 1. Minority report: 1857-8 (2292) Vol. XIX. 233. A number of documents illustrating the history of the purchase system are in the appendix to the main report.

406. REPORT OF THE COMMISSIONERS appointed to inquire into the regulations affecting the sanitary condition of the army, the organization of military hospitals, and the treatment of the sick and wounded. 1857-8 (2318) Vol. XVIII. 1.

407. REPORT OF THE COMMISSIONERS appointed to inquire into the question of promotion and retirement in the higher ranks of the army commencing with the rank of major. 1857-8 (2418) Vol. XIX. 241.

408. REPORT OF THE COMMISSIONERS appointed to inquire into
the organization of the Indian army. 1859 (2515) Vol.
V. 1. Inquired into the changes revealed to be
needed following the Mutiny.

409. REPORT FROM THE SELECT COMMITTEE on military organization. 1860 (441) Vol. VII. 1. The minutes of evidence
are a valuable source of information. The commission,
under Sir James Graham, examined especially the relationship between the secretary for war and the commander-in-
chief.

410. REPORT OF THE COMMISSIONERS appointed to inquire into
the present system of recruiting in the army. 1861 (2762)
Vol. XV. 1. Established to attempt to resolve the long
standing problem of obtaining an adequate supply of
soldiers in peacetime.

411. ROYAL COMMISSION on the condition of the volunteer
force in Great Britain. 1862 (3035) Vol. XXVII.

412. REPORT OF THE COMMITTEE appointed to inquire into the
condition as to provision, pay and allowances of the
regimental quartermasters of Her Majesty's service.
1865 (123) Vol. XXXII. 617.

413. REPORT FROM THE SELECT COMMITTEE on the system of retirement from the three non-purchase corps of Royal artillery,
engineers and marines. 1867 (482) Vol. VII. 1. Appointed
to devise methods of improving the rate of promotion in
these corps where it was notoriously slow.

414. REPORT OF THE SELECT COMMITTEE appointed to inquire into
the duties performed by the British army in India and the
colonies. 1867 (478) Vol. VII. 199; Further report:
1867-8. (197) Vol. VI. 789.

415. REPORT FROM THE SELECT COMMITTEE on military reserve funds.
1867 (453) Vol. VII. 713; Further report 1867-8 (298)
Vol. VI. 809. Two reports on what was considered by some
to be a particularly iniquitous feature of the purchase
system.

416. REPORT OF THE COMMISSIONERS appointed to inquire into the
recruiting for the army. 1867 (3752) Vol. XV. 1.

417. ROYAL COMMISSION on courts-martial and military punishments. 1868-9 (4114) Vol. XII.

418. FIRST REPORT OF THE ROYAL COMMISSION on the present
     state of military education, and training of candidates
     for commissions. 1868-9 (4221) Vol. XXII. 1. Minutes of
     evidence: 1870 (25) (251) Vol. XXIV. 1. 585. Second
     report: 1870 (214) *Ibid*. 701.

419. REPORT OF A COMMITTEE appointed to inquire into the
     arrangements in force for the conduct of business in the
     army departments. 1870 (54) Vol. XII. 1. The reorgan-
     ization of the War Office, and the allocation of overall
     responsibility for army business to the secretary for war
     followed the committee's report.

420. REPORT OF COMMISSIONERS appointed to inquire into over
     regulation payments on promotion in the army. 1870 (201)
     Vol. XII. 199. An inquiry into the illegal and covert
     aspects of the sale of officers' commissions.

421. REPORT OF COMMITTEE appointed to inquire into the
     promotion and retirement of the officers of the Ordnance
     corps. 1870 (206) Vol. XII. 611.

422. REPORT OF A COMMITTEE on the education of artillery
     officers. 1871 (258) Vol. XIV. 1.

423. REPORT TO THE SECRETARY OF STATE FOR WAR on army agency.
     1871 (391) Vol. XXXIX. 13. Provides useful information
     on the officially recognized functions of the army agent.

424. REPORT OF ROYAL COMMISSION on the supersession of colonels
     of the British army. 1871 (276) Vol. XXXIX. 827. The
     career prospects of British and Indian army colonels are
     examined.

425. REPORT OF A COMMITTEE on the organization of the various
     military land forces of the country. 1872 (493). Vol.
     XXXVII. 386.

426. REPORT OF THE ADJUTANT GENERAL upon the organization of
     the Royal artillery. 1872 (561) Vol. XIV. 69.

427. REPORT OF THE COMMISSIONERS appointed to inquire into
     certain memorials from officers in the army in reference
     to the abolition of purchase. 1874 (1018) Vol. XII. 1.
     The commission considered the injustices claimed to have
     arisen from the abolition of purchase.

428. REPORT OF THE ROYAL COMMISSION on army promotion and
     retirement. 1876 (1569) Vol. XV. 77. The commission's
     basic instruction was to refine and improve the system of
     promotion devised to replace the purchase system.

429. REPORT OF THE COMMITTEE appointed to enquire into
the subject of boys' enlistment appointed by the
Secretary of State for War. 1877 (1677) Vol.XVIII.
1.

430. REPORT OF THE COMMITTEE appointed by the Secretary
of State for War to enquire into certain questions that
have arisen with respect to the militia and the present
brigade depot system. 1877 (1654). Vol. XVIII. 29.

431. REPORT FROM THE SELECT COMMITTEE on mutiny and marine
mutiny acts and into the law relating to those acts . . .
1878 (316) Vol. X. 253.

432. REPORT OF THE COMMITTEE on the pay, promotion, and the
conditions of service and retirement of officers of the
ordnance corps. 1881. (2816) Vol. XX. 41.

433. REPORT OF THE COMMITTEE appointed by the Secretary of
State for War to consider the conditions of a soldier's
service, as affected by the introduction of the short
service system and other matters in connection therewith.
1881. (2817) Vol.XX. 343. Recommended changes in the
short service system and localization scheme.

434. REPORT OF COMMITTEE on the formation of territorial
units as proposed by Colonel Stanley's committee. 1881.
(2793) Vol.XX 367.

435. REPORT OF A COMMITTEE of general and other officers of
the army on army reorganization. 1881 (2791) Vol.XXI. 1.

436. REPORT AND OTHER DOCUMENTS relating to army organization.
1881. (2792) Vol.XXI. 1.

437. REPORT OF COMMITTEE on artillery localization. 1882.
(3168) Vol. XVI. 1.

438. REPORT of the cavalry organization committee. 1882 (3167)
Vol. XVI. 15.

439. REPORT OF THE COMMITTEE on the organization of the Royal
artillery. 1888 (5491) Vol. XXV. 207.

440. REPORT OF THE COMMITTEE appointed to inquire into the
pay, status, and conditions of service, of medical officers of the army and navy. 1889. (5810) Vol.XVII 137.

441. PRELIMINARY AND FURTHER REPORTS of the Royal Commission appointed to inquire into the civil and professional administration of the naval and military departments and the relation of those departments to each other and to the Treasury. 1890 (5979) Vol.XIX. 1. The Royal Commission, under the chairmanship of Lord Hartington, recommended major reforms in army administration.

442. REPORT OF COMMITTEE appointed by the Secretary of State for War to consider the terms and conditions of service in the army. 1892   (6582) Vol. XIX.1. Known as the Wantage report, it advocated conscription if other measures to obtain an adequate supply of recruits failed.

443. REPORT OF THE COMMITTEE appointed to enquire into the entrance examinations (in non military subjects) of candidates for commissions in the army. 1894 (7373) Vol. XIX. 1.

444. REPORT OF A COMMITTEE appointed by the Secretary of State for War to consider the decentralization of War Office business. 1898 (8934) Vol. XIII. 123.

445. REPORT OF THE COMMITTEE appointed to enquire into War Office organization. 1901.   (580)Vol.XI. 179. Evidence. 1901. (581) 207. Recommended changes proved necessary by events connected with the South African war.

446. REPORT OF THE COMMITTEE APPOINTED to consider the education and training of officers of the army. 1902. (982) Vol.X. 93. Provides some of the reasons for the continuing lack of professionalism among the bulk of the officers of the army.

447. REPORT OF THE COMMITTEE appointed by the Secretary of State to consider the reorganization of the army medical services. 1902 (791). Vol. X. 131.

448. REPORT OF THE COMMITTEE appointed by the Secretary of State for War to inquire into the nature of the expenses incurred by officers of the army, and to suggest measures for bringing commissions within reach of men of moderate means. 1903. (1421) Vol. X. 535.Gives valuable detailed information on the levels of private income needed by officers in various branches of the army.

449. REPORT OF THE COMMISSIONERS appointed to inquire into
     the military preparations and other matters connected
     with the war in South Africa. 1904. (1789) Vol. XL. 1.
     Evidence Vol. I: 1904 (1790) Ibid. 325. Vol. II: (1791)
     XLI. 1. Appendices (1792) XLII. 1. A long report, with
     a mass of evidence, on some of the reasons for the poor
     performance of the army in the Boer war.

450. REPORT OF THE WAR OFFICE RECONSTITUTION COMMITTEE 1904
     (1932) Vol. VIII, 101; (1968) Ibid. 121; (2002) Ibid.
     157. The Esher Committee, as it was called, was
     established to devise a reformed organizational structure
     at the War Office, taking the Admiralty system of higher
     administration as the basis of its investigation. Its
     three reports were of profound importance, and the
     committee established the basic elements of War Office
     organization and the general staff, which have existed
     ever since.

451. REPORT OF THE WAR OFFICE COMMITTEE on promotion to
     colonel and general. 1906. (2995) Vol. LXVII. 419.

452. INTERIM REPORT OF THE WAR OFFICE COMMITTEE on the
     provision of officers for service with the regular army
     in war and for the auxiliary forces. 1907. (3294). Vol.
     XLIX. 549.

11.   HISTORICAL MANUSCRIPTS COMMISSION REPORTS

     The reports published by the Historical Manuscripts
Commission since 1870 on a wide number of manuscripts in the
possession of private owners and corporate bodies contain
much material relating to the history of the army. Little
material has so far been published, however, which is of
value for the period after 1815.

     The earliest reports give few details of the particular
collections inspected, beyond a very general description of the
fields they cover and their main use is indicating the existence
of particular sources. For various reasons, after the publication of the first few reports, the appendices to the
Commissioners' Reports to the Crown, which contained the reports
to the Commissioners by the Inspectors whom they employed, began
to contain more detailed accounts of the contents of the collections. From 1885, these appendices were issued separately
from the reports, although they were still considered as
attached to the particular report which had given a general
description of their contents. Some of these appendices cover a
number of collections while others relate to a single collection
only. From this period information may be found which can be
used without reference to the originals, although in many cases

all that is provided is an indication of where the information may be found. Since 1900 the Inspectors' reports have been issued separately rather than as appendices to the commissioners' reports, and since then they have become full abstracts, giving all the more important documents verbatim so that access to the originals is unnecessary.

There is no complete guide to the reports. The most useful are listed below, as are the few articles relating to the material on the army contained in the reports.

(a)   Guides

453. HISTORICAL MANUSCRIPTS COMMISSION. INDEX. Part I. Topographical. 1914. A selective index down to 1911.

454. -- Part II. Persons. 2 Vols. 1935-8.

455. GUIDE TO THE REPORTS OF THE HISTORICAL MANUSCRIPTS COMMISSION. 1911-1957. Ed. by A.C.S.Hall. 3 Vols. 1966.

456. ROBERTS, R.A. The reports of the Historical Manuscripts Commission. 1920.

457. ATKINSON, C.T. 'Material for military history in the reports of the Historical Manuscripts Commission'. J.S.A.H.R. Vol. XXI no. 81, spring 1942, 17-34. The only index of its kind, particularly valuable for students of regimental history.

458. ------- 'The Chequers Court MSS. Some extracts relating to the Foot Guards, 1742-48'. Ibid. Vol. XXIII no. 95, autumn 1945, 114-118. From the letters of Col. Charles Russell.

459. OMAN, SIR C.W.C. 'Book review - supplementary report on the manuscripts of Robert Graham of Fintry'. Ed. by C.T. Atkinson. Ibid. Vol. XXII no. 85, spring 1943, 36-7.

(b)   The reports

The following list indicates the more important reference to the army to be found in the reports, but it is not intended to be a comprehensive guide. The list is in alphabetical order of the title of the collection on which a report has been published. The number of the report is indicated by an arabic numeral immediately after the title of the collection: parts of reports are indicated by roman numerals. Following the arabic numeral is the serial number: volumes relating to one collection are grouped together by the Commission under the same serial number.

460. ABERGAVENNY MSS. 10 VI, 15. Letters to Lord North during the American war of Independence.

461. AILESBURY MSS. 15 VII, 43 A few letters relating to the early part of the Napoleonic wars.

462. ANCASTER MSS. ————, 66. For material on King William's Campaigns, 1692-4, see pp 422-6.

463. ATHOLL MSS. 12 VIII, 26. Contains account by Lord Orkney of the battle of Blenheim. For earlier references to King William's campaigns, see pp. 37-44, 48, 53.

464. BAGOT, J.F., MSS. 10 IV, 13. References to British troops in France, 1674 (p.328) and to Blenheim (p.337) and Ramillies (p.340).

465. BATH MSS. —————, I,II, and III, 58. An important source containing letters to and from Marlborough, as well as material on several other wars.

466. BATHURST. MSS. —————,76. Contains inter alia, the letters of Henry, 3rd Earl Bathurst Secretary for War 1812-27, and as such is an invaluable source for the period of the Napoleonic wars, and after.

467. BEAUFORT MSS. 4—, 3 ; 12 IX, 27. For the letters of Sir W. Lockhart from France, see Vol. I pp. 237 ff.

468. BRAYBROOKE MSS. 8—, 7. A number of letters of Lord Cornwallis, 1779-1781 are noted, but not reproduced verbatim.

469. BUCCLEUCH MSS. (Drumlanrig Castle). 15 VIII, 44. See Vol. II, pp. 77 et. seq. for Monmouth's rising, and pp. 264-297 for some letters of John Graham of Claverhouse, Viscount Dundee.

470. BUCCLEUCH MSS. (Montagu House). —————, 45. An important source, (Vols. I-II) containing information on the major wars up to the mid-eighteenth century.

471. BUCKINGHAMSHIRE MSS. 14 IX, 38. For material on the War of Austrian succession see pp. 85-151 and for the Forty Five, pp. 130-146.

472. CAMPBELL, SIR H. HUME, MSS. 14 III, 34. An account of Sheriffmuir, in the 'Fifteen is in the collection, and reproduced in this report.

473. CHARLEMONT MSS. 12 X, 28. See Vol. I, for some letters,
particularly those of Lord Pembroke, during the Seven
Years' War.

474. CLEMENTS, M.L. MSS. Var. Coll. VIII, 55. A few letters
concerning Marlborough's campaign in Flanders are printed
in this report. More important is the order book of
British forces in northern Germany, 1758-9 on pp. 418-568.

475. COWPER MSS. 12 I, II, III, 23. Contains a number of
letters from regimental officers who served in the army
during the War of Spanish Succession.

476. DARTMOUTH MSS. 11V, 14II, and 15I, 20. A major source
containing information on Monmouth's rising, the
revolution of 1668, the American War of independence and
the Mahratta war, 1779. Also includes the duke of
Ormonde's correspondence, 1712.

477. DE LA WARR MSS. 4—, 3. Includes Lord G. Sackville's
letters, 1745-6.

478. DENBIGH MSS. ——,68. A few letters on the revolution
of 1688, and the war of Austrian succession.

479. DE ROS MSS. 4—, 3. See letters relating to the army
in Ireland (pp.317 et. seq.).

480. DONOUGMORE MSS. 12 IX, 27. Some material on the relief
of Gibraltar, 1782.

481. DOWNSHIRE MSS. ——, 75. Vol. I important for the
period to 1714.

482. DU CANE MSS. ——, 61. Some material on the Forty
Five and the Seven Years War.

483. EGMONT MSS. ——, 63. A few letters, including one
from Marlborough on the conduct of the war.

484. ELPHINSTONE MSS. 9—8. Letters of Lord Moira, 1814-1817.

485. FINCH, A.G. MSS. ——, 71. Letters of Sir R. Southwell,
1690: the army in Ireland.

486. FITZHERBERT, SIR W. MSS. 13 VI. 32. Useful material for
the Forty-Five.

487. FLEETWOOD-WESTON-UNDERWOOD MSS. 10I, 10. See for the
Forty Five and the Seven Years' War.

488. FORTESCUE, J.B. MSS. 13I, 14V, 30. An important source
of background information for the period 1793-1815: the
letters of the Grenville family.

489. FRANKLAND-RUSSELL-ASTLEY, MRS, MSS. ------.52. Contains
the important collection of letters of Col. Charles
Russell written during the war of Austrian succession.
See also, (458) above. The papers reported on here are
also known as the Chequers Court MSS.

490. GRAHAM, SIR F. MSS. 7--, 6. For the period up to 1688.

491. GRAHAM, R. MSS. -----, 81. Much useful material on
the campaign in the Peninsula, and the Netherlands
1813-14.

492. HARE, T.J. MSS. 14 IX, 38. Contains some letters of
Archdeacon Hare, Marlborough's chaplain-general in the
Blenheim campaign and after.

493. HASTINGS, R. RAWDON, MSS. -----,78. Vol. III, Lord
Rawdon's letters during service in America, 1775-6. See
the same volume for his letters (as Lord Moira) during
the Napoleonic Wars.

494. HODGKIN, J.E. MSS. 15 II, 39. Some information on the
period before 1714.

495. HOME, COL. MILNE, MSS. -----,57. Letters on Minden, and
Warburg.

496. KENYON MSS. 14 IV, 35. Letters on the Forty Five.

497. KETTON, R.W. MSS. 121X, 27. Letters on the war of
Spanish succession (pp. 198 et.seq.).

498. KNOX, CAPT. H.V., MSS. Var. Coll. VI, 55. Useful for
the American war of Independence.

499. LAING MSS. -----,72. Vol. II useful for the Forty Five
(pp. 352 et.seq.) and the American war of Independence
(pp. 470-1, 491, 495-7).

500. LE FLEMING, S.H. MSS. 12 VII, 25. An important source
for the period before 1714. See, inter alia, pp. 152-6
for the British in the Netherlands, 1678; pp. 203-231
for the revolution of 1688, and pp. 234-327 for news-
letters with information on the army in Ireland.

501. LEYBORNE-POPHAM, F.W., MSS. -----,51. Some material on
the wars of William III in Ireland.

502. LONSDALE MSS. 13 VIII, 33. See for Peninsula war letters
on pp. 23, 244.

503. LORDS, HOUSE OF, MSS. 11 II, 12 VI, 13V, 14 VI, 17; <u>Independent Series</u>, Vols. I-VIII. Important for the wars of William III and Queen Anne, and includes the report of, and numerous documents presented to, the committee which investigated the campaigns of Lord Peterborough in Spain. (Vol. VII N.S.)

504. LOTHIAN MSS. ———, 62. See for letters relating to the American War of independence. pp. 295 <u>et.seq.</u>, and esp. 396-410, and for miscellaneous references to the army.

505. MAR AND KELLIE MSS. ———, 60. Marlborough's campaigns in 1702, 1706 and 1708.

506. MENZIES, SIR R. MSS. 6—, 5. Includes some Letters of Major-General Hugh Mackay 1689-90. (pp.700-2) Commander in Chief of the forces in Scotland.

507. MORRISON,A., MSS. 9 VIII, 8. Some letters from Lord Peterborough in Spain (pp. 467-8).

508. NORTHUMBERLAND MSS. 3—, 2. Useful for Monmouth's rising, pp. 96-9.

509. ORMONDE MSS. 7—, 6. 14 VII, 36; ———36. A collection of importance for the period down to 1713: there is much information on regiments in Ireland between 1660-1713.

510. PALK MSS. ———, 74. See for the Mysore War in India, 1767-1770.

511. POLWARTH MSS. ———, 67. See for the 'Fifteen and Glenshiel.

512. PORTLAND MSS. 13I and II, 14 II, 15 IV, 29. See for Monmouth's rising, the wars of William and Anne. Particularly useful are the letters from 1705 of Col. James Cranstoun of the Cameronians published in this series. See also Vol. X of the Portland MSS. for a 'Calendar of military papers' pp. 61-95.

513. ROYAL INSTITUTION MSS. ———, 59. Summaries of many documents relating to the War of American Independence: the headquarters papers of British Commanders in chief in America 1775-82.

514. RUTLAND MSS. 12 II, V, 14I, 24. Volume II contains many letters of Lord Granby.

515. SACKVILLE, MRS. STOPFORD, MSS. ------.49. An important
collection with information on Monmouth's rising and
the Seven year's war, and letters from Lord George
Sackville on the war of the Austrian succession.

516. SOMERSET MSS. 15 VII, 43. The campaign in Spain during
the War of Spanish succession.

517. STIRLING-HOME-DRUMMOND-MORAY MSS. 10 I, 10. Miscellaneous
letters relating to military affairs in Scotland.

518. SUTHERLAND MSS. 5--, 4. Includes letters of Cornelius
Wood, 3rd Dragoon Guards, 1706-9.

519. TOWNSHEND MSS. 11 IV, 12. See for letters relating to
the War of Spanish succession.

520. WOOD, HON. F.L. MSS. Var. Coll. 8---, 55. Material on
recruiting in Queen Anne's reign, and the Jacobite
rebellions.

521. WYKEHAM-MARTIN, C. MSS. Var. Coll. 6---,55. Contains
letters of Lord Cornwallis.

2.   JOURNALS AND PERIODICALS

522. ADMIRALTY AND HORSE GUARDS GAZETTE. Weekly. 1884-1901.

523. AMERICAN HISTORICAL REVIEW. American Historical Assoc.
N.Y. 1895+. Quarterly. Regular lists of articles dealing with English history are published.

524. THE ANNUAL REGISTER: a review of public events at home
and abroad. 1758+.

525. ARMY AND NAVY GAZETTE. 1860-1921. Weekly. An important
newspaper with conservative viewpoint.

526. ARMY AND NAVY MAGAZINE. 1880-1888. Then merged in the
United Service Magazine listed below (564).

527. ARMY AND NAVY REGISTER AND WOOLWICH GAZETTE. 1841-1855.

528. ARMY QUARTERLY. 1920+. Index Vols. 1-100 1920-1970.
1970. Many historical articles, of varied quality.

529. THE ARMY REVIEW. 1911-1914.

530. BROAD ARROW. 1868–1917. Weekly. Written from a liberal viewpoint at least in its early years. Merged with the Army and Navy Gazette in April, 1917.

531. BRITISH MILITARY LIBRARY OR JOURNAL, comprehending a complete body of military knowledge, 1799–1801. An early periodical with many valuable articles.

532. BULLETIN OF THE INSTITUTE OF HISTORICAL RESEARCH. 1923+. Three times a year. Publishes information on the location of MSS. and summaries of theses, in addition to articles and documents.

533. BULLETIN OF THE MILITARY HISTORICAL SOCIETY. 1950+. Specialist articles usually published, often on uniforms and equipment.

534. CANADIAN HISTORICAL REVIEW. Toronto. 1920+. Occasional articles of interest.

535. THE ECONOMIST. 1843+. Weekly. Useful articles on the army throughout the nineteenth century.

536. ENGLISH HISTORICAL REVIEW. 1886+. Quarterly. Index. Useful documents and review articles have appeared relating to the army.

537. FIGHTING FORCES. 1924+. Relevant material sometimes published.

538. GENTLEMAN'S MAGAZINE 1731–1907. Monthly. Contains useful biographical information on lesser known officers.

539. GUNNER: official organ of the Royal Artillery association. Woolwich. 1919+.

540. HISTORICAL JOURNAL. Camb. 1957+. Known as the Cambridge Historical Journal, 1925–1956.

541. HISTORY: the quarterly journal of the Historical Assoc. 1916+.

542. HISTORY TODAY. 1951+. Monthly. Often contains relevant illustrated articles.

543. ILLUSTRATED NAVAL AND MILITARY MAGAZINE. 1884–1890.

544. IRISH SWORD: the journal of the Military History Society of Ireland. Dublin. 1949/50+.

545. JOURNAL OF BRITISH STUDIES. Hertford, Conn. 1961+. Published by the Conference on British Studies.

546. JOURNAL OF THE ROYAL ARTILLERY. Woolwich. 1858+.
    Quarterly. See, Index of subjects and authors, 1940-
    1959 Vols. 67-86.

547. JOURNAL OF THE ROYAL UNITED SERVICE INSTITUTION. 1857+.
    Originally published monthly, but now quarterly. See,
    Robin Higham and K.C. Wing eds. The consolidated author
    and subject index to the journal of the Royal United
    Service Institution, 1857-1933. Ann Arbor. 1964. The
    J.R.U.S.I. was known as the United Service Institution
    Journal, between 1857-59. Mainly valuable now for
    reviews of new books, as there have been few historical
    articles published in recent years.

548. JOURNAL OF THE SOCIETY FOR ARMY HISTORICAL RESEARCH.
    1921+. Quarterly. General Index to Vols. 1-XL, 1921-
    1962. 1969. An indispensable work of reference for all
    concerned with the history of the army: particularly
    useful for articles on uniforms and equipment.

549. MILITARY AFFAIRS: journal of the American Military
    Institute. Washington. 1937+. Vols. 1-2 published as
    the Journal of the American Military History Foundation
    and Vols. 3-4 as the Journal of the American Military
    Institute.

550. MINUTES OF PROCEEDINGS OF THE ROYAL ARTILLERY INSTITUTION.
    1858-1905. Continued as Journal of the Royal Artillery,
    (546).

551. NATIONAL DEFENCE. 1908-12.

552. NATIONAL SERVICE JOURNAL. 1903-7. Continued as Nation
    In Arms. 1907-14.

553. NAVAL AND MILITARY GAZETTE 1833-1886. Merged in the
    Broad Arrow (530).

554. NAVAL AND MILITARY MAGAZINE. 1827-1828. Continued as the
    United Service Magazine (564).

555. NAVAL AND MILITARY RECORD. 1886-1936.

556. NOTES AND QUERIES. 1849+.Weekly. Contains much useful
    miscellaneous information. Each series of this publicat-
    ion has been indexed.

557. PROCEEDINGS OF THE UNITED SERVICE INSTITUTION OF INDIA
    1873-8. Renamed, Journal of the United Service Institut-
    ion of India, 1878+.

558. RECENT PUBLICATIONS OF MILITARY INTEREST. 1907–1911.
Continued by the _Army Review_, listed above.

559. ROYAL ENGINEERS JOURNAL. 1879–1911.

560. ROYAL MILITARY CHRONICLE, or, the British Officer's
monthly register, chronicle and military mentor.
1810–1817.

561. SCOTTISH HISTORICAL REVIEW. Glasgow. 1903–1928, 1947+.
Quarterly. Not published 1928–1947.

562. SOLDIER: THE BRITISH ARMY MAGAZINE. 1945+. Popular
publication, with some useful reviews and articles.

563. TRANSACTIONS, ROYAL HISTORICAL SOCIETY LONDON. 1869+
Annual.

564. UNITED SERVICE MAGAZINE. 1829–1920.Monthly. Published
as _United Service journal_,1829–1843; as _Colburn's United
Service Magazine_, 1843–1890; and _United Service
Magazine_, 1890–1920. In 1920 it was incorporated in
the _Army Quarterly_, listed above. An invaluable source
for determining the evolution of military thought, and
there are many historical articles particularly in the
later period.

565. VICTORIAN STUDIES. Bloomington, Ind. 1957+. Useful
bibliographical notes are included.

PART III   ORGANIZATION, MANAGEMENT, AND PERSONNEL

13.   ORGANIZATION OF THE ARMY.

(a)   Central administration and institutions

566. ALLEN, F.S. The supreme command in England, 1640-1780.
     N.Y. 1966. This inadequately researched and ill-written
     short work indicates an area where further investigation
     is urgently needed.

567. ---------. 'Towards a theory of civil-military control
     in England, 1670-80'. J.S.A.H.R. Vol. XL no. 162,
     June 1962, 95-102. Some of the material here was
     incorporated in his book listed immediately above.

568. ANDERSON, OLIVE. 'The role of the army in parliamentary
     management during the American War of Independence'.
     Ibid. Vol. XXXIV. no. 140, December 1956, 146-9.
     Discusses the influence of the army in parliamentary
     decision making.

569. BAKER, NORMAN. The Treasury administration of contracts
     for the supply of the British armies in North America
     and the West Indies, 1775-83. University of London.
     Unpublished Ph. D. thesis. 1967.

570. ---------. 'The Treasury and open contracting 1778-1782'.
     H.J. Vol. XV, September 1972, 433-54.

571. BOUGHEY, JOHN. The elements of military administration
     and military law. 1874.

572. BROOMFIELD, J.H. 'Some hundred unreasonable parliament
     men. A study of military representation in the eighteenth
     century British parliament'. J.S.A.H.R. Vol. XXXXI no.
     158, June 1961, 91-102. Army officers as M.P.s, their
     role and influence.

573. BURTON, I.F. 'The Committee of Council at the War Office:
     an experiment in cabinet government under Anne'. H.J. Vol.
     IV, 1961, 78-84.

574. ---------. The Secretary at War and the administration
     of the army during the war of the Spanish Succession.
     University of London. Unpublished Ph. D. thesis. 1960.
     Identifies changes in military administration produced
     by the exigencies of war.

575. BUXTON, J.W. The elements of military administration.
     Pt. I - Permanent system of administration. Ed. by Col.
     C.B. Brackenbury. 1883.

576. CAILLARD, MAURICE. 'The War Office fifty years ago'. **A.Q.** Vol. LXXI no. 1, October 1955, 56-63. Personal reminiscences and history of the War Office in the late nineteenth century.

577. CALLWELL, SIR CHARLES EDWARD. 'War Office reminiscences'. **Blackwood's Mag.** Vol. CXC no. mcl, August 1911, 154-70. A rare and interesting account of life and work in various branches of the War Office from the 1880's.

578. CORBETT, SIR J.S. 'Queen Anne's defence committee'. **Monthly Rev.** 1904, 55-65.

579. DE WATTEVILLE, H.G. 'The commander-in-chief of the army'. **A.Q.** Vol. XXXVII no. 1, October 1938, 57-66. The story of the abolition of the office.

580. D'OMBRAIN, NICHOLAS. War machinery and high policy: defence administration in peacetime Britain, 1902-1914. Oxf. 1973. Discusses the major reforms introduced following the Boer war.

581. 'E and OE'. 'How the army lost its commander-in-chief'. **A.Q.** Vol. XXXVI no. 2, July 1938, 310-13. Gives some of the reasons for the abolition of the post in 1904, and the retirement of its last incumbent, Lord Roberts.

582. EHRMAN, JOHN. Cabinet government and war, 189-1940. Camb. 1958. The story of the development of new institutional structures to meet changing needs of defence with some earlier historical material.

583. ELLISON, SIR GERALD. 'Army administration'. **A.Q.** Vol.III no. 1, January 1922, 9-22. A summary from Cromwell's time.

584. GOOCH, JOHN. The plans of war. The general staff and British military strategy c. 1900-1916. 1974. The first scholarly survey of the role of the general staff.

585. GORDON, HAMPDEN. The War Office. 1935. A narrative account which is more a survey of the development of the army than a history of the War Office. There is a complete list of secretaries for war for the period from 1794 when the office was first created.

586. GREENLEAF, W.H. 'The commission of military enquiry 1805-12'. **J.S.A.H.R.** Vol. XLI no. 168, December 1963, 171-181. The background to the protracted enquiry into the operation of British army administration during the Napoleonic wars. See (386) above for the reports.

587. HALIBURTON, ARTHUR LAWRENCE, LORD Army administration
in three centuries. 1901. Written under the pseudonym
'Constitutionalist'.

588. HAMER, W.S. The British army: civil-military relations,
1885-1905. Oxf. 1970. A scholarly account of higher
central administration of the army, civil and military.
There is a full bibliography.

589. HOGG, O.F.G. 'Forerunners of the army council'.
J.S.A.H.R. Vol. XI no.43, July 1932, 101-48. Early
policy-making bodies of the army, and their membership.

590. HUNTINGTON, S.P. The soldier and the State. Camb.,
Mass. 1957. Includes some material on England, while
expounding his rather controversial theory of civil-
military relations.

591. JOHNSON, F.A. Defence by committee; the British committee
of Imperial Defence, 1885-1959. 1960. The standard account, with a lengthy bibliography.

592. JONES, K.R. 'Cox and Co: army agents Craig's Court: the
nineteenth century'. J.S.A.H.R. Vol. XL no. 164, December
1962, 178-86. The foremost army agents of the period.

593. KIER, SIR DAVID LINDSAY. Constitutional history of
modern Britain. 1935. See pp. 304-6 for a summary of
administration of the eighteenth century army.

594. LESLIE, J.H. 'The honourable the board of Ordnance
1299-1855'. J.S.A.H.R. Vol. IV no. 17, July-September
1925, 100-4.   The first of a series of articles
due to have been published but which did not appear.
Continued by Hogg's article listed above in this section.

595. MACKINTOSH, J.P. 'The role of the C.I.D. before 1914'.
E.H.R. Vol. LXXVII. 1962, 490-503. The origin and early
role of the Committee of Imperial Defence.

596. OBSERVATIONS ON ARMY ADMINISTRATION. By a general officer.
1868.

597. OMOND, J.S. Parliament and the army. 1642-1904. Camb.
1933. A historical examining the changing relationship
between the Crown, parliament and the army.

598. SCOULLER, MAJOR R.E. 'Secretaries at War to Queen Anne'.
J.S.A.H.R. Vol. XXXVIII no. 153, March 1960, 3-10. Useful discussion of the early history of the office. See
also his article 'Queen Anne's Secretaries at War' A.Q.
Vol. LVII no.2, January 1949, 215-20.

599. SKENTELBERRY, N. A history of the Ordnance Board. 1968. A short official account.

600. STOCQUELER, J.H. A personal history of the Horse Guards from 1750 to 1872. 1873. A mainly anecdotal account, and as such valuable. It contains information not readily available elsewhere, and is highly readable.

601. SWEETMAN, JOHN. '"Chaos" A just description of British army administration before the Crimean War?' A.Q. Vol. LXXXXV no.2 January, 1968, 225-30.

602. TURNER, J.D. 'Army agency'. J.S.A.H.R. Vol. XIII no. 49, spring 1934, 27-37. A good short history of army agents, and their functions.

603. WHEELER, OWEN. The War Office past and present. 1914. The best account of its kind, but still only a superficial survey of a subject which needs much more research.

604. WILLIAMSON, JOHN. A treatise on military finance; containing the pay, subsistence, deductions, and arrears, of the forces on the British and Irish establishments... with an enquiry into the method of clothing and recruiting the army. 1782. The most useful work of its kind, outside parliamentary reports.

(b)   Military law

    See also the works on punishment listed below (929) (933) (941) and (952).

605. ADYE, S.P. A treatise on courts martial, to which is added an essay on military punishments and rewards. 1769.

606. BENNETT, R.W. 'Military law in 1839'. J.S.A.H.R. Vol. XLVIII no. 196, winter 1970, 225-241. Extracts from an interesting work by Lieut. General Sir George C. D'Aguilar Observations on the practice and the forms of courts martial and courts of enquiry etc., first published in 1839.

607. BRUCE, ALEXANDER. The institution of military law, ancient and modern; wherein the most material questions and cases relating to martial discipline are fully examined and cleared from the principles of civil Law. Edin. 1717. An important early text which distinguishes between military and civil law.

608. BULLOCK, H. 'The Judge Advocate'. A.Q. Vol. XVIII no. 2. July 1929, 369-73. The origin of the office.

609. BURKE, PETER. Celebrated naval and military trials. 1876. See especially the chapters entitled 'Soldiers and civilians in the service of William III' and 'Lord George Sackville', and the material on Sir Robert Wilson.

610. CLODE, CHARLES MATTHEW. The administration of justice under military and martial law. 1872. Fully documented.

611. ————. The statutes relating to the War Office and to the army. 1880.

612. DESCRIPTIONS OF COURTS MARTIAL and Articles of War in several European countries to 1586 and a bibliography 1532-1746. P.R.O. W.O. 93/6. In MSS.

613. FINLASON, W.F. Treatise upon military law, as allowed by the law of England, in time of rebellion: with practical illustrations drawn from the official documents in the Jamaica case and the evidence taken by the Royal Commission of Inquiry, with comments, constitutional and legal. 1866.

614. FORD, ARTHUR. A concise text book on military law. Woolwich. 1875.

615. GORHAM, C.A. Textbook of military law as applicable to persons subject to the Army Discipline Act; to which is added military law as applicable to persons subject to the Indian articles of war. 1880.

616. GUNTER, EDWARD. Outlines of military law and customs of war, with new tables and examples. 1897.

617. HOUGH, WILLIAM. Military law authorities. Chronological exposition of the opinions of the several writers on military law. 1839.

618. ————. Precedents in military law: including the practice of courts martial; the mode of conducting trials: and the duties of officers at military courts of inquests, courts of inquiry, courts of requests, etc. 1855. A standard reference work.

619. ————. The practice of courts martial, also the legal exposition and military explanation of the mutiny act and articles of war. 1834.

620. LATHBURY, D.C. 'Military courts-martial'. Home and Foreign Rev. Vol. IV, January 1864, 19-37.

621. MANUAL OF MILITARY LAW. War Office 1914. 1914. First published in 1884, it was the first comprehensive official guide to military law. Apart from the detailed rules of procedure contained in Part II, there are a number of more general chapters on various aspects of military law, including its history, and on the evolution of the military forces of the crown. There is a useful short bibliography.

622. McARTHUR, JOHN. Principles and practice of naval and military courts martial, with an appendix illustrative of the subject 2 Vols. 1806.

623. THE MILITARY LAW OF ENGLAND, with all the principal authorities, adapted to the general use of the army, in its various duties and relations, and the practice of courts martial. 1810.

624. PRATT. S.C. Military law, its procedure and practice. 1910. rev.edn.

625. SCOTT, ROBERT BISSET. The military law of England with all the principal authorities adapted to the general use of the army, in its various duties and relations, and the practice of courts-martial. 1810. Includes an appendix of precedents.

626. SCOULLER, MAJOR R.E. 'The mutiny acts'. J.S.A.H.R. Vol. L no. 201, spring 1972, 42-5. Between 1689 and 1713.

627. SIMMONS, THOMAS FREDERICK. Remarks on the constitution and practice of courts martial; with a summary of the law of evidence, as connected with such courts; also some notice of the criminal law of England, with reference to the hundred and second article of war. 1830. In the absence until 1884 of an official guide to military law, this book was regarded as the standard text on courts-martial, and much of it was incorporated into the official War Office manual listed above.

628. STUART-SMITH, JAMES. 'Military law: its history, administration and practice'. Law Quarterly Rev. Vol. 85, October 1969, 478-504. A short introduction to the subject, mainly on the modern period, but with a historical background.

629. SULLIVAN, R.G. Thoughts on martial law, with a mode recommended for conducting the proceedings of general courts martial. 1784.

630. TOVEY, R.E. Military law, with a chapter on the military law of foreign states. Chatham. 1887.

631. TULLOCH, SIR ALEXANDER BRUCE. Elementary lectures
on military law. 1873.

632. TURNER, SIR JAMES. Pallas armata: military essays of
the ancient and modern art of war. 1683. Describes the
articles of war, and courts-martial.

633. TYTLER, A.F. An essay on military law and the practice
of courts martial. Edin. 1800.

(c) Military education

No comprehensive single volume survey of the development
of military education in England has yet been produced.

634. BARNETT, CORELLI. 'The education of military elites'.
Journal of Contemporary History. Vol. II. no. 3, July
1967, 15-35. Higher education of the upper echelons
of the officer corps in France and Germany as well as
England.

635. BENSON, R.H.R. 'Military College of Science'. Journal
of the R.A. Vol. LX1. no.1, April 1934, 1-11. Includes
remarks on the Military Society of Woolwich, founded 1772.

636. BOND, BRIAN. The Victorian army and the Staff College
1858-1914. 1972. A scholarly account of the Staff
College, and its impact on the performance in the army,
based on a wide range of MS. sources.

637. BOWYER-BOWER, T.A. 'Some early educational influences in
the British Army'. J.S.A.H.R. Vol. XXXIII no. 133,
spring 1955, 3-11. From Cromwell to the Napoleonic wars.

638. THE BRITISH ARMY: or the present system of education for
officers. 1884.

639. BUCHANAN-DUNLOP, H.D. Records of the Royal Military
Academy, 1741-1892. 1893. A useful early history of
'The Shop'.

640. DE ROS, W.L.L.F.,LORD. Remarks on the new examination
system for the army. 1859. A critical review of changes
introduced following the Crimean debacle.

641. FITZGERALD, LUCAS. 'The making of Sandhurst, the Royal
Military College, in 1812'. U.S.M. Vol. CLXIX. 1914,
299-309. Documents are included.

642. GOODWIN-AUSTEN, MAJOR A.R. The Staff and the Staff
College. 1927. Not entirely superseded by Bond's work
noted above (636) as it contains a mass of material and
anecdotes not found elsewhere. There is a bibliography.

643. GUGGISBERG, F.G.   'The shop': the story of the Royal
     Military Academy. 1900.

644. HARVEY, A.J.W. 'Army schools III.   The school of
     artillery' A.Q.   Vol. LXVIII no.2, July 1954, 198-208.
     One part of a series on the lesser known army educational
     institutions.

645. JONES, W.D.   Records of the Royal Military Academy,
     1741-1840. Woolwich. 1851.   From the foundation of the
     College in 1741.

646. LAMBERT, J.M. 'Army schools II. Past and present at the
     school of military engineering, Chatham.' A.Q. Vol.LXVIII
     no. 1, April 1954, 66-74.

647. LOCHEE, LEWIS.   An essay on military education. 1776.
     The author was master of the military academy, Little
     Chelsea, at the time this pamphlet was written.

648. MAGUIRE, T. MILLER. Military education in England. 1903.

649. MOCKLER-FERRYMAN, LIEUT COL. A.F.   Annals of Sandhurst:
     a chronicle of the Royal Military College from its
     foundation to the present day, with a sketch of the
     history of the Staff College. 1900.   Mainly personal
     records and registers.

650. NEWSOME, DAVID.   History of Wellington college. 1959.
     The definitive history.

651. OTLEY C.B. 'Public school and army'. New Society,
     17 November 1966, 754-7.   The connection between public
     schools and the officer corps, and the influence of the
     former on the values of the latter.

652. SMYTH, SIR JOHN.   Sandhurst.   The history of the Royal
     Military Academy, Woolwich, the Royal Military College,
     Sandhurst, and the Royal Military Academy, Sandhurst.
     1741-1961. 1961.   The best study available, although
     the definitive scholarly account of Sandhurst remains to
     be written.

653. SPERMAN, J.M.   Notes on military education. 1852.

654. THE STORY OF ARMY EDUCATION. 1946.   Includes notes on
     the Corps of Army Schoolmasters from 1846, and the Queen's
     Army Schoolmistresses.

655. THOMAS, HUGH.   The story of Sandhurst. 1961.   Not a very
     satisfactory study, based on a limited range of sources.

656. WARD, B,R. The school of military engineering, 1812–
1909. 1909.

657. WHITE, A.C.T. The story of army education, 1643–1963.
1963. The development of the education of the soldier
and the role of the Royal Army Education Corps. Only
the first two chapters deal with the period before 1914.

658. WILLIAMS, N.T. St.J. Tommy Atkins' children: the story
of the education of the army's children, 1675–1970. 1971.

659. YOUNG, F.W. The story of the Staff College. Camberley.
1958. A pamphlet produced for the centenary of the
College.

14. REGIMENTAL ORGANIZATION AND HISTORIES

(a) Regimental histories: general studies.

    See White (62), (63); Leslie (35); (67), under heading
'England army'. Useful lists are also in (74) and (77).

660. ADAM, FRANK. The clans, septs and regiments of the
Scottish highlands. Edin. 1965. new edn. One part is
devoted to the military forces of the highlands.

661. ADAMS, W.H.D. Famous regiments of the British army:
their origin and services. With a sketch of the rise
and progress of the military establishment of England
and brief memoirs of eminent British generals. 1864.
A narrative of the campaigns of the army, and the
regiments who served in them. The biographical sketches
are also of interest even if they do not make any
contribution to knowledge.

662. ATKINSON, C.T. 'Foreign regiments in the British army,
1793–1802'. J.S.A.H.R. Vol. XXI no.48, winter 1942, 175–
81; Vol. XXII no. 49, spring 1943, 2–14; no. 50, summer
1943, 45–52; no. 51, autumn 1943, 107–15; no. 52, winter
1943, 132–42; no.53 spring 1944, 187–97; no.54 summer 1944
234–50; no. 55, autumn 1944, 365–76; no. 56, winter 1944,
313–24. An important survey.

663. BALDRY, W.Y. and WHITE, A.S. 'Disbanded regiments'.
J.S.A.H.R. Vol. I. no. 3, March 1922, 90–2; no. 5, September 1922, 205–10. Articles on the 100th and 104th Foot.

664. BARNES, R.M. A history of the regiments and uniforms of the British army. 1950. An account of the history of the army through the achievements of the regiments. There are also a number of illustrations with full notes on the uniforms depicted.

665. ―――――― and ALLEN, C.K. The uniforms and history of the Scottish regiments. Britain ‑ Canada ‑ Australia‑ New Zealand ‑ South Africa 1625 to the present day. 1956. A valuable general history with appendices entitled 'abbreviated regimental histories'.

666. BRANDER, MICHAEL. The Scottish highlanders and their regiments. 1971. Popular, adding little new.

667. CANNON, RICHARD. Historical records of the British army, comprising the history of every regiment in His Majesty's service. 71 Vols. 1835‑53. The first attempt at regimental history on any scale, these volumes were compiled officially. Not always accurate, but often useful sources of information.

668. CAREW, TIM. How the regiments got their nicknames. 1969. A less serious military work, with illustrations.

669. CHICHESTER, H.M. and BURGES‑SHORT, GEORGE. The records and badges of every regiment and corps in the British army. 1895.repr. 1969. A summary of Cannon's Historical records, listed above.

670. DICKINSON, R.J. Life and customs in the regiments. Tunbridge Wells. 1973.

671. EDWARDS, T.J. 'The origin of British light infantry regiments'. A.Q. Vol. XXXII no. 2. July 1936, 300‑8; Vol. XXXIII no. 1, October 1936, 101‑8. This study and the article below have been largely superseded by the reference works now available on this subject.

672. ―――――――. 'The origin of existing British regiments and corps' Ibid. Vol. XXIX no.2, January 1935, 232‑45; Vol. XXX no.1, April 1935, 94‑106.

673. FAMOUS REGIMENTS. 1967+. Over fifty volumes giving concise histories of individual regiments have so far been published. Although of varying quality, they provide useful short introductions to regimental history. Authors and titles are not listed separately here.

674. FARMER, JOHN S.   The regimental records of the British army.   A historical resume chronologically arranged of the titles, campaigns, honours, uniforms, facings, badges, nicknames, etc. 1901.   Listed under individual regiments, and each regimental entry contains a bibliographical note.

675. FIRTH, SIR C.H. and DAVIES, GODFREY.   The regimental history of Cromwell's army.   2 Vols. Oxf. 1940.   An exhaustive guide, which gives much information necessary for an understanding of the later development of the standing army.

676. FREDERICK, J.B.M.   Lineage book of the British army. Mounted corps and infantry 1660-1968. N.Y. 1970.   A useful and accurate reference guide.

677. GRIFFITHS, ARTHUR.   Famous British regiments. 1900.

678. LAFFIN, JOHN.   Scotland the brave.   The story of the Scottish soldier. 1963.   A popular survey of the history of the Scottish regiments.

679. MACLENNAN, JOHN.   Scots of the line . . . an account of some heroes of the Scottish regiments. 1953.

680. MAXWELL, SIR HERBERT E.   ed.   The lowland Scots' regiments: their origin, character and services previous to the great war of 1914. Glasgow. 1918.   A number of essays on the lowland Scots regiments, and also on disbanded Scots regiments, and regimental music.

681. MURRAY, A.K.   History of the Scottish regiments in the British army. 1862.

682. PAUL, W.P.   History of the Scottish regiments. Glasgow 1960.

683. ───────.   The highland regiments: tigers in tartan. Aberdeen. 1971. Popular.

684. ───────.   The lowland regiments: lions rampart. Aberdeen. 1972.

685. RAFTER, MICHAEL.   The guards: or, the household troops of England. 1852.

686. RICHARDS, WALTER.   Her Majesty's army.   A descriptive account of the various regiments now comprising the Queens forces from their first establishment to the present time. 2 Vols. 1892.

687. ——————. Her Majesty's army. Indian and colonial forces. A descriptive account of the various regiments now comprising the Queen's forces in India and the colonies. 1892.

688. SEWELL, A.E. 'The extinct regiments of the British army'. J.R.U.S.I. Vol. XXXI, January 1887, 1-44. A valuable guide.

689. STEWART, CHARLES H. The service of British regiments in Canada and North America. Ottawa.1962. A systematic survey of regiments, their service in North America, and details of their principal actions.

690. SWINSON, ARTHUR. A register of the regiments and corps of the British army: the ancestry of the regiments and corps of the regular establishment. 1972. The standard scholarly work.

691. WHITE, A.S. 'The order of precedence of regiments' J.S.A.H.R. Vol. V no. 19, January-March 1926, 17-23.

692. YAPLE, R.L. 'The auxilaries: foreign and miscellaneous regiments in the British army 1802-1817' Ibid. Vol. L. no. 201, spring 1972, 10-28.

(b)   Branches of the army.

See also section 17.

Artillery.

693. KANE, JOHN. List of officers of the Royal regiment of artillery, as they stood in the year 1763 with a continuation to the present time. 1815.

694. FRAZER, COL. SIR AUGUSTUS SIMON. Remarks on the organization of the corps of artillery in the British service. 1818.

695. BROWNE, J.A. England's artillerymen. An historical narrative of the service of the Royal Artillery, from the formation of the regiment to the amalgamation of the Royal and Indian artilleries in 1862. 1865.

696. HEAD, SIR FRANCIS B. The Royal Engineer. 1869. Training and establishments of the Royal Engineers in the mid-nineteenth century.

697. DUNCAN, FRANCIS. History of the royal regiment of artillery compiled from the original records. 2 Vols. 1879. A valuable source, from earliest times, which contains much detail, and prints extracts from original documents.

698. CLEAVELAND COL. F.D. Notes on the early history of the Royal Regiment of Artillery. 1892. Covers the period down to 1757. Many important documents printed in full.

699. HIME, H.W.L. History of the Royal Regiment of Artillery, 1815-1853. 1908. Discusses, inter alia, the reductions after the Napoleonic wars, equipment, and war services. Part of the official history.

700. JOCELYN, J.R.J. The history of the Royal Artillery. 1911. The Royal Artillery in the Crimea period. It is a continuation of the volume by Hime listed above in this section.

701. CALLWELL, SIR CHARLES EDWARD AND HEADLAM, SIR JOHN. The history of the Royal Artillery from the Indian Mutiny to the Great War. 3 Vols. 1931-40. The standard history.

702. LAWS, M.E.S. 'Foreign artillery corps in the British service'. 'I the French Emigrant artillery'. '2 the Dutch immigrant artillery'. '3 The Royal foreign artillery' Journal of the R.A. Vol. LXV no. 3. October 1938, 356-67; Vol. LXXIII no. 3, July 1946, 250-60; Vol. LXXV no. 2, April 1948, 57-63.

703. HOBDAY, E.A.P. 'The history and traditions of the Royal Artillery'. Ibid. Vol. LXVIII no. 2, April 1941, 179-208. A useful summary.

704. LAWS, M.E.S. Battle records of the Royal artillery, 1716-1859. 1952. A standard reference work.

705. MAURICE-JONES, K.W. The history of the coast artillery in the British army. 1959.

706. HOGG, O.F.G. English artillery 1326-1714 being the history of artillery in this country prior to the formation of the Royal Regiment of Artillery. 1963. Supersedes Duncan for the period, and is the standard work.

CAVALRY.

707. NOLAN, LOUIS EDWARD. Cavalry: its history and tactics. 1853. An important work by a noted theorist on the role of the cavalry in war.

708. BAKER, VALENTINE. The British cavalry: with remarks
on its practical organization. 1858.

709. DENISON, GEORGE. A history of cavalry from the earliest
times with lessons for the future. 1877. A general
survey, not limited to England.

710. WOOD, SIR HENRY EVELYN.   Achievements of cavalry.
1897. The role of cavalry in various battles and
campaigns.

711. TYLDEN, GEOFFREY. 'Lancers'. J.S.A.H.R. Vol. XIII no.
94, summer 1945, 44-6. A short summary of their role,
not confined to England.

712. COOPER, LEONARD. British regular cavalry 1644-1914. 1965
A short popular account, useful because it is the only
work of its kind.

713. ROGERS, COL. H.C.B. The mounted troops of the British
army 1066-1945. 1967. A popular survey of the cavalry
in England.

714. ANGLESEY, MARQUESS OF. A history of the British cavalry
1816 to 1919. 2 Vols. 1973-5. The first two of four
planned volumes of what is likely to be the definitive
account of the role of the cavalry in the period it
considers. Full consideration is given to the organization and personnel of the cavalry, as well as to the many
campaigns in which it was involved.

    Engineers

715. CONSIDERATIONS ON THE ESTABLISHMENT OF THE BRITISH
ENGINEERS. 1768.

716. CONNOLLY, T.W.J. History of the Royal sappers and
miners. 2 Vols. 1855. An interesting early account by
the quartermaster sergeant of the corps, from its
formation in March, 1772.

717. PORTER, W. and WATSON, C.M. History of the corps of
the Royal engineers 3 Vols. 1889-1915. The standard
approved history.

    Infantry

718. STUART, H.B. A history of infantry from the earliest
times to the present. 1862.

719. LLOYD, E.M. A review of the history of infantry. 1908.
A standard account of its tactical role, which has not
been superseded.

720. FERRAR, M.L. 'The reorganization of the infantry of the line 1 July 1881.' J.S.A.H.R. Vol. X no. 40, October 1931, 208-10. Includes remarks on the facings which were adopted by the combined regiments.

Military chaplains.

721. DOW, A.C. Ministers to the soldiers of Scotland. A history of the military chaplains of Scotland prior to the war in the Crimea. 1962. Scholarly.

722. SMYTH, SIR JOHN. In this sign conquer: the story of the army chaplains. 1968. The only work of its kind, it is a useful summary.

Military medicine.

See the bibliographical essay by F.N.L. Poynter in R. Higham (30).

723. PRINGLE, JOHN. Observation on the diseases of the army in camp and garrison. 1752. A classic text by one of the founders of military medicine.

724. BROCKLESBY, RICHARD. Economical and medical observations on military hospitals and camp diseases. 1764.

725. MONRO, DONALD. Observation on the means of preserving the health of soldiers and of conducting military hospitals. 1769.

726. SINNOTT, N. Observations, tending to show the mismanagement of the medical department of the army. 1796.

727. NIGHTINGALE, FLORENCE. Notes on matters affecting the health efficiency, and hospital administration of the British army founded chiefly on the experience of the late war. 1858.

728. PARKES, E.A. A manual of practical hygiene prepared especially for use in the medical service of the army. 1864. Parkes was the first Professor of Hygiene at the Army Medical School which was established as a result of Florence Nightingale's efforts.

729. GORE, A.A. The story of our services under the crown. A historical sketch of the army medical staff. 1879. Reprinted from Colburn's United Service Magazine.

730. GARRISON, F.H. Notes on the history of military medicine. Wash. 1922. A general survey.

731. STEWART, DAVID. 'Military surgeons in the sixteenth and seventeenth centuries'. <u>J.S.A.H.R</u>. Vol. XXVI no. 108, winter 1948, 151-7. The pay and conditions of military medical officers.

732. LOVEGROVE, PETER. Not least in the crusade. A short history of the Royal Army Medical Corps. Aldershot. 1951. A brief illustrated account.

733. HAY, IAN. One hundred years of army nursing. 1953. A history of British army nursing services from the time of Florence Nightingale.

734. LAFFIN, JOHN. Surgeons in the field. 1970. A popular general account, with much material on Britain.

Military music

See also (47)

735. FARMER, HENRY GEORGE. Memoirs of the Royal Artillery band, its origins, history and progress. An account of the rise of military music in England. 1904. Farmer pioneered the study of military music in England.

736. ----------. The rise and development of military music. 1912. A general history.

737. FFOULKES, CHRISTOPHER. 'Notes on early military bands'. <u>J.S.A.H.R</u>. Vol. XVII no. 68, winter 1938, 188-200. A fine short survey from earliest times until the eighteenth century.

738. FARMER, HENRY GEORGE. 'The Royal Artillery band. Fresh light on its history'. <u>Ibid</u>. Vol. XXIII no. 95, autumn 1945, 90-7.

739. ----------. Military music. 1950. A simple short introduction.

740. ----------. History of the Royal Artillery band, 1762-1953. 1954. A completely rewritten account adding much new material to the history originally published under a different title in 1904.

741. BURNS, P.L. A hundred years of military music being the story of the Royal Military School of Music, Kneller Hall. Gillingham, Dorset. 1959.

742. FARMER, HENRY GEORGE. 'Bands in the Crimean War. A criticism of a blunder'. <u>Ibid</u>. Vol. XLI no. 165, spring 1963, 19-26.

743. WINSTOCK, LEWIS. Songs and music of the redcoats.
A history of the war music of the British army, 1642-
1902. 1970. The best modern account.

Transport, ordnance and supply.

744. REPORT OF A COMMITTEE on the administration of the
transport and supply depots of the army. 1867.
(3848) Vol. XV. 343.

745. FORBES, ARTHUR. A history of the army ordnance
services. 3 Vols. 1929. The official account.

746. FORTESCUE, HON. SIR J.W. and BEADON, CAPT. R.H. The
Royal army service corps: a history of supply and
transport in the British army. 2 Vols. Camb. 1930-1.
Vol. II covers the period from the Boer war.

747. WHITEHEAD, ALAN. 'The development of British military
transport'. Fighting Forces Vol. XXV no. 1, April
1948, 50-2.

748. HOGG, O.F.G. The Royal arsenal: its background,
origin and subsequent history. 2 Vols. 1963. The fully
documented definitive history, not likely to be replaced.

749. RYAN, ERNEST. 'Army horse transport: general service,
ambulance, and other vehicles from the Crimean war to
mechanization'. J.S.A.H.R. Vol. XLII no. 171,
September 1964, 121-131.

Volunteer forces

750. AN EXAMINATION of all the statutes respecting the
volunteers; in which the appointment of the officers,
the right to resign, and their exemptions and obligations
are fully considered. 1804.

751. HAY, COL. GEORGE JACKSON. An epitomized history of the
militia ('the constitutional force') together with the
origins, periods of embodied service, and special
services (including South Africa 1899-1902) of militia
units existing October 31, 1905. 1906. A history from
earliest times, with many useful references.

752. SEBAG-MONTEFIORE, CECIL. A history of the volunteer
forces from the earliest times to the year 1860, being
a recital of the citizen duty. 1908.

753. RICHARDS, WALTER. His Majesty's territorial army. A descriptive account of the yeomanry, artillery, engineers and infantry, with the army service and medical corps, comprising "The King's Imperial army of the second line". 4 Vols. 1910-11. Brief accounts of the regiments and corps.

754. BALDRY, W.Y. 'Order of precedence of militia regiments'. J.S.A.H.R. Vol. XV no. 57, spring 1936, 5-16.

755. TEICHMAN, O. 'The yeomanry as an aid to civil power, 1795-1867' J.S.A.H.R. Vol. XIX no. 74, summer 1940, 75-91; no. 75, autumn 1940, 127-43. A pioneering scholarly study.

756. VIGMAN, F.K. 'A 1745 plan for a national militia in Great Britain and America'. American Military Institute Jour. Vol. IX no. 4, winter 1945, 355-60.

757. McANALLY, SIR HERY. The Irish militia, 1793-1816. A social and military study. 1949. A standard work, with a valuable bibliography.

758. ROSE, BARRIE. 'The volunteers of 1859'. J.S.A.H.R. Vol. XXXVII no. 151. September 1959, 97-110. A study of the volunteer movement.

759. WESTERN, J.R. The English militia in the eighteenth century. The story of a political issue, 1660-1802. 1965. A fully documented study, and a major contribution to the subject.

760. McGUFFIE, T.H. 'The Lord Bradford militia documents in the Shirehall, Shrewsbury, Salop'. J.S.A.H.R. Vol. XLIV no. 179, September 1966, 135-46. A large collection dealing mainly with the period 1803-1820.

761. COUSINS, GEOFFREY. The defenders: a history of the British volunteer. 1968.

762. WILLIAMS, G. Citizen soldiers of the Royal engineers transportation and movements and of the R.A.S.C. 1859-1965. Aldershot, 1969.

(c)   Regimental histories.

A field with a vast literature, very varied in character. Included here is a selection of the standard authorities, with some of the more important articles; for other works, including the many short accounts written for a wider audience, see the bibliographies listed above, particularly that by A.S. White (63).

763. BEAMISH, N. LUDLOW. History of the King's German Legion. 2 Vols. 1832.

764. PACKE, E. An historical record of the Royal Regiment of Horse Guards or Oxford Blues. 1834. In the series by Cannon, but not officially compiled.

765. CADELL, CHARLES. Narrative of the campaigns of the 28th regiment since their return from Egypt in 1802. 1835.

766. MACKINNON, DANIEL. Origin and services of the Coldstream Guards. 2 Vols. 1835.

767. HIGGINS, R.T. ed. The records of the King's Own Borderers, or old Edinburgh regiment. 1873. The fullest account available for the period before 1914.

768. HAMILTON, SIR F.W. The origin and history of the First or Grenadier Guards. 3 Vols. 1874.

769. NOAKES, GEORGE. A historical account of the services of the 34th and 55th regiments, the linked battalions in the 2nd or Cumberland and Westmorland Sub-District Brigade, from the periods of the formation until the present time. Carlisle. 1875.

770. BRODIGAN, FRANCIS. Historical records of the 28th North Gloucestershire regiment, from 1692 to 1882. 1884.

771. THE HISTORY OF THE SECOND, Queen's Royal Regiment, now the Queen's (Royal West Surrey) regiment. Vols. 1-6 by John Davies. Vol. 7 by H.C. Wylly. 7 Vols. 1887-1925.

772. EVERARD, H.E.E. History of Thos. Farrington's regiment, subsequently designated the 29th (Worcestershire) Foot, 1694 to 1891. 1891. Uses MS. material.

773. LIDDELL, R.S. The memoirs of the tenth Royal Hussars (Prince of Wales's Own). Historical and social. 1891.

774. SWINEY, G.C. Historical records of the 32nd (Cornwall) Light Infantry, now the 1st Battalion Duke of Cornwall's Light Infantry, from the formation of the regiment in 1702 down to 1892. 1893.

775. O'DONNELL, H. Historical records of the 14th regiment now the Prince of Wales's Own (West Yorkshire Regiment) from its formation in 1685 to 1892. 1893.

776. WOOLLRIGHT, H.H. History of the 57th (West Middlesex) regiment of Foot 1755-1851. 1893.

777. FORTESCUE, HON. SIR J.W. A history of the 17th Lancers
     (duke of Cambridge's Own). 1895. Based mainly on
     external evidence as almost all the early records have
     been destroyed.

778. FYLER, A.E. The history of the 50th or (the Queen's
     Own) regiment from the earliest date to the year 1881.
     1895.

779. FORBES, ARCHIBALD. The 'Black Watch'. The record of
     an historic regiment. 1896.

780. BIDDULPH, COL. JOHN. The nineteenth and their times;
     being an account of the four cavalry regiments in the
     British army that have borne the number nineteen and
     of the campaigns in which they served. 1899.

781. GARDYNE, C. GREENHILL. The life of a regiment: the
     history of the Gordon Highlanders from its formation
     in 1794 to 1816. 1901. Three further volumes by the
     same author carry the history down to 1914. 1903-1929.
     There are long extracts from regimental and War Office
     records.

782. HISTORICAL RECORD OF THE 14th (KING'S) HUSSARS FROM AD
     1715 to AD 1900. By Col. H.B. Hamilton. Vol II (1900-
     1922) by J.G. Browne and E.J. Bridges. 1901-1932.

783. FALKINER, C.L. 'Irish guards 1661-1798'. Proc. Royal
     Irish Academy Vol. XXIV 1902-4, 7-30.

784. GROVES, PERCY Historical record of the 7th or Royal
     Regiment of Fusiliers, now known as the Royal Fusiliers
     (the City of London regiment) 1685-1903. Guernsey. 1903.

785. HENNELL, SIR REGINALD. The history of the King's body
     guard of the Yeoman of the Guard . . . the oldest
     permanent body guard of the sovereigns of England,
     1485 to 1904. 1904.

786. HISTORICAL RECORDS OF THE BUFFS, East Kent regiment,
     3rd Foot, formerly designated the Holland regiment and
     Prince George of Denmark's regiment. 1572-1914. Vol. I
     (1572 - 1704) by H.R. Knight; Vol. II by C.R.B. Knight
     (2 pts) 1905-35.

787. WOOLLRIGHT, H.H. Records of the Seventy-Seventh (East
     Middlesex), the duke of Cambridge's Own regiment of Foot,
     now the second battalion the duke of Cambridge's Own
     (Middlesex regiment). 1907.

788. ALMACK, EDWARD. The history of the second dragoons
'Royal Scots Greys'. 1908.

789. WILLIAMS, TREVELYAN. The historical records of the
11th Hussars, Prince Albert's Own. 1908.

790. ARTHUR, SIR GEORGE. The story of the Household Cavalry.
2 Vols. 1909

791. HISTORICAL RECORDS OF THE QUEEN'S OWN CAMERON HIGHLANDERS.
7 Vols. Edin. 1909-61.

792. JACKSON, E.S. The Inniskilling Dragoons. The records
of an old heavy cavalry regiment. 1909.

793. BARRETT, C.R.B. History of the XIII Hussars. 2 Vols.
Edin. 1911.

794. THE CAMPAIGNS AND HISTORY OF THE ROYAL IRISH REGIMENT
from 1684 to 1902, by G. le M. Gretton, Edin. 1911.
See also Vol. II by S. Geoghegan for the period 1910-
1922. Edin. 1927.

795. FERRAR, M.L. A history of the services of the 19th
regiment, now Alexandra, Princess of Wales' Own
(Yorkshire regiment) from its formation in 1688 ... 1911.

796. LEE, ALBERT. The history of the Tenth Foot (the
Lincolnshire regiment). 2 Vols. Aldershot.1911.

797. WEBB, E.A.H. A history of the 17th (the Leicestershire)
regiment, containing an account of the formation of the
regiment in 1688, and of its subsequent services. 1911.

798. GRAHAM, HENRY. History of the Sixteenth, the Queen's
Light Dragoons (Lancers), 1759 to 1912. Devizes.1912.

799. VERNER, W.W.C. History and campaigns of the Rifle
Brigade. 2 Vols. 1912-19. A fine, but unfinished study
covering the period 1800-13.

800. BULLOCH, J.M. The Gordon Highlanders. The history of
their origin together with a transcript of the first
official muster. Banff.1913. The muster was in 1793.

801. BUTLER, LEWIS. et.al. The annals of the King's Royal
Rifle Corps. 4 Vols. 1913-29. One of the finest regimental histories, it is scholarly and has many valuable
appendices. See also the separately published, Appendix
dealing with uniform, armament, and equipment, by S.M.
Milne and A. Terry. 1913.

802. BARRETT, C.R.B.   The 7th (Queen's Own) Hussars.   2 Vols.
1914.

803. LAURIE, G.B.   History of the Royal Irish Rifles.   1914.

804. WEBB, E.A.H.   History of the 12th (The Suffolk)
regiment, 1685-1913.   Including a brief history of the
east or west Suffolk militia, the latter being now the
3rd battalion the Suffolk regiment.   1914.

805. WYLLY, H.C.   XVth (the King's) Hussars, 1759 to 1913.
1914.

806. LEASK, J.C. and McCANCE, H.M.   The regimental records
of the Royal Scots (the first or the Royal Regiment of
Foot).   Dublin.   1915.

807. NEWBOLT, SIR HENRY.   The story of the Oxfordshire and
Buckinghamshire Light Infantry (the old 43rd and 52nd
regiments).   1915.

808. PURDON, H.G.   A historical sketch of the 64th (Second
Staffordshire) regiment and of the campaigns through
which they passed.   1915.

809. PEARSE, H.W.   History of the 31st Foot, Huntingdonshire
regiment - 70th Foot, Surrey regiment, subsequently first
and second battalions the East Surrey regiment.   1916.
Vol. I covers the period 1702-1914.

810. WALKER, H.M.   A history of the Northumberland Fusiliers
1674-1902.   1919.

811. ANDERSON, W.H.   The history of the Twenty Second Cheshire
regiment 1689-1849.   1920.

812. CARY, A.D.L. and McCANCE, S.   Regimental records of the
Royal Welch Fusiliers (late the 23rd Foot).   2 Vols.
1921-3.   Covers the period 1689-1914.

813. KINGSFORD, C.L.   The story of the Royal Warwickshire
regiment formerly the Sixth Foot.   1921.

814. LEE, ALBERT.   History of the Thirty-third Foot, Duke of
Wellington's (West Riding) regiment.   Norwich.   1922.

815. BANNATYNE, NEIL.   History of the Thirtieth regiment, now
the first battalion East Lancashire regiment 1689-1881.
Liverpool.   1923.

816. CAPE, J.R. The history of the 5th (Royal Irish)
     Regiment of Dragoons from 1689 to 1799, afterwards the
     5th Royal Irish Lancers from 1858 to 1921. Aldershot.
     1923.

817. JONES, J.P. A history of the South Staffordshire
     Regiment (1705-1923).1923.

818. WYLLY, H.C. History of the Manchester regiment (late
     the 63rd and 96th Foot).2 Vols. 1923-5.

819. FIELD, COL. CYRIL. Britain's sea soldiers: a history
     of the Royal Marines and their predecessors and of
     their services in action, ashore and afloat, and upon
     sundry other occasions of moment. 2 Vols. Liverpool.
     1924. The standard, fully documented, account, useful
     for the period down to 1755, when the marines were
     reconstituted under the Admiralty.

820. JOURDAIN, H.F.N. and FRASER, EDWARD. The Connaught
     Rangers. 3 Vols. 1924.

821. PETRE, F.L. The history of the Norfolk regiment, 1685-
     1918. 2 Vols. 1924.

822. POMEROY, HON. R.L. The story of a regiment of horse;
     being the regimental history from 1685 to 1922 of the
     5th Princess Charlotte of Wales' dragoon guards. 2 Vols.
     Edin. 1924.

823. BUCHAN, JOHN. The history of the Royal Scots Fusiliers
     1678-1918. 1925.

824. PETRE, F.L. The Royal Berkshire regiment (Princess
     Charlotte of Wales') 49th-66th Foot. 2 Vols. Reading.
     1925.

825. WYLLY, H.C. History of the King's own Yorkshire light
     infantry. 2 Vols. 1926.

826. AUBREY-FLETCHER, H.L. A history of the Foot Guards to
     1856. 1927.

827. BRUCE, C.D. History of the Duke of Wellington's
     regiment (first and second battalions) 1881-1923. 1927.

828. McCANCE, S. History of the Royal Munster Fusiliers.
     2 Vols. Aldershot. 1927.

829. MURRAY, R.H. The history of the VIII Kings Royal Irish
     Hussars, 1693-1927. 2 Vols. 1928.

830. THE ROYAL INNISKILLING FUSILIERS, being the history of the regiment from December 1688 to July 1914. 1928.

831. WHITTON, F.E. A short history of the Prince of Wales's volunteers (South Lancashire). Aldershot.1928.

832. HALL, SIR JOHN. The Coldstream Guards 1885-1914. Oxf. 1929.

833. WYLLY,H.C. History of the 1st and 2nd battalions the Sherwood Foresters Nottinghamshire and Derbyshire regiment 1740-1914. 45th Foot. - 95th Foot. 2 Vols. Frome. 1929.

834. WHYTE, FREDERIC and ATTERIDGE, A.H.A. History of the Queen's Bays (the 2nd dragoon guards) 1685-1929. 1930.

835. WYLLY, H.C. The York and Lancaster regiment 1758-1919 65th Foot - 84th Foot. 2 Vols. 1930.

836. MAURICE, SIR FREDERICK. The 16th Foot. A history of the Bedfordshire and Hertfordshire regiment. 1931.

837. WHITEHOUSE, A.C. The history of the Welch regiment. Cardiff. 1932. Vol. I covers the period 1719-1914.

838. WYLLY, H.C. The Royal North Lancashire regiment. 2 Vols. 1933.

839. HILLS, R.J.T. A short history of the Life guards. Aldershot. 1933.

840. ATKINSON, C.T. History of the Royal Dragoons.Glasgow. 1934.

841. EVERETT, SIR. H. The history of the Somerset Light Infantry (Prince Albert's) 1685-1914. 1934.

842. MAURICE, SIR FREDERICK. The history of the Scots guards from the creation of the regiment to the eve of the great war. 2 Vols. 1934.

843. GURNEY, RUSSELL. History of the Northamptonshire regiment, 1742-1934. 1935.

844. LUMLEY, L.R. History of the Eleventh Hussars (Prince Alberts Own) 1908-1934. 1936.

845. ATKINSON, C.T. The South Wales Borderers 24th Foot 1689-1937. Camb. 1937.

846. COWPER, L.I. The King's Own. The story of a royal regiment. 2 Vols. Oxf. 1939. A scholarly study.

847. SHEPPARD, E.W. The Ninth Queen's royal lancers 1715-1936. Aldershot. 1939.

848. ATKINSON, C.T. The Dorsetshire regiment the Thirty Ninth and Fifty fourth and the Dorset Militia and Volunteers. 2 Vols. Oxf. 1947.

849. STEWART, P.T. The history of the XII Royal Lancers (Prince of Wales's). Oxf. 1950.

850. ATKINSON, C.T. Regimental history the Royal Hampshire regiment 2 Vols. Glasgow. 1950-2. Makes full use of official military records.

851. DANIELL, DAVID SCOTT. Cap of honour. The story of the Gloucestershire regiment (the 28th/61st Foot) 1694-1950. 1951. A good clear summary.

852. TAYLOR, J. The Devons. A history of the Devonshire regiment. 1685-1945. Bristol. 1951.

853. CUNLIFFE, MARCUS. The Royal Irish fusiliers 1793-1950. Oxf. 1952. A scholarly survey.

854. OATTS, L.B. Proud heritage. The story of the Highland light infantry. 3 Vols. 1953-61. A well written account from the raising of the first battalion in 1777.

855. MARTINEAU, G.D. A history of the Royal Sussex regiment: a history of the old Belfast regiment and the regiment of Sussex 1701-1953. Chichester.1955.

856. McGUFFIE, T.H. 'The short life and sudden death of an English regiment of foot. An account of the raising, recruiting, mutiny and disbandment of the 113th regiment of Foot, or 'Royal Birmingham Volunteers' (April, 1794 to September, 1795)'. J.S.A.H.R. Vol. XXXIII no. 133, spring 1955, 16-25; no. 134, summer 1955, 48-55. Based on the extant records of the regiment.

857. CROOKENDEN, ARTHUR. Twenty second footsteps, 1849-1914; an account of life in the 22nd (Cheshire) regiment in those years. 1956.

858. THE HISTORY OF THE CAMERONIANS (Scottish Rifles) 26th and 90th. 1689-1933.2 Vols. 1957-61. Vol. I by S.H.F. Johnston and Vol. II by Col. H.H. Story.

859. JONES, R.J. A history of the 15th (East Yorkshire) regiment (the Duke of York's Own) 1685 to 1914. Beverley. 1958.

860. CHAPLIN, H.D. The Queen's Own Royal West Kent Regiment. 1881-1914. Maidstone. 1959.

861. DANIELL, D.S. 4th. Hussar: the story of the Queen's Own Hussars, 1685-1958. Aldershot. 1959.

862. McGUFFIE, T.H. 'The life of a light cavalry regiment. A report on the Anglesey papers dealing with the 7th Light Dragoons (Hussars)'. J.S.A.H.R. vol. XXXVIII no. 154, June 1960, 69-74; no. 155, September 1960, 127-134; no. 156, December 1960, 175-83; vol. XXXIX no. 157, March 1961, 20-6; no. 158, June 1961, 75-85; no. 159, September 1961, 113-25; no. 160, December 1961, 198-204.

863. MUIR, AUGUSTUS. The first of Foot: the history of the Royal Scots (the Royal regiment). Edin. 1961.

864. SYM, JOHN. Seaforth Highlanders. Aldershot. 1962.

865. BOLITHO, HECTOR. The galloping third: the story of the 3rd, the King's Own Hussars. 1963. A readable account constructed from a wide variety of sources in view of the lack of almost any regimental records.

866. KENRICK, N.C.E. The story of the Wiltshire regiment (Duke of Edinburgh's) the 62nd and 99th Foot (1756-1959) the militia and the territorials, the service battalions and all those who have served or been affiliated with the Moonrakers. Aldershot. 1963.

867. RAY, CYRIL. Regiment of the line. The story of the XX the Lancashire Fusiliers. 1963.

868. WARD, S.P.G. Faithful: the story of the Durham Light Infantry. 1963.

869. McGUFFIE, T.H. 'The 7th Hussars in 1813. Duties of a light cavalry regiment in London'. J.S.A.H.R. vol. XLII no. 169, March 1964, 4-15. Extracts from a book of daily orders.

870. OATTS, L.B. I serve: regimental history of the 3rd Carabiners (Prince of Wales's Dragoon Guards). Chester. 1966. The only comprehensive study apart from the work in the Cannon series. Covers wider issues than purely regimental activities, because of the dearth of material.

71. VALE, W.L. History of the South Staffordshire regiment.
    Aldershot. 1966.

72. BRYANT, SIR ARTHUR. Jackets of green. A study of the
    history, philosophy and character of the Rifle
    brigade. 1972.

73. SUTHERLAND, DOUGLAS. Tried and valiant; the history
    of the Border regiment (the 34th and 55th regiments of
    Foot) 1702-1959. 1972.

5. PERSONNEL

a) The Officer Corps.

74. THE ARMY LIST. List of all officers of the army and
    royal marines. 1756-1881. Issued by the War Office.
    It then became, Monthly army list. 1881. See also,
    the new annual army list, 1839-1915, which, known as
    Hart's army list, included the militia. Also published
    was the official army list, June 1880 – January 1913,
    which became the quarterly army list, 1913-1922.

75. THE ARMY LIST OF 1740. Reprinted by the Society for
    Army Historical Research. Special issue no. 3. 1931.
    A useful reprint of an otherwise not easily obtainable
    document.

76. BAMFIELD, VERONICA. On the strength. The story of the
    British army wife. 1975. A history of army wives
    during peace and war since the Restoration.

77. BIDDULPH, BRIG. GENERAL H. 'The era of army purchase'.
    J.S.A.H.R., Vol. XII. no. 48. Winter, 1933, 221-33.
    Based partly on the papers of his father, General Sir
    Robert Biddulph, Cardwell's private secretary, it gives
    a number of interesting examples of the effect of
    purchase on individual officers.

78. BRUCE, A.P.C. The system of purchase and sale of
    officers' commissions in the British army and the campaign
    for its abolition, 1660-1871. University of Manchester.
    Unpublished Ph.D. thesis. 1974. A comprehensive survey
    of the sale of commissions in the army from its medieval
    origins to 1871, when Cardwell secured its abolition.

79. BURNE, ALFRED H. The Woolwich mess. Aldershot. 1954.
    A comprehensive history, with interesting material on
    social life.

880. DALTON, CHARLES. The Blenheim roll. 1704. 1899.

881. ————————. English army lists and commission registers
1661-1714. 6 Vols. 1892-1902. The product of many
years work, this and the other works listed here by
Dalton are the standard guide to the officers of the
army at this time. There are very detailed references
to many individual officers.

882. ————————. George the first's army 1714-1727. 2 Vols.
1910-12. A continuation of the lists noted immediately
above, this work includes a general introductory survey
of the army during George's reign.

883. ————————. Irish army lists 1661-1685. 1907.

884. ————————. The Scots army 1661-1688. 1909.

885. ————————. The Waterloo roll call. 1904. Second rev. edn.
Biographical details and anecdotes of officers who
served at Waterloo. Includes N.C.O.'s and men who served
and subsequently received commissions.

886. D'ALTON, J. Illustrations, historical and genealogical,
of King James's Irish army list (1689). 1855.

887. DICKINSON, R.J. Officers' mess: a history of mess origins
and customs from military records, anecdotes and the
progress of Charles Oswald Littlewart from 2nd lieutenant
to Major General. Tunbridge Wells. 1973.

888. DODWELL, EDWARD AND MILES, JAMES SAMUEL. Officers of the
Indian army.1838. A comprehensive guide to East India
company officers.

889. DREW, SIR ROBERT, et.al. Roll of commissioned officers
in the medical services of the British army, 1660-1960.
2 Vols. 1968. Vol. II is entitled 'Roll of officers in
the Royal Army Medical Corps 1898-1960'.

890. EDMONDS, R.F. Roll of officers of the corps of Royal
Engineers from 1660-1898. Compiled from the ms. volumes
of the late Capt. T.W.J. Connolly R.E. and brought up to
date in the office of the R.E. Institute. Chatham. 1898.

891. EDWARDS, T.J. 'British field marshals'. A.Q. Vol. LII
no. 2. July 1946, 244-7. The origin and definition of
the rank.

892. ————————. 'The field marshal's baton' A.Q. Vol.LIII
no.1., October 1946, 100-4. List of all the holders of
the rank from its creation by George II in 1736.

893. FIREBRACE, C.W.   The Army and Navy Club 1837–1933. 1934.

894. GLOVER, MICHAEL. 'Purchase, patronage and promotion in the army at the time of the Peninsular war'. A.Q. Vol. 103 no.2, January 1973, 211–215; no.3, April 1973, 355–62.   An analysis of statistics collected from the London Gazette during a selected period of the Peninsular war.

895. GRENFELL, CMDR. RUSSELL.   The men who defend us. 1938. Contains two historical chapters on the pay of officers and men.

896. GROSE, FRANCIS.   Advice to the officers of the British army. 1782.   A satire on the lives of eighteenth century army officers.

897. HAYES, J.W. 'Scottish officers in the British army. 1714–1763'. S.H.R.   Vol. 37, April 1958, 23–33.   A short review of the career patterns and qualities of Scottish officers, and of the more notable individuals from Scotland who served in the army.

898. —————————. The social and professional background of the officers of the British army 1715–1763. University of London. Unpublished M.A. thesis. 1956. A pioneering work. Similar detailed studies of the officer corps, based on statistical data, are needed for other periods.

899. JACKSON, SIR L.C.   History of the United Service Club. 1937.   This famous club was founded in May, 1815.

900. JOHNSTON, WILLIAM. Roll of commissioned officers in the medical service of the British army, who served on full pay within the period between the ascension of George II and the formation of the Royal Army Medical Corps, 20 June 1727 to 23 June 1898 with an introduction showing the historical evolution of the corps. Aberdeen, 1917.

901. LESLIE, J.H. 'Old printed army lists'. J.S.A.H.R. Vol. I. no. 1. September 1921, 6–9; no.2, December 1921, 56–9; no.4, June 1922, 142–5; Vol. II no. 10, October 1923, 164–7; Vol. III no. 11, January 1924, 22–25; no. 12, April 1924, 85–9; no.13, July 1924, 166–172; Vol. IX no. 37, July 1930, 144–146.   Reprint of the army lists for 1661, and 1684.

902. LESLIE, N.B. The succession of colonels of the British army from 1660 to the present day. S.A.H.R. special publication no. 11. 1974.   A comprehensive list of British army colonels.

903. MILES, W. 'When promotion was slower still. The commission of enquiry in 1838'. J.S.A.H.R. Vol. XII no. 48, winter 1933, 213-221. The royal commission on army and navy promotion which reported in 1840 (393),and recommended changes to increase the rate of promotion in both services.

904. NEAVE-HILL, W.B.R. 'Brevet rank' Ibid. Vol. XLVIII no. 194, summer 1970, 85-104. A scholarly account of the origin and history of this rank.

905. --------------. 'The rank titles of brigadier and brigadier general'. Ibid. Vol. XLVII no. 190, summer 1969, 96-116.

906. O'DOWD, SIR J.C. Army reform. A few words on the purchase system and regimental organization, with some practical suggestions from their improvement. 1866. An important defence of the purchase system.

907. OTLEY, C.B. The origins and recruitment of the British army elite, 1870-1959. University of Hull. Unpublished Ph.D. thesis. 1965. A full survey of the educational and family backgrounds, and career patterns of general officers at selected periods, and the implications for their collective political behaviour as military officers. A summary of the arguments in this thesis can be found in his article, 'Militarism and the social affiliations of the British army elite'. In Armed forces and society: sociological essays. Ed. by J. van Doorn. The Hague. 1969, 84-108.

908. PHILIPPART, JOHN. The royal military calendar. Containing the services of every general officer in the British army from the date of their first commissions.2 Vols. 1815. Details of the careers of general officers, with fuller accounts of the services of the most distinguished soldiers.

909. ---------------. The royal military calendar: or, army service and commission book. Containing the services and progress of promotion of the generals, lieutenant generals, major generals, colonels, lieutenant colonels, and majors of the army, according to seniority. 5 vols. 1820.

910. PIGGOTT, F.S.G. 'Promotion by brevet' A.Q. Vol. LIX no.1, October 1949, 97-104. A short survey of the history of the rank, with some interesting examples.

911. PRENDERGAST, HARRIS. The law relating to officers in
the army. 1855. A comprehensive guide to the law,
civil and military, relating to the officer corps, with
many important cases quoted and discussed at length.

912. RAZZELL, P.E. 'Social origins of officers in the Indian
and British home army, 1758-1962'. British journal of
Sociology, Vol. 14, no. 3, 1963, 248-60. A survey of
the proportion of members of the aristocracy and gentry
in the officer corps, and the reasons for changes in it
during the period under review.

913. READER, W.J. Professional men : the rise of the professional classes in nineteenth century England. 1966.
There is a valuable chapter on the growth of professionalism in the army.

914. 'RELATIVE RANK in the Royal Navy and the Army'. J.S.A.H.R.
Vol. IX no. 36, April 1930, 110-112. An Admiralty letter
of 1747 on the subject is reproduced.

915. ROBSON, ERIC. 'Purchase and promotion in the British
army in the eighteenth century'. History, Vol. XXXVI,
February 1951, 55-72. A scholarly analysis, based on War
Office records, mainly of the role and influence of Lord
Barrington during his periods as Secretary at War.

916. SOCIAL LIFE IN THE BRITISH ARMY. By a British Officer.
1900. Valuable information on the many expenses incurred
while holding a commission, at the end of the nineteenth
century.

917. THE SUCCESSION OF COLONELS to all His Majesty's land
forces from their rise to 1742. Precedence of each
regiment, with dates of promotions, removes, deaths, etc.
1742. Sometimes erroneously described as an army list,
this is a register of colonels only.

918. SULLIVAN, A.E. 'The rise and fall of the purchase system'.
A.Q. Vol. LVIII no. 2, July 1949, 233-9. A short popular
survey.

919. TEAGARDEN, E.M. 'Lord Haldane and the origins of officer
training corps'. J.S.A.H.R. Vol. XLV. no. 182, summer
1967, 91-6. Haldane's development of a reserve supply
of officers.

920. TURNER, E.S. Gallant gentlemen. A portrait of the British officer, 1660-1956. 1956. A popular, but the only
full length, survey of the officer corps. Contains some interesting material, but there is little analysis or explanation. A scholarly study of the officer corps is needed.

921. WAR OFFICE. Army lists. Index of the names of
officers who appear in the Army lists (hitherto
unindexed) from 1702 to 1752. 1897.

922. WESTERN, J.R. 'Roman catholics holding military
commissions in 1798: notes and documents'. E.H.R.
vol. LXX, July 1955, 428-432. Examples of the evasion
of the anti-catholic legislation which barred Roman
Catholics holding commissions in England (but not after
1793 in Ireland) at this time.

(b)   Rank and file

923. ASCOLI, DAVID. A village in Chelsea. An informal
account of the Royal Hospital. 1974. A history of the
in-pensioners of the Royal Hospital, which incidentally
reveals much about the changing status of the soldier.

924. BALDRY, W.Y. 'Notes on the early history of billeting'.
J.S.A.H.R. vol. XIII no. 50, summer 1934, 71-3.

925. BLANCO. R.L. 'Army recruiting reforms, 1861-1867'.
Ibid. Vol. XLVI no. 188, winter 1968, 217-224. A
fully documented account of the ultimately successful
attempts to change the terms of service and improve
recruiting of soldiers.

926. ------- 'Attempts to abolish branding and flogging
in the army of Victorian England before 1881'. Ibid.
Vol. XLVI no. 187, autumn 1968, 137-145. The protracted
campaign to end corporal punishment, not finally
successful until 1881.

927. BOND, BRIAN. 'Recruiting the Victorian army, 1870-92'.
V.S. vol. V no. 4, June 1962, 331-8. A study of the
continuing problem of recruiting soldiers, and the
attempts of government to devise solutions.

928. BROWNE, D.G. Private Thomas Atkins, a history of the
British soldier from 1840-1940. 1940.

929. CLAVER, SCOTT. Under the lash. A history of corporal
punishment in the British armed forces. 1954. A popula
survey, with a valuable bibliography.

930. DAVIES, F.J. The sergeant-major: the origin and histor
of his rank, with notes on military customs and habits
of former times. 1886.

931. DAVIES, GODFREY. 'Recruiting in the reign of Queen Anne'. J.S.A.H.R. Vol. XXVIII no. 116, winter 1950, 146-59. A detailed account of the methods used, and their effectiveness.

932. DE WATTEVILLE, H.G. The British soldier. His daily life from Tudor to modern times. 1954. A widely used history which is, however, very inadequately documented.

933. ----------------. 'The reign of the lash' A.Q. Vol. XXIV no. 1, July 1932, 308-322. The material here was largely incorporated in the book listed immediately above.

934. DON, W.G. 'Recruits and recruiting'. J.R.U.S.I., Vol. XXXIII. 1889, 827-53.

935. EDWARDS, T.J. 'The sergeant-major'. Ibid. Vol. LXXIV. no. 495, August 1929, 594-6. Origin of the rank is considered.

936. FEATHERSTONE, DONALD F. All for a shilling a day. 1966. A semi fictional account of recruits from enlistment in the 16th Queen's Lancers to the charge at Aliwal.

937. FORTESCUE, HON. SIR J.W. The county lieutenancies and the army, 1803-1814. 1909. A valuable study of the complex subject of recruiting, during the Napoleonic wars.

938. HARGREAVES, REGINALD. 'Promotion from the ranks'. A.Q. Vol. LXXXVI no. 2, July 1963, 200-10. A brief survey of the whole period, with some interesting examples.

939. KENDALL, J.M. 'The Lancepessade and the history of the "Lance" rank'. J.S.A.H.R. Vol. V no. 20, April-June 1926, 81-6.

940. LAFFIN, JOHN. Tommy Atkins: the story of the English soldier. 1966. A widely read competent popular survey. There is a limited use of MS. sources, but little analysis.

941. MARSHALL, HENRY. A historical sketch of military punishments, in as far as regards non-commissioned officers and private soldiers. n.d.

942. ------------. Military miscellany: comprehending a history of the recruiting of the army. 1846.

943. ------------. On the enlisting, the discharging, and the pensioning of soldiers: with the official documents on these branches of military duty. 1832.

944. McGUFFIE, T.H. 'Early barrack life'. <u>A.Q.</u> Vol. LIV
no. 1, April 1947, 65-8. Organization and condition of
barracks in the late eighteenth and early nineteenth
century.

945. --------- ed. Rank and file: the common soldier in
peace and war. 1642-1914. 1964. Extracts from a number
of soldiers' reminiscences, including some in ms.,
arranged by subject.

946. ----------. 'Recruiting the ranks of the regular army
during the French wars. Recruiting, recruits, and methods
of recruitment'. <u>J.S.A.H.R.</u> Vol. XXXIV no. 138, June
1956, 50-8; no. 139, September 1956, 123-132. An
important, scholarly survey.

947. MOORE, WILLIAM. The thin yellow line. 1974. A discussion of attitudes to cowardice in battle, mainly on the
period since 1914, although there is some material in
the early part of the book on the situation from 1632.

948. PAY, ALLOWANCES AND STOPPAGES of privates of infantry
from 1660 to 1891. 1891. A useful official source of
reference.

949. SCOULLER, MAJOR R.E. 'Recruiting: a familiar problem'.
<u>A.Q.</u> Vol. LXXI no. 1, October 1955, 105-112. Recruiting
during the war of Spanish Succession.

950. SEELY, J.E.B. The private soldier in modern war:
with some considerations on his training and enlistment
under a voluntary system. 1904.

951. SULLIVAN, A.E. 'Married quarters - a retrospect'. <u>A.Q.</u>
Vol. LXIII no. 1, October 1951, 113-9.

952. THOMSON, HENRY. 'Punishments in the army'. <u>Blackwood's
Mag.</u> Vol. XV, April 1824, 399-406.

16. <u>BIOGRAPHIES, MEMOIRS AND UNPUBLISHED PERSONAL PAPERS.</u>

(a) Collected biography

953. ADAMS, W.H.D. Eminent soldiers. A series of biographical sketches of great military commanders, English and
foreign. 1880. Includes essays on Marlborough,
Wellington and C.J. Napier.

954. ASHLEY, MAURICE. Cromwell's generals. 1954. See especially the chapter entitled 'General George Monck and the Restoration'.

955. CHAMBERS,R. ed. Biographical dictionary of eminent Scotsmen. Edin. 1855.

956. CHESNEY. COL. C.C. Essays in modern military biography. 1874. See for essays on Lord Cornwallis in India, Sir William Gordon, and on Chinese Gordon and the Taiping rebellion.

957. CLARK, C. British soldiers 1550-1906. 1907. Twelve sketches of soldiers.

958. COLE, J.W. Memoirs of British generals distinguished during the Peninsular war. 2 vols. 1856. Chapters on Moore, Baird, Anglesey, Paget, Beresford, Craufurd, Cole, Picton, Lynedoch, Hopetoun, Hill, Le Marchant, Ross, and Pakenham.

959. CUST, GENERAL THE HON. SIR EDWARD. Lives of the warriors who have commanded fleets and armies' before the enemy. Vol. III. Warriors of the seventeenth century - Part I. 1869. Monck, William III, and Graham of Claverhouse.

960. DICTIONARY OF NATIONAL BIOGRAPHY. Ed. by Sir Leslie Stephen and Sir Sidney Lee. 63 Vols. 1885-1900. Further volumes published for the periods, 1901-1911, and 1912-1930. An invaluable source of reference but should be used with caution.

961. DICTIONARY OF NATIONAL BIOGRAPHY, CORRECTIONS AND ADDITIONS, cumulated from the Bulletin of the Institute of Historical Research. Boston, Mass. 1966.

962. FERGUSON, JAMES. Two Scottish soldiers - a soldier of 1688 and Blenheim, a soldier of the American revolution - and a jacobite laird and his forbears. 1888. Studies of James Ferguson, and Patrick Ferguson who patented what is claimed to have been the first breech loading rifle.

963. FITCHETT, W.H. Wellington's men. Some soldier autobiographies. 1900. Extracts from some of the more obvious published accounts. Introductory chapter on 'the soldier in literature'.

964. FORREST, G.W. Sepoy generals: Wellington to Roberts. Edin. 1901. Sketches of Wellington, C.J. Napier, Sir H.B. Edwardes, Sir T. Munro, Sir David Baird, General John Jacob, Sir D. Stewart, Sir W. Lockhart, Lord Roberts.

965. FORTESCUE, HON. SIR J.W. Following the drum. Edin.
1931. Essays on Wolseley, Kitchener, and Horace Smith-
Dorrien.

966. ------------. A gallant company or deeds of duty and
discipline from the story of the British army. 1927.
Essays on Rollo Gillespie, Lord Lake, Burrard, Moore,
Lord Raglan, and Sir Harry Smith.

967. ------------. The last post. Edin. 1934. Essays on Hugh,
1st Viscount Gough, Sir Edward Pakenham and the Napiers
are included in this collection.

968. ------------. Six British soldiers. 1928. Includes
assessments of Marlborough, Abercromby, Moore, Stuart,
and Wellington.

969. GLEIG, REV. GEORGE ROBERT. Lives of the most eminent
British military commanders. 3 vols. 1831-2. Long
essays on Marlborough, Peterborough, Wolfe, Clive, Cornwallis, Abercromby, and Moore.

970. HAWKES, C.P. Authors-at-arms: the soldiering of six
great writers. 1935. Richard Steele, Edward Gibbon,
Coleridge, Scott, Savage Landor, and Byron.

971. HAYES, JAMES. ed. 'Two soldier brothers of the eighteenth
century'. J.S.A.H.R. Vol. XL. no. 163, September 1962,
150-161. Letters of Lieut. General Cuthbert Ellison
and his younger brother Robert, who died in North America
in 1755, preserved among the Carr Ellison manuscripts in
Gateshead public library.

972. HOLMES, T.R.E. Four famous soldiers: Sir Charles
Napier, Hodson of Hodson's horse, Sir William Napier,
and Sir Herbert Edwardes. 1889.

973. HUDLESTON, F.J. Warriors in undress. 1925. Anecdotal
accounts of Wellington, Frederick, Duke of York, Major
General H.E. Lloyd, and John Shipp.

974. KING, G.J.S. 'Britain's war secretaries' A.Q. Vol.
LIV no. 1, April 1947, 42-8; no. 2, July 1947, 199-205.
Biographical details of holders of the office of
Secretary of State for War.

975. LOW, CHARLES R. Soldiers of the Victorian age. 2 Vols.
1880. A number of biographies, including those of Sir
James Outram, Lord Strathnairn, and Lord Clyde.

976. ------------. Our greatest living soldiers. 1900.
Includes Wolseley, Buller, Roberts, White, Kitchener,
Sir Hector Macdonald, et.al.

977. MACPHERSON, W.C. ed. Soldiering in India, 1764-1787.
Extracts from journals and letters left by Lieut. Col.
Allan Macpherson and Lieut. Col. John Macpherson of
the East India Company's service. Edin. 1928.

978. MITCHELL, MAJOR-GENERAL JOHN. Biographies of eminent
soldiers of the last four centuries. Edin. 1865.
See for the account of Marlborough.

979. MORRIS, W. O'CONNOR. Great commanders of modern times
and the campaign of 1815. 1891. Includes Wellington
and Marlborough.

980. PEARSE, HUGH. 'Marlborough's men'. Cornhill Magazine.
Vol. XXX (N.s.), 1911, 67-75.

981. RICKWOOD, G.O. 'Military gleanings from the Cheveley
papers. Two Essex officers: eighteenth century militia
and nineteenth century volunteers'. J.S.A.H.R. Vol. XL
no. 163, September 1962, 125-42.

982. ROBINSON, C.N. ed. Celebrities of the army, 1900.

983. SCUDAMORE, CYRIL. English officers of the nineteenth
century .1913. Includes Lawrence, Seaton, Wellington,
Gordon, Church, Nicholson, and Clyde.

984. SHAND, A.I. Wellington's lieutenants. 1902. Essays on
Lord Hill, Craufurd, Thomas Picton, Beresford, Lynedoch,
Hopetoun, Anglesey, Combermere.

985. SMALL, E.M. ed. Told from the ranks: recollections of
service during the Queen's reign by privates and non-
commissioned officers of the British army. 1897.

986. THORNTON, L.H. Campaigners, grave and gay. 1925. There
are essays on Peterborough and Wolfe.

987. ----------. and FRASER, PAMELA. The Congreves, father
and son: General Sir William Norris Congreve, V.C. Bt.
Major William La Touche Congreve, V.C. 1930.

988. TOWER, CHARLEMAGNE. Essays political and historical.
Philadelphia, Pa. 1914. See for Lord Cornwallis in
America, and General Howe's campaign in the revolutionary
war.

989. WHITWORTH, LIEUT-COL. REX H. 'Amherst and Wolfe'. A.Q.
Vol. LXXIII no. 1, October 1956, 66-73.

990. WILKIN, W.H. Some British soldiers in America. 1914.
There are chapters on Howe, Carleton, Clinton, Rawdon,
Sir William Medows and Lord Harris, and some letters
of Lieut Hale are printed.

991. WILKINSON, MAJOR-GENERAL OSBORN and WILKINSON, MAJOR-
GENERAL JOHNSON. The memoirs of the gemini generals.
Personal anecdotes, sporting adventures, and sketches
of distinguished officers. 1896. Autobiographies by
these two officers.

992. WILKINSON, SPENCER. ed. From Cromwell to Wellington:
twelve soldiers. 1899. Includes essays by various
authors on Marlborough, Peterborough, Wolfe, Lord
Heathfield, and Sir Ralph Abercromby.

993. YONGE, C.D. England's great generals. 1892. Essays
on Marlborough, Clive, Wellington, Gough, C.J. Napier,
Clyde.

(b)   Political leaders

     Also included in this section are biographies of other
civilians concerned with the army. Published biographical
studies are listed here only if they throw light on the
subjects' role in relation to the army.

ARNOLD-FORSTER, H.O.

994. Arnold Forster, M. Rt. Hon. Hugh Oakeley Arnold
Forster: a memoir. 1910.

995. Papers: B.M. Add. MSS. 50275-50357.

BARRINGTON, WILLIAM WILDMAN, VISCOUNT

996. Barrington, Shute. The political life of William
Wildman, Viscount Barrington, compiled from original
papers. 1815. Not a critical account, and is mainly
valuable for the extracts from Barrington's correspondence and papers which are printed in it. It has not
proved possible to locate the present whereabouts of
Lord Barrington's papers.

BLATHWAYT, WILLIAM.

997. Jacobsen, G.A. William Blathwayt: a late seventeenth
century English administrator. Oxf. 1933. Detailed
coverage of his long administration of the army.

998. Papers: B.M. Add. MSS. 9719-9736, 9741-9749, 9752-9755,
9764.

BOLINGBROKE, HENRY ST. JOHN, VISCOUNT.

999. Dickinson, H.T. Bolingbroke. 1970. The best modern
account: see pp. 44-62 for his period as secretary at
war. Earlier biographies are listed in the excellent
bibliography at the end of this work.

1000. Dudley, G.A. The early life of Henry St. John.
Unpublished Ph.D. thesis. University of California.
1955-6. For his period of office as secretary at war,
see pp. 117-278.

CALCRAFT, JOHN.

1001. Pemberton, W. Baring. 'John Calcraft, army agent'.
A.Q. Vol. XXXIX no. 2, January 1940, 333-40.

CAMPBELL-BANNERMAN, SIR HENRY.

1002. Spender, J.A. Life of Sir Henry Campbell-Bannerman.
2 Vols. 1923.

1003. Wilson, John. 'C.B.' The life of Sir Henry Campbell-
Bannerman. 1973. A fine work, with fully documented
accounts of his periods at the War Office.

1004. Papers: B.M. Add. Mss., 41206-41252, 52512-52521.

CARDWELL, EDWARD, VISCOUNT.

1005. Erickson, Arvel. Edward T. Cardwell: Peelite. Trans.
of the American Philosophical Soc. Vol. 49 Pt. 2. 1959.
Contains many errors of fact and interpretation. A
definitive biography is urgently required.

1006. Papers: P.R.O. 30/48. Many letters from his period as
secretary for war have been preserved.

CHANDOS, JAMES BRYDGES, DUKE OF

1007. Robinson, J.R. The princely Chandos: a memoir of James
Brydges, paymaster-general to the forces abroad . . .
1705-11, afterwards the first duke of Chandos. 1893.
For his papers, see (115) above.

CHATHAM, WILLIAM PITT, EARL OF

1008. Williams, B. William Pitt, earl of Chatham. 2 Vols.
1913. The standard account.

1009. Freemantle, Alan. 'Britain's greatest war minister'.
Contemporary Review. Vol. CLXI, March 1942, 163-7.

CHILDERS, H.C.E.

1010. Childers, E.S.E. The life and correspondence of the
Rt. Hon. Hugh C.E. Childers, 1827-1896. 1901.

1011. Papers: P.R.O. 30/48. For his correspondence with Edward Cardwell. Many of his political papers were destroyed in a fire.

COX, RICHARD.

1012. Jones, K.R. 'Richard Cox, army agent and banker'. J.S.A.H.R. Vol. XXXIV no. 140, December 1956, 178-81.

CRAGGS, JAMES, the elder.

1013. Papers: Devon R.O.

CRANBROOK, GATHORNE HARDY, LORD.

1014. Gathorne Hardy, first earl of Cranbrook: a memoir with extracts from his diary and correspondence. Ed. by the Hon. A.E. Gathorne Hardy. 2 Vols. 1910.

1015. Papers: Suffolk C.R.O.

DALHOUSIE, FOX MAULE, BARON PANMURE AND EARL OF.

1016. The Panmure papers, being a selection from the correspondence of Fox Maule, second Baron Panmure, afterwards eleventh earl of Dalhousie. Ed. by Sir George Douglas and Sir George Ramsay. 2 Vols. 1908. A useful selection from the collection listed immediately below.

1017. Papers: S.R.O., the Dalhousie muniments. Contains a valuable collection of official military papers, some of which are not in the P.R.O., from Panmure's period as secretary of state for war from February 1855.

DEVONSHIRE, SPENCER COMPTON CAVENDISH, MARQUESS OF HARTINGTON AND DUKE OF.

1018. Papers: Chatsworth House, Derbyshire. Useful for his two periods as secretary for war.

ELLICE, EDWARD, the elder.

1019. Papers: N.L.S. For the period 1816-1863.

ESHER, REGINALD, VISCOUNT.

1020. Brett, M.V. ed. Journals and letters of Reginald, Viscount Esher. 4 Vols. 1934-38.

1021. Papers: Watlington Park, Watlington, Oxf.

GLADSTONE, W.E.

1022. Papers: B.M. Add.Mss. 44086-44835. Many official papers, and correspondence and notes by Gladstone on military questions.

GRANVILLE, GEORGE LEVESON GOWER, EARL.

1023. Private correspondence, 1781-1821. Ed. by Countess
      Castalla Granville.2 Vols. 1916.

1024. Papers: P.R.O. 30/29, the Granville papers. The papers
      of later members of the family also include many items
      of interest.

GREY, CHARLES, 2ND EARL.

1025. Papers: University of Durham. A comprehensive index
      listing individual items has been produced by the
      custodians.

HALDANE, RICHARD BURDON, VISCOUNT.

1026. Baker, H.T. 'Lord Haldane'. A.Q. Vol. XVII no. 1,
      October 1928, 13-22. Baker was financial secretary to
      the War Office from 1912 to 1915.

1027. Harris, Sir Charles. Lord Haldane. 1928.

1028. Maurice, Sir Frederick. Haldane 1856-1915. The life of
      Viscount Haldane of Cloan. 2 Vols. 1937-39. Still the
      best account of his administration of the army.

1029. Summer, Dudley. Haldane of Cloan. His life and times.
      1856-1928. 1960. A good scholarly account.

1030. Bond, Brian. 'Richard Burdon Haldane at the War Office
      1905-1912' A.Q. Vol. LXXXVI no. 1, April 1963, 33-43.
      A summary of Haldane's transformation of the organization
      of the army, with a select bibliography.

1031. Koss, S.E. Lord Haldane. Scapegoat for liberalism.
      N.Y. 1969. Brief description of his time at the War
      Office.

1032. Papers: N.L.S.

HALIBURTON, ARTHUR LAWRENCE, LORD.

1033. Atlay, J.B. Lord Haliburton: a memoir of his public
      service. 1909.Haliburton was permanent under secretary
      of state for war, 1895-7, and an army reformer.

HARDINGE, SIR HENRY, VISCOUNT.

1034. Hardinge, Charles. Viscount Hardinge. 1891. The only
      biography of Lord Hardinge who served in the Peninsula,
      and was secretary at war, and commander-in-chief.

1035. Papers: McGill University. Many military papers are in
      this collection. For details see P. Howitt, The Hardinge
      papers A preliminary report on the letters of the first
      Viscount Hardinge, n.d. (unpublished).

HARDWICKE, PHILIP YORKE, 2ND EARL.

1036. Papers: B.M. Add. MS. 35349-36278. Includes many
military papers.

HERBERT, SIDNEY, LORD.

1037. Stanmore, Lord. Sidney Herbert: a memoir. 2 Vols. 1906.
Includes many selections from his papers relating to
his periods as Secretary at War, and Secretary of State
for War.

1038. Papers: Wilton House, Salisbury, Wilts. Contains
material relating to the Crimean war, and later attempts
to reform the army.

HERRIES, J.C.

1039. Papers: B.M. Add. MSS. 57366-57469. Relating to the
commissariat, and to his short term of office as
Secretary at War.

LANSDOWNE, H.C.K. PETTY-FITZMAURICE, MARQUESS OF.

1040. Newton, Lord. Lord Lansdowne. A biography. 1929. See
pp. 127-94 for his period as Secretary for War.

1041. Papers: Bowood Park, Calne, Wilts.

LEWIS, SIR GEORGE CORNWALL

1042. Papers: N.L.W. The papers are not, as yet, listed.

LIVERPOOL, CHARLES JENKINSON, 1ST EARL.

1043. Papers: B.M. Add. MSS. 38190-38489. There are many papers
relating to his period as Secretary at War.

LONDONDERRY, ROBERT STEWART, VISCOUNT CASTLEREAGH, MARQUESS OF.

1044. Londonderry, Marquess of ed. Correspondence, despatches
and other papers of Viscount Castlereagh, second Marquess
of Londonderry. 12 Vols. 1848-53. Vol. VIII covers his
period as Secretary of State for War, 1804-9.

1045. Bartlett, C.J. Castlereagh. 1966. The most useful
modern biography with material on his tenure as Secretary
for War.

1046. Papers: In the possession of Lady Bury, Mountstewart,
Co. Down, Northern Ireland.

MACAULAY, THOMAS BABBINGTON, LORD.

1047. Trevelyan, Sir George. The life and letters of Lord
Macaulay. 2 Vols. 1876. Includes some information on
his unremarkable period at the War Office.

MELVILLE, HENRY DUNDAS, VISCOUNT.

1048. Furber, Holden. Henry Dundas, first Viscount Melville, 1742-1811. 1931. Based on his private correspondence.

1049. Papers: S.R.O.

MIDDLETON, WILLIAM ST. J. BRODRICK, EARL OF.

1050. Records and reactions 1856-1939. 1939.

1051. Papers: B.M. Add. MSS. 50072-50077.

NEWCASTLE, HENRY PELHAM, FIFTH DUKE OF.

1052. Martineau, John. The life of Henry Pelham, fifth Duke of Newcastle 1811-64. 1908.

1053. Papers: University of Nottingham.

NIGHTINGALE, FLORENCE.

1054. Cook, Sir Edward. Florence Nightingale. 2 Vols. 1913. Still the best account, with a valuable bibliography: see Appendix A 'List of writings by Miss Nightingale and Appendix B for works about her. On this subject see also W.J. Bishop and S. Goldie <u>A bio-bibliography of Florence Nightingale</u>. 1962.

1055. Woodham-Smith, Cecil. Florence Nightingale. 1950. A sound introduction to her life and achievements.

1056. Papers: B.M. Add. MSS. 43393-43403, 45750-45889, 46385, 47714-47767.

ORFORD, SIR ROBERT WALPOLE, EARL OF.

1057. Coxe, William. Memoirs of the life and administration of Sir Robert Walpole. 3 Vols. 1798. Many useful papers are printed.

1058. Plumb, J.H. Sir Robert Walpole. 2 vols. 1972. repr. See Vol. I, pp. 129-162 for his period as secretary at war. The standard biography.

1059. Papers: Cholmondeley (Houghton) MSS. Houghton, Norfolk.

PALMERSTON, HENRY JOHN TEMPLE, 3RD VISCOUNT.

1060. Bell, H.C.F. Lord Palmerston. 2 Vols. 1936. Contains in Vol. I, a full account of his long period as secretary at war.

1061. Ridley, Jasper. Lord Palmerston. 1970. A good modern account, with bibliography of earlier biographies.

1062. Papers: B.M. Add. MSS. 48417-48589; 49963-49969. (letter books); The Trustees of the Broadlands Archives.

PULTENEY-MURRAY, SIR JAMES.

1063. Papers: Pierpoint Morgan Lib. N.Y.

RICHMOND, CHARLES LENNOX, THIRD DUKE OF.

1064. A.G. Olson. The radical duke: career and correspondence of Charles Lennox, third duke of Richmond. 1961. The duke was master general of the ordnance.

RIPON, G.F.S. ROBINSON, EARL DE GREY AND MARQUESS OF.

1065. Wolf, Lucien. Life of the first Marquess of Ripon. 2 Vols. 1921. Prints extracts from his correspondence.

1066. Denholm, Anthony. 'Lord de Grey and army reform, 1859-1866'. A.Q. Vol. 102, no. 1, October 1971, 57-64.

1067. Papers: B.M. Add. Mss. 43510-43644.

RUSSELL, SIR WILLIAM HOWARD.

1068. Atkins, J.B. The life of Sir William Howard Russell: the first special correspondent. 1911.

1069. Furneaux, Rupert. The first war correspondent. William Howard Russell of the Times. 1944.

SMITH, W.H.

1070. Chilston, Lord. W.H. Smith. 1965. For Smith's two periods at the War Office, see pp. 192 ff.

1071. Papers: P.R.O. WO/110. Official papers as secretary of state for war.

STANHOPE, EDWARD.

1072. Papers: Chevening, Sevenoaks.

WILKINSON, HENRY SPENCER.

1073. Thirty five years 1874-1909. 1933. The reminiscences of an important Victorian military thinker and writer.

1074. Papers: Army Museums Ogilby Trust.

WINDHAM, WILLIAM.

1075. The Windham Papers. The life and correspondence of the Rt. Hon. William Windham . . . including hitherto unpublished letters from George III, the dukes of York and Gloucester, Pitt, Fox, Burke, Canning, Lords Grenville, Minto, Castlereagh and Nelson, Malone, Cobbett, Dr. Johnson, Dr. Burney, etc. Intr. by Earl of Rosebery. 2 Vols. 1913. Selection from his papers in the British Museum.

1076. Papers: B.M. Add. Mss. 37842-37935, 50851.

(c)   Military officers and men

        (i) 1660-1793

     Reminiscences relating to, or particularly useful for, specific campaigns or battles are listed in Part V below.

ABERCROMBIE, JAMES.

1077. Papers: Huntington Library, San Marino, Calif.

ALBEMARLE, GEORGE MONCK, DUKE OF.

1078. Corbett, Sir Julian S. Monk. 1889. A good summary of his life.

1079. Davies, J.D.G. Honest George Monck. 1936.

1080. Warner, O.M.W. Hero of one restoration. 1936. A popular account.

ALBEMARLE, WILLIAM ANNE VAN KEPPEL, SECOND EARL OF.

1081. The Albemarle papers: being the correspondence of William Anne, second earl of Albemarle, commander-in-chief in Scotland, 1746-47, with an appendix of letters . . . 1746-48. 2 Vols. Aberdeen. 1902.

1082. Papers: East Suffolk R.O. See also, collection in National Library of Scotland, for his activities as commander-in-chief after the '45.

AMHERST, JEFFREY, LORD.

1083. Mayo L.S. Jeffrey Amherst: a biography. N.Y. 1916. Superseded by later research.

1084. Long, J.C. Lord Jeffrey Amherst: a soldier of the King. N.Y. 1933. Based on thorough research in the main manuscript collections.

1085. Webster, J.C. ed. The journals of Jeffrey Amherst, recording the military career of General Amherst in America from 1758 to 1763. Toronto and Chicago. 1931.

1086. Des Cognets, Louis. Amherst and Canada. New Jersey. 1962.

1087. Papers: Military papers P.R.O. W.O. 34; papers, 1758-1764, W.L. Clements Lib., Ann Arbor; papers, 1759-82, Amherst College Library, U.S.A. See also (989).

AYTOUN, JAMES.

1088. 'A private soldier in the eighteenth century'. <u>Cornhill Magazine</u>. Vol. LIV (N.s.), 1923, 653-664. Extracts from Aytoun's notebook written while a soldier in the 58th Foot.

BERNARDI, JOHN.

1089. A short history of the life of Major John Bernardi,
written by himself. 1729. Useful for the period he
was with James II in Ireland.

BISHOP, MATTHEW.

1090. The life and adventures of Matthew Bishop of Deddington
in Oxfordshire. Containing an account of several
actions by sea, battles and sieges by land, in which
he was present from 1701 to 1711, interspersed with
many curious incidents, entertaining conversations
and judicious reflections. 1744. A valuable account
by a private soldier.

1091. Atkinson, C.T. 'One of Marlborough's men: Matthew
Bishop of Webb's'. J.S.A.H.R. vol. XXIII no. 96,
winter 1945, 157-169.

BLACKADER, LIEUT. COL. JOHN.

1092. The life and diary of Lieut. Col. John Blackader of the
Cameronian regiment. . . Ed. by A. Crichton. Edin. 1824.
Of some use for the Flanders campaign during the war of
Spanish succession, although the author is rather
preoccupied with personal religious thoughts.

BRADDOCK, EDWARD.

1093. Maccardell, Lee. Ill-starred general. Braddock of the
Coldstream Guards. Pittsburgh. 1958. The only full
length account, it is scholarly and has a full
bibliography.

1094. Pargellis, Stanley. 'Braddock's defeat'. A.H.R. Vol.
XLI, 1936, 251-9.

BROWNE, PHILIP.

1095. 'Letters of Captain Philip Browne, 1737-1746'. J.S.A.H.R.
Vol. V no. 20, April-June 1926, 49-65; no. 21, July-
September 1926, 97-111; no. 22, October-December 1926,
145-55. 54 letters of Philip Browne who served as
cornet in the King's Own Regiment of Horse, and exempt
and captain in the 3rd Troop of Horse Guards. Useful
for military life in England, and the war of Austrian
succession.

BURGOYNE, GENERAL JOHN.

1096. De Fonblanque, Edward B. Political and military episodes
in the latter half of the eighteenth century derived from
the life of the Rt. Hon. John Burgoyne, general, states-
man, dramatist. 1876. Prints much valuable family and
other correspondence.

1097. Hudleston, F.J. Gentleman Johnny Burgoyne: misadventures of an English general in the revolution. 1928. Popular, but valuable.

1098. Paine, Lauren. Gentleman Johnny. The life of General John Burgoyne. 1973. A popular account which adds little new.

CAMPBELL, THE HON. SIR JAMES.

1099. Burn, W.L. 'A Scots fusilier and dragoon under Marlborough: Lieut General the Hon. Sir James Campbell, K.B. of Lawers'. J.S.A.H.R. Vol. XV. no. 58, summer 1936, 82-97.

CARLETON, GEORGE.

1100. Memoirs of Captain Carleton. Ed. by C.H. Hartmann.1929. First published in 1728 as, Military memoirs of Captain George Carleton, from the Dutch war, 1672 . . . 1713, the authorship of the work has been often questioned. Believed by some to have been written by either Defoe or Swift, Hartmann and others have defended it as an authentic account.

CARLETON, SIR GUY.

1101. Records of British army headquarters in America during 1775-1783: P.R.O. 30/55.

CLINTON, SIR HENRY.

1102. Willcox, W.B. Portrait of a general. Sir Henry Clinton in the War of Independence. N.Y. 1964. A valuable work, with a useful general assessment of Clinton in the final chapter.

1103. Papers: William L. Clements Library.

CLIVE, ROBERT, LORD.

1104. Malcolm, Sir John.Life of Clive. 3 Vols. 1836. Largely superseded by later works.

1105. Forrest, G.W. The life of Lord Clive.2 Vols. 1918. The best account, based on a wide selection of manuscript material.

1106. Davies, A.M. Clive of Plassey. 1939. A popular account.

1107. Papers: India Office Library; B.M. Add. MSS. 29131, 44061.

CODRINGTON, CHRISTOPHER.

1108. Harlow, V.T. Christopher Codrington, 1668-1710 Oxf. 1928. Life of a soldier who served in Flanders, and the West Indies during the reign of William III.

COLVILLE, HON. CHARLES.

1109. 'Military memoirs of Lieut. General the Hon. Charles Colville'. Ed. by J.O. Robson. J.S.A.H.R. Vol. XXV no. 102, summer 1947, 54-62; Vol. XXVI no. 107, autumn 1948, 117-120; Vol. XXVII no. 110, summer 1949, 70-8; no. 111, autumn 1949, 96-104; no. 112, winter 1949, 144-153; Vol. XXVIII no. 113, spring 1950, 2-12; no. 114, summer 1950, 70-81; no. 115, autumn 1950, 101-5. Extracts from his papers, 1710-1748 covering a number of campaigns.

COOTE, SIR EYRE.

1110. Wylly, H.C. A life of Lieut. General Sir Eyre Coote, K.B. Oxf. 1922. Valuable for numerous extracts from unpublished documents; there are appendices of letters.

1111. Sheppard, E.W. Coote Bahadur. A life of Lieut. General Sir Eyre Coote, K.B. 1956.

1112. Papers: N.A.M.

CORNWALLIS, CHARLES, MARQUIS.

1113. Correspondence of Charles, first Marquis Cornwallis. Ed. by Charles Ross. 3 Vols. 1859. Vol. I deals partly with the American war; Vols. II and III with his administration in India.

1114. Guedalla, Philip. 'Portrait of a red-faced general: Lieut. General Earl Cornwallis'. Harper's Monthly Mag. Vol. CLII. 1925, 102-106.

1115. Winkwire, Franklin and Mary. Cornwallis in America. 1971. A detailed treatment, but not well written. A full length biography of Cornwallis has not yet appeared.

1116. Papers: P.R.O. 30/11. See for American War, 1780-2, as master general of the ordnance, 1795-8, and for Indian military administration, 1786-1797. See also, the collection of his letterbooks, 1782-1805 at the N.A.M.

CRAUFURD, JOHN LINDSAY, EARL OF.

1117. Memoir of the life of John, earl of Craufurd . . . compiled from his worship's own papers, and other authentic memoirs. 1769.

CUMBERLAND, WILLIAM AUGUSTUS, DUKE OF.

1118. MacLachlan, A.N.C. William Augustus, duke of Cumberland: being a sketch of his military life and character chiefly as extracted in the general orders of H.R.H., 1745-1747. 1876. Contains little beyond the valuable extracts from Cumberland's orderly books.

1119. Charteris, Hon. Evan. William Augustus, duke of Cumberland: his early life and times, 1721-1748. 1913.

1120. ------------, William Augustus, duke of Cumberland, and the seven years' war. 1925. These two volumes by Charteris form the standard work on Cumberland based on his private papers.

1121. Papers: Royal Archives, Windsor Castle.

DAVENPORT, RICHARD.

1122. "To Mr. Davenport", being letters of Major Richard Davenport, (1719-1760) to his brother during service in the 4th troop of Horse Guards and 10th Dragoons, 1742-1760. Ed. by C.W. Frearson. S.A.H.R. Special publication no. **9**. 1968.

DAVIES, MRS. CHRISTIAN.

1123. The life and adventures of Mrs. Christian Davies, commonly called Mother Ross. 1740. Ed. by Hon. Sir J.W. Fortescue. 1928. The largely fictional adventures of a woman soldier.

DELACHEROIS, NICHOLAS.

1124. 'The letters of Capt. Nicholas Delacherois, 9th regiment J.S.A.H.R. Vol. LI. no. 205, spring 1973, 5-14. Throws some light on the daily life of a junior officer in the mid-eighteenth century.

DUNDEE, JOHN GRAHAM OF CLAVERHOUSE, VISCOUNT OF

1125. Letters of John Graham of Claverhouse, Viscount of Dundee . . . 1678-1689. Ed. by G. Smythe. Edin. 1826. A major source.

1126. Napier, Mark. Memorials and letters illustrative of the life and times of John Graham of Claverhouse, Viscount of Dundee. 3 Vols. Edin. 1859-62. The standard biography with many letters from the Queensbury archives.

1127. Terry, C.S. John Graham of Claverhouse, Viscount of Dundee 1648-1689. 1905. The best short biography.

1128. Barrington, M.J. Graham of Claverhouse, Viscount of Dundee. 1911. Contains excellent portraits, and a facsimile letter.

1129. Daviot, Gordon. Claverhouse. 1937. Adds little new.

GAGE, HON. THOMAS.

1130. The correspondence of General Thomas Gage with the secretaries of state and with the War Office and the Treasury. Ed. by C.E. Carter. 2 Vols. New Haven. 1933-34.

1131. Alden, J.R. General Gage in America, being principally a history of his role in the American revolution. Baton. Rouge. 1948.

1132. Papers: W.L. Clements Library, Ann Arbor, Mich.
The documents relate to his service in North America,
1754-83.

GATLIFF, JAMES.

1133. Stations, gentlemen. Memoirs of James Gatliff.
Epitome or biographical sketch of my own life, written
- calamo veritatis - at the request of my son, John,
who will preserve it as a record which would not have
been penned to oblige any other being on earth - the
Lady Diana Strongellotti excepted. Ed. by H.E.
Gatliff. 1938. Valuable for his account of service
in England and social life in the army, from his
appointment in 1782 to a first commission in the 52nd
regiment. He served in India and China.

GERMAIN, GEORGE SACKVILLE, FIRST VISCOUNT.

1134. The trial of the Rt. Hon. Lord George Sackville, at a
court-martial held at the Horse Guards . . . with his
Lordship's defence. 2 Vols. 1760.

1135. Marlow, Louis. Sackville of Drayton. 1948. The
first biography, which remains the best account.

1136. Sullivan, A.E. 'Was Lord George Sackville guilty?'.
A.Q. Vol. LXXIII no. 2, January 1957, 242-50. A
review of his court-martial.

1137. Valentine, Alan. Lord George Germain. Oxf. 1962.
Not a balanced account.

1138. Papers: William L. Clements Library. These papers
relate to the War of Austrian Succession, correspondence
with Amherst and Wolfe, but mainly concerned with the
American War of Independence.

GRAHAM, SAMUEL.

1139. Memoir of General Graham. Ed. by James John Graham.
Edin. 1862.

GRANBY, JOHN MANNERS, MARQUIS OF.

1140. Manners, W.E. Some account of the military, political
and social life of . . . John Manners, Marquis of
Granby. 1899. A useful biography, with much
correspondence printed, of a fine cavalry officer, who
was commander-in-chief.

GRANT, JAMES.

1141. Grant, A.M. General James Grant of Ballindalloch, 1720-
    1806: being an account of his long services in
    Flanders, America, and the West Indies, with original
    letters throwing sidelights on many strange and ancient
    customs in the Highlands, on early days of road making
    and the recruitment and equipment of the first highland
    regiments. 1930. A short study but with many
    unpublished letters reproduced.

HAMILTON, R.

1142. Barnsley, R.E. 'The life of an eighteenth century army
    surgeon'. J.S.A.H.R. Vol. XLIV. no. 179, September
    1966, 130-4. Extracts from,and comments on,a book of
    reminiscences written by R. Hamilton, M.D. first
    published in 1787 as The duties of a regimental surgeon
    considered.

HARRIS, GEORGE, LORD.

1143. Lushington, S.R. Life and services of General Lord
    Harris, G.C.B. during his Campaigns in America, the
    West Indies and India.1840. By his private secretary.

HERVEY, GENERAL THE HON. WILLIAM.

1144. Journal of the Hon. William Hervey in North America and
    Europe 1755-1814, with orderly books at Montreal 1760-
    1763. With a memoir and notes. Ed. by S.H.A. Hervey.
    1894.

HASTINGS, FRANCIS RAWDON, MARQUESS OF.

1145. Sheppard, E.W. 'Little known soldiers of the past. II
    The Marquess of Hastings (1754-1826)' A.Q. Vol. LXXXIV
    no. 1, April 1962, 70-9. A fuller account of his
    distinguished military career is needed.

HOWE, SIR WILLIAM.

1146. Partridge, Bellamy. Sir Billy Howe. N.Y. 1932.

HUGHES, THOMAS.

1147. A journal by Thomas Hughes. For his amusement, and
    designed only for his perusal by the time he attains the
    age of fifty if he lives so long 1778-1789. Camb. 1947.
    Served in the 53rd regiment in America, and as A.D.C.
    to Arthur Wellesley at the capture of Seringapatum.

JOHNES, JOHN.

1148. 'The diary of an infantry subaltern, 1787'. Ed. by
    M.E.S. Laws. A.Q. Vol. LIV. no. 1. April 1947, 138-42.
    Diary of an ensign which clearly indicates the lack of
    professionalism in the officer corps at the time.

KEITH, SIR. ROBERT MURRAY.

1149. Papers: John Rylands Library, University of Manchester, among the collection of the Earl of Crawford and Balcarres.

KIRK, PERCY.

1150. Jackson, J.H. 'Lieutenant-General Percy Kirk, 1646-91'. A.Q. Vol. LXXXVIII no. 2, July 1964, 215-20. A balanced survey of a maligned soldier whose reputation was tarnished during his period in Tangiers.

KNIGHT, JOHN.

1151. Calvert, E.M. and Calvert, R.T.C. Sergeant Surgeon John Knight, surgeon general 1664-1680. 1939. Knight was surgeon general during the Dutch wars.

LAMB, ROGER.

1152. An original and authentic journal of occurrences during the late American war, from its commencement to the year 1783. Dublin. 1809. This, and the memoir listed immediately below, are two of the most important example of a soldier's reminiscences of which there are few extant from this period.

1153. Memoir of his own life. By R. Lamb. Formerly a sergeant in the Royal Welch Fusiliers. Dublin. 1811.

LAWRENCE, STRINGER.

1154. Biddulph, Col. John. Stringer Lawrence, the father of th Indian army. 1901. The first commander in chief in Indi

LIGONIER, JOHN LOUIS, LORD.

1155. Whitworth, Lieut. Col. Rex. H. Field Marshal Lord Ligon ier: a study of the British army, 1702-1770. Oxf. 1958. The standard work.

1156. Papers: are among the Add. MSS. in the British Museum.

LISTER, JEREMY.

1157. Innes, R.A. 'Jeremy Lister, 10th regiment, 1770-1783'. J.S.A.H.R. Vol. XLI. no. 165 March 1963', 31-41; no. 156, June 1963, 59-63. Service in North America.

LLOYD, HENRY.

1158. Fuller, J.F.C. 'Major General Henry Lloyd adventurer and military philosopher'. A.Q. Vol. XII no. 2, July 1926, 300-14. A good summary of what is known about his life.

LOUDOUN, JOHN CAMPBELL, EARL OF.

159. Papers: Henry E. Huntington Library; B.M. Add Mss. 44063-44084. See also, (1845).

MACKAY, HUGH.

160. Mackay, John. Life of Lieut. General Hugh Mackay of Scoury, commander-in-chief of the forces in Scotland, 1689 and 1690, colonel commandant of the Scots Brigade in the service of the States General, and a privy counsellor in Scotland. Edin. 1836. See also, Hugh Mackay, Memoirs of the war carried on in Scotland and Ireland. Ed. by John Mackay. Edin. 1833.

MACLEOD, DONALD.

161. Memoirs of the life and gallant exploits of the old highlander, Sergeant Donald Macleod. Int. by J.G. Fife. Edin. 1933. Sergeant Macleod joined the Black Watch in 1700, and served in many campaigns, but unfortunately little detailed information about them is given in this autobiography.

MARLBOROUGH, JOHN CHURCHILL, DUKE OF.

162. Lediard, Thomas. Life of John, duke of Marlborough. 3 Vols. 1736. Many documents are printed.

163. Coxe, William. Memoirs of the duke of Marlborough, with his original correspondence. 3 Vols. 1818-19. Valuable now for the original material printed from the Blenheim archives. The best early biography.

164. Murray, General Sir George. ed. Letters and dispatches of John Churchill, duke of Marlborough, from 1702-1712. 5 Vols. 1845. A major source of information for the period.

165. Alison, Sir Archibald. The military life of John, duke of Marlborough; with some account of his contemporaries and of the War of Succession. 2 Vols. 1852. This is the second enlarged edn.

166. Wolseley, Garnet Joseph, Viscount. The life of John Churchill, duke of Marlborough to the accession of Queen Anne. 2 Vols. 1894. An unfinished work, it is not very reliable.

167. Atkinson, C.T. Marlborough and the rise of the British army. 1921. Useful for his military career, and also for bibliographical note, pp. vii-xii.

168. Fortescue, Hon. Sir J.W. Marlborough. 1932. A short popular work.

1169. Churchill, Sir Winston S. Marlborough: his life and times. 4 Vols. 1934-38. A vigorous defence of Marlborough combined with a detailed survey of his career. There is a full bibliography.

1170. Esson, D.M.R. 'The character of John Churchill, duke of Marlborough'. A.Q. Vol. LXXXI no. 1, October 1960, 45-51.

1171. Snyder, H.E. 'The duke of Marlborough's request of his captain-generalcy for life: a re-examination'. J.S.A.H.R. Vol. XLV no. 182, summer 1967, 67-83.

1172. Burton, I.F. The captain-general. The career of John Churchill, duke of Marlborough from 1702 to 1711. 1968. Based on published sources it incorporates the results of recent research.

1173. Chandler, David. Marlborough as military commander. 1972. His qualities as a military leader, with background information on the art of war during the period.

1174. Scouller, Major R.E. 'Marlborough - the international commander'. A.Q. Vol. 102 no. 4, July 1972, 438-450. A discussion of his historical reputation.

1175. Barnett, Corelli. Marlborough. 1974. A valuable essay accompanied by numerous fine illustrations.

1176. Papers: Blenheim Palace, Oxfordshire. Transcripts of documents at Blenheim made by W. Coxe for his biography are in the British Museum. They were a major source for many years when the Blenheim archives were closed.

MILLER, JAMES.

1177. Leslie, J.H. 'The diary of James Miller, 1745-50'. J.S.A.H.R. Vol. III no. 14, October 1924, 208-226. Diary of a soldier in the army of Prince Charles Stuart, and later that of the crown.

MILLNER, JOHN.

1178. A compendious journal of all the marches, famous battles sieges and other most noteworthy, heroic and ever memorable actions of the triumphant armies of the ever-glorious confederate high allies. 1733. A detailed account of service during Marlborough's campaigns.

MOODIE, JOHN.

1179. Cadell, Sir Patrick. 'John Moodie, military medical writer of the eighteenth century'. J.S.A.H.R. Vol. XXII no. 88, winter 1943, 148-53. Moodie was the author of a history of the Malabar campaign, 1782-84.

MURRAY, HON JAMES.

1180. Mahon, R.H. The life of General the Hon. James Murray, a builder of Canada. 1921. The life of one of Wolfe's brigadiers at Quebec.

NOYES, SAMUEL.

1181. Johnston, S.H.F. 'Letters of Samuel Noyes, chaplain of the Royal Scots, 1703-4'. J.S.A.H.R. Vol. XXXVII no. 149, March 1959, 33-40; no. 150, June 1959, 128-35; no. 152, December 1959, 145-52.

OGLETHORPE, GENERAL JAMES EDWARD.

1182. Ettinger, Amos A. James Edward Oglethorpe, imperial idealist. Oxf. 1936. The best account of his military career, which was mainly spent in North America.

PETERBOROUGH, CHARLES MORDAUNT, EARL OF.

1183. Freind, J. Account of the earl of Peterborough's conduct in Spain, chiefly since the raising of the siege of Barcelona, 1706 ... with original papers. 1707. A defence of Peterborough by a participant.

1184. Warburton, G.D. A memoir of Charles Mordaunt, earl of Peterborough, with selections from his correspondence. 2 Vols. 1853. Useful for the letters that are printed, but very critical of Lord Peterborough.

1185. Russell, F.S. The earl of Peterborough and Monmouth. 2 Vols. 1187. Contains additional information, but is not a good biography.

1186. Stebbing, William. Peterborough. 1890. Probably the best extant life, which while short, gives a fair assessment of a controversial figure.

1187. Ballard, Colin Robert. The great earl of Peterborough. 1929. A popular survey, which adds little new although the author has used Ms. sources.

1188. Dickinson, H.T. 'The recall of Lord Peterborough'. J.S.A.H.R. Vol. XLVII no. 191, autumn 1969, 175-187. The end of his controversial campaign in Spain.

ROBERTSON, ARCHIBALD.

1189. Lydenberg, H.M. ed. Archibald Robertson, lieutenant-general Royal Engineers, his diaries and sketches in America, 1762-1780. N.Y. 1930.

ST. PIERRE, COL. DE.

1190. Military journal of Col. de St. Pierre, Royal Dragoons, and other manuscripts relating to the war of the Spanish Succession, 1703-13. Ed. by J.E. Renouard James. Chatham. 1882. Deals with operations in Spain and Portugal.

STAIR, JOHN DALRYMPLE, SECOND EARL OF.

1191. Graham, J.M. Annals and correspondence of the Viscount
and the first and second earls of Stair. Edin. 1879.
The only full study of this neglected soldier's
remarkable career.

TOWNSHEND, GEORGE, FIRST MARQUESS.

1192. Townshend, C.V.F. Military life of F.M. George, first
marquess Townshend, 1724-1807. 1901. Includes extracts
from his journal kept during service at Dettingen,
Fontenoy, Culloden and Quebec.

TURNER, SIR JAMES.

1193. Memoirs of his own life and times, by Sir James Turner,
MDCXXXII-MDCLXX, from original manuscript. Edin.1829.
The author served in the Scots guards, 1662-1668,
rising to the rank of lieut. col.

WOLFE, JAMES.

1194. Wright, Robert. The life of Major-General James Wolfe,
founded on original documents and illustrated from his
correspondence. 1864. Family letters are printed.

1195. Willson, Beckles. The life and letters of James Wolfe.
1909. Prints much correspondence.

1196. Paine, J. 'James Wolfe'. A.Q. Vol. XIV no. 1, April
1927, 89-99. Bibliographical comments, and notes on
the location of relics of Wolfe.

1197. Findlay, J.T. Wolfe in Scotland in the '45 and from
1749 to 1753. 1928.

1198. Waugh, W.T. James Wolfe, man and soldier. 1928. Perhaps the best single account, which analyses his personality.

1199. Reilly, Robin. The rest to fortune. The life of Major
General James Wolfe. 1960. Based on manuscript sources.

1200. Grinnell-Milne, Duncan. Mad is he? The character and
achievement of James Wolfe. 1963. A popular defence of
Wolfe.

(ii) 1793-1914.

ABERCROMBY, SIR RALPH.

1201. Dunfermline, James Abercromby, Lord. Lieut. General Sir
Ralph Abercromby. 1861.

1202. Paine, J. 'Sir Ralph Abercromby, the bicentenary of a
famour soldier'. J.R.U.S.I. Vol. LXXIX no. 515,
August 1934, 574-80. Useful bibliographical remarks.

1203. Gordon, T.C. Four notable Scots. 1960. Includes an
essay on Abercromby.

ADAM, GENERAL SIR FREDERICK.

1204. Papers: 1797-1833, including his accounts of the
battles of Castilla and Waterloo: Adam of Blair Adam
Mss., Kinross, Scotland.

ADAMS, PRIVATE BUCK.

1205. The narrative of Private Buck Adams, 7th (Princess
Royal's) Dragoon Guards on the eastern frontier of the
Cape of Good Hope, 1843-48. Ed. by A. Gordon Brown.
Cape Town. 1941.

ADDINGTON, HON. CHARLES JAMES.

1206. 'The Crimean and Indian mutiny letters of the Hon.
Charles James Addington, 38th regiment'. Ed. by the
Hon. Mrs. Hiley Addington. J.S.A.H.R. vol. XLVI
no. 187, autumn 1968, 156-180; no. 188, winter 1968,
206-216.

ADYE, LIEUT. GENERAL SIR JOHN.

1207. Soldiers and others I have known. Recollections from
the Afghan campaign to the Great War. 1925. He was
the son of Sir John Miller Adye.

ADYE, GENERAL SIR JOHN MILLER.

1208. Recollections of a military life. 1895. Service in the
Crimea and India of an artillery officer well known as
an author of several campaign histories.

AIREY, RICHARD, LORD.

1209. Papers: Hereford C.R.O. relating to the Crimean war. No
biography of General Airey has yet been written.

ALDERSON, E.A.H.

1210. With the mounted infantry and the Mashonaland Field
Force. 1898.

ANDERSON, LIEUT. COL. JOSEPH.

1211. Recollections of a Peninsular veteran. 1913. Account
of his service in the Peninsula, West Indies and India.

ANGLESEY, HENRY WILLIAM PAGET, EARL OF UXBRIDGE AND MARQUESS OF.

1212. Anglesey, Marquess of. One-leg. The life and letters
of Henry William Paget, 1st Marquess of Anglesey. 1961.
The standard account based on his private papers which
remain in the family's possession.

ANTON, JAMES.

1213. Retrospect of a military life during the most eventful periods of the last war. Edin. 1841. One of
the more important accounts of the period by a
participant.

ARDAGH, MAJOR-GENERAL SIR JOHN.

1214. Malmesbury, Susan Harris, Countess of. The life of
Major-General Sir John Ardagh. 1909. A useful account
by his wife.

1215. Papers: 1862-1908: P.R.O. 30/40.

ARTHUR, SIR GEORGE C.A.

1216. Not worth reading. 1938. Perhaps known best now for
his writings on military subjects.

AUSTIN, THOMAS.

1217. 'Old stick-leg': extracts from the diaries of Major
Thomas Austin. Ed. by H.H. Austin. 1926. He served
in the Walcheren expedition and in the American war of
1812.

BACON, GENERAL ANTHONY.

1218. Boger, A.J. The story of General Bacon: being a short
biography of a Peninsula and Waterloo veteran. 1903.

BADEN-POWELL, GENERAL ROBERT S.S., LORD.

1219. Adventures and accidents. 1934. See particularly for
his useful essay 'Bluffing at Mafeking'.

1220. Carter, M.E. Life of Baden-Powell. 1956. A good
short account. There are also a number of other
biographical studies most of which concentrate on his
later achievements.

1221. Papers: there are collections in the Bodleian Library,
the N.L.W., the N.A.M., and the B.M. (including Add.Mss.
50255, relating to the siege of Mafeking), and elsewhere

BAIRD, SIR DAVID.

1222. Hook, T.E. Life of General the Rt. Hon. Sir David
Baird. 2 vols. 1832. A rather partisan defence of
Baird.

1223. Wilkin, W.H. The life of Sir David Baird. 1912. A
more balanced study than that by Hook, but only
secondary sources have been used.

BARKER, SIR GEORGE DIGBY.

224. Letters from Persia and India, 1857-1859: a subaltern's
experiences in war. By the late General Sir George
Digby Barker. Ed. by Lady K.W. Barker. 1915.

BAYLY, RICHARD.

225. Diary of Colonel Bayly, 12th regiment. 1796-1830.
1896.

BEAUCHAMP-WALKER, GENERAL SIR C.P.

226. Diary of a soldier's life. Being letters written...
during active service in the Crimean, Chinese, Austro-
Prussian, and Franco-German wars. 1894.

BELL, GENERAL SIR GEORGE.

227. Rough notes by an old soldier during fifty years service.
2 vols. 1867. A shortened version has been published
as: Soldier's glory, being 'rough notes of an old
soldier'. Ed. by Brian Stuart. 1956. Details of his
long army service from 1811 in the Peninsula, India,
Canada, and the Crimea.

BELL, WILLIAM.

228. The letters of William Bell, 89th Foot 1808-1810. Ed.
by B.W. Webb-Carter. J.S.A.H.R. vol. XLVIII no. 194,
summer 1970, 66-84; no. 195, autumn 1970, 147-164.
These letters give a fascinating account of the daily
life of a subaltern in a marching regiment in the early
years of the nineteenth century.

BERESFORD, ROBERT BALLARD LONG, LORD.

229. Peninsula cavalry journal (1811-1813) of Lieut. General
R.B. Long, Lord Beresford. Ed. by T.H. McGuffie.
1951. This work is included in this section because of
the brief memoir of Beresford produced by the editor:
surprisingly, perhaps, no full length biography of
Beresford has yet been written.

BEVAN, MAJOR HENRY.

230. Thirty years in India, or a soldier's reminiscences of
native and European life in the Presidencies from 1808
to 1838. 2 vols. 1839.

BLAKENEY, ROBERT.

231. A boy in the Peninsular war: the services, adventures
and experiences of Robert Blakeney; subaltern in the
28th regiment. An autobiography. Ed. by J. Sturgis.
1899. To be used with caution, as it was written
twenty-five years after the end of the war.

BLAKISTON, JOHN.

1232. Twelve years military adventures in three quarters of
      the globe; or memoirs of an officer who served in the
      armies of his Majesty and of the East India company
      between the years 1802 and 1814, in which are contained
      the campaigns of the duke of Wellington in India and
      his last in Spain and the south of France. 2 vols.
      1829. An engineers officer who served in the Indian
      and British armies.

BRACKENBURY, GENERAL SIR HENRY.

1233. Some memories of my spare time. Edin. 1909. Covers
      the period between 1856–1885.

1234. Papers: Royal Artillery museum, Woolwich.

BRAGGE, WILLIAM.

1235. Peninsula portrait: the letters of Captain William
      Bragge, Third (King's Own) Dragoons. Ed. by S.A.C.
      Cassels. 1963. One of the few personal records from
      a cavalry regiment covering nearly the whole of its
      period on active service in the Peninsula.

BROADFOOT, GEORGE.

1236. Broadfoot, William. The career of Major George
      Broadfoot...compiled from his personal papers. 1888.
      Useful particularly for the Afghan war, 1838–40, where
      he served with distinction. He was killed at the
      battle of Ferozeshah, 1845.

BROCK, SIR ISAAC.

1237. Tupper, Ferdinand Brock. The life and correspondence
      of Major General Sir Isaac Brock. 1847. See also
      H.J. Eayrs, Sir Isaac Brock. Toronto. 1924. Useful
      for his important role in the war of 1812 with America.

BROWN, DAVID.

1238. Diary of a soldier, 1805–1827. Ardrossan. 1934.

BROWN, GENERAL SIR GEORGE.

1239. Papers concerning the Crimean war: N.L.S.

BROWNE, GENERAL SIR JAMES FRANKFORT MANNERS.

1240. Innes, James J. Life and times of General Sir James
      Browne. 1905.

BROWNRIGG, GENERAL SIR ROBERT.

1241. Papers as quartermaster general 1803–11: N.A.M. Papers
      as military secretary to the commander-in-chief, and as
      governor of Ceylon, 1811-20: P.R.O. W.O. 133.

BULLER, SIR REDVERS.

1242. Jerrold, Walter. Sir Redvers H. Buller, V.C. The
      story of his life and campaigns. 1900. Not of much
      value now.

1243. Butler, Lewis. Sir Redvers Buller. 1909. A rather
      uncritical study, originally published in the King's
      Royal Rifle Corps Chronicle.

1244. Melville, C.H. Life of General the Rt. Hon. Sir
      Redvers Buller. 2 vols. 1923. Based on Buller's
      surviving papers and the recollections of his
      contemporaries.

1245. Paine, J. 'General Sir Redvers Buller, V.C. The
      centenary of a great leader'. J.R.U.S.I. vol. LXXXIV
      no. 535, August 1939, 578-82. Includes useful bibliog-
      raphical notes.

1246. Papers: P.R.O. W.O. 132. Mainly official correspondence
      for the period 1872-1901.

BURGOYNE, FIELD MARSHAL SIR JOHN FOX.

1247. Military opinions of Sir John Burgoyne. Ed. by Lieut.
      Col. the Hon. George Wrottesley. 1859. Includes
      selections from his writings. The editing is not
      generally of a high standard.

1248. Wrottesley, Lieut. Col. the Hon. George. Life and
      correspondence of Sir John Burgoyne. 2 vols. 1873.
      The basic source for his long and distinguished career.

1249. Papers: Royal Engineers museum, Chatham. Most of the
      correspondence in this collection has already been
      published in Wrottesley's Life listed immediately above.

BURNABY, FREDERICK.

1250. Wright, Thomas. The life of Colonel Fred. Burnaby.
      1908.

BUTLER, GENERAL SIR W.F.

1251. Sir William Butler: an autobiography. Ed. by Eileen
      Butler. 1911. A classic account.

1252. McCourt, Edward. Remember Butler: the story of Sir
      William Butler. 1967. A concise biography of a
      soldier who was a prolific author.

CALLADINE, SERGEANT GEORGE.

1253. The diary of Colour-Sergeant George Calladine, 19th
      Foot, 1793-1837. Ed. by M.L. Ferrar. 1922. The
      author served in Ceylon and later in England and
      Ireland, and gives a useful picture of life in the
      peacetime army after the Napoleonic wars.

CALLWELL, SIR CHARLES EDWARD.

1254. Service yarns and memories. 1912. Callwell was a
cadet at Woolwich and served mainly in India and South
Africa. Perhaps best remembered now for his pioneering
analysis Small wars (1636). See also his later book
Stray recollections.2 vols. 1923.

CALVERT, SIR HARRY.

1255. The journals and correspondence of General Sir Harry
Calvert comprising the campaigns in Flanders and
Holland in 1793-4 with an appendix containing his
plans for the defence of the country in case of
invasion. Ed. by Sir Harry Verney. 1853.

1256. Jones, K.R. 'General Sir Harry Calvert'. A.Q. vol.
LXXVIII no. 2, July 1959, 238-40. Calvert was adjutant
general under the duke of York.

1257. Papers: Claydon House, Bucks.

CAMBRIDGE, GEORGE, DUKE OF.

1258. Verner, W.W.C. The military life of H.R.H. George,
duke of Cambridge. 2 vols. 1905. Still the best
account, with extracts from his correspondence and
official papers.

1259. Sheppard, J.E. George, duke of Cambridge: a memoir
of his private life based on the journals and correspondence of His Royal Highness. 2 vols. 1906. A
useful supplement to Verner's biography.

1260. Sullivan, A.E. 'The last commander-in-chief: George,
duke of Cambridge'. A.Q. vol. LXI no. 1, October 1950,
88-94.

1261. Bond, Brian. 'The retirement of the duke of Cambridge'.
J.R.U.S.I. vol. 106, November, 1961, 544-53. Examines
the circumstances surrounding the duke of Cambridge's
departure from office.

1262. St. Aubyn, Hon. G.R. The royal George, 1819-1904. The
life of H.R.H. Prince George, duke of Cambridge. 1963.
Based on unpublished sources, this popular work adds
little new of interest.

1263. Papers: Windsor Castle, Bucks. A major collection,
which still has not been fully used.

CARDIGAN, JAMES THOMAS BRUDENELL, EARL OF.

1264. Compton, Piers. Cardigan of Balaclava. 1972. A popular
account.

1265. Thomas, Donald. Charge! Hurrah! Hurrah! A life of Cardigan of Balaclava. 1974. Presents a convincing portrait of this controversial soldier inspite of the title. Further information on his career is in the scholarly family history by Joan Wake, The Brudenells of Deene, 1953.

CHAMBERLAIN, SIR NEVILLE.

1266. Forrest, G.W. Life of F.M. Sir Neville Chamberlain. 1909. The military life of an officer who distinguished himself in India during 44 years military service.

CHELMSFORD, FREDERICK AUGUSTUS THESIGER, LORD.

1267. Papers: N.A.M. See also (2121) which gives the details of his career in the army.

CHILDS, SIR WYNDHAM.

1268. Episodes and reflections: being some records from the life of Major-General Sir Wyndham Childs. 1930. Served in the Boer war, and India before World War I.

CLARKE, HON. SIR ANDREW.

1269. Vetch, R.H. Life of Lieut. General the Hon. Sir Andrew Clarke. 1905. Clarke was Inspector General of Fortifications 1882-1886.

CLARKE, JOHN.

1270. Adventures of a Leicestershire veteran. By colour sergeant John Clarke of Loughborough, with the 17th Foot, 1829-52. Leicester. 1893.

CLYDE, FIELD MARSHAL COLIN CAMPBELL, LORD.

1271. Shadwell, Major-General Lawrence. The life of Colin Campbell, Lord Clyde. 2 vols. 1881. Much use is made of Campbell's diary and papers.

COBBETT, WILLIAM.

1272. The progress of a ploughboy to a seat in parliament. Ed. by William Reitzell. 1933. Includes a detailed account by Cobbett of his early life in the army.

COCKBURN, GENERAL SIR GEORGE.

1273. Papers: BM Add. Mss. 48312-48339. Served with the army of occupation in Sicily during the Napoleonic wars.

CODRINGTON, GENERAL SIR WILLIAM JOHN.

1274. Entrybooks of correspondence and orders and memoranda kept by Sir William Codrington as governor of Gibraltar. PRO 30/31. Papers: N.A.M.

COGHILL, N.J.A.

1275. Coghill, Patrick. Whom the gods love. A memoir of
      Lieut. Nevill Josiah Alymer Coghill, V.C., the 24th
      Regiment, 1852-1879. Halesowen. 1968.

COLE, GENERAL THE HON. SIR GALBRAITH LOWRY.

1276. Cole, M.L. and Gwyn, Stephen. Memoirs of Sir Lowry
      Cole. 1935. The memoirs of one of Wellington's most
      trusted and capable subordinates.

1277. Papers: P.R.O. 30/43, as commander of the 4th Division,
      and elsewhere.

COMBERMERE, STAPLETON COTTON, VISCOUNT.

1278. Memoirs and correspondence of F.M. Viscount Combermere.
      Ed. by Lady Combermere and W. Knollys. 2 vols. 1866.
      Useful for the correspondence which is printed.

COMPTON, RICHARD.

1279. Turner, E.H. 'Letters from a soldier, 1856'. A.Q.
      vol. LXXV no. 1, October 1957, 113-7. Compton was a
      trooper in the 12th Royal Lancers, and he served in
      England and India.

COOKE, SIR JOHN HENRY.

1280. Memoirs of the late war. 1831.

COOPER, JOHN SPENCER.

1281. Rough notes of seven campaigns in Portugal, Spain,
      France, and America during the years 1809-10-11-12-13-
      14-15. 1869.

CORBETT, A.F.

1282. Service through six reigns, 1891 to 1953. Norwich. 1953

COSTELLO, EDWARD.

1283. The adventures of a soldier; or memoirs of Edward
      Costello, formerly a non-commissioned officer in the
      Rifle Brigade; comprising narratives of the campaigns
      in the Peninsula under the duke of Wellington. 1841.
      A vivid portrait of his service in the army from 1806.

COWANS, SIR JOHN.

1284. Chapman-Huston, W.W.D.M. and Rutter, Owen. General
      Sir John Cowans, the quartermaster-general of the Great
      War. 2 vols. 1924.

COWELL, SIR JOHN STEPNEY.

1285. Leaves from the diary of an officer of the Guards. 1854.
Later known as Sir John Stepney, he served as a young
officer in the Peninsula war.

CRAUFURD, ROBERT.

1286. Craufurd, A.H.G. General Craufurd and his light division.
With many anecdotes, a paper and letters by Sir John
Moore, and also letters from the Rt. Hon. W. Windham,
the duke of Wellington, Lord Londonderry and others. 1891.
An accurate account of one of Wellington's most able
divisional commanders.

1287. Spurrier, M.C. 'The career of Robert Craufurd in the
75th Foot'. J.S.A.H.R. vol. XLIV no. 177, March 1966,
3-10. Served in 75th between 1787 and 1793, mainly
in India. The article is based on letters between
Craufurd and his brother.

CROMER, EVELYN BARING, LORD.

1288. Zetland, L.J.L.D. Ronaldshay, earl of. Lord Cromer
being the authorised life of Evelyn Baring, first earl
of Cromer. 1932. Useful for his early military career,
and activities as a military reformer.

DAVEY RICHARD.

1289. 'A Sussex soldier of Wellington's. The letters of an
old campaigner: 1811-1816'. Ed. by W.A. Woodward.
Sussex County Mag. vol. II, 1928, 48-55, 88-92, 126,
134-140.

DENT, WILLIAM.

1290. Woodford, L.W. 'War and peace - the experiences of an
army surgeon 1810-27'. J.S.A.H.R. vol. XLIX no. 97,
spring 1971, 43-58. Service in Gibraltar, the Peninsula,
Waterloo, and later in the West Indies.

DICKSON, SIR ALEXANDER.

1291. The Dickson manuscripts. Being diaries, letters, maps,
account books, with various other papers of... Major
General Sir Alexander Dickson...series "C" - from 1809
to 1818. Ed. by J.H. Leslie. 2 vols. 1905-12.
Mainly useful for the role of the artillery in the
Peninsula war.

DON, GENERAL SIR GEORGE.

1292. Papers: B.M. Add Mss. 46702-46711, 46883-46884. Includes
documents relating to service in Flanders, 1793-5.

DONALDSON, SERGEANT JOSEPH.

1293. Recollections of the eventful life of a soldier.
1856. Some useful observations by an intelligent
n.c.o.

1294. Scenes and sketches of a soldier's life in Ireland.
1826.

DOUGLAS, SIR HOWARD.

1295. Fullom, S.W. Life of General Sir Howard Douglas from
his notes, conversations and letters. 1863. Douglas
served with Sir John Moore, and with Wellington in
the Peninsula.

DUNDAS, GENERAL SIR DAVID.

1296. Papers as quartermaster-general, 1796-1803: N.A.M.
There are some other papers among the Add Mss. in the
B.M., relating to his time as commander-in-chief
after the duke of York's resignation.

DUNDONALD, D.M.B.H. COCHRANE, EARL OF.

1297. My army life. 1926. Dundonald participated in the
Gordon relief expedition, and was involved in the
reform of the army after the Boer war.

DURAND, SIR HENRY MARION.

1298. Durand, Sir Henry Mortimer. Life of Major-General Sir
Henry Marion Durand. 1885.

D'URBAN, SIR BENJAMIN.

1299. The Peninsula journal of Major General Sir Benjamin
D'Urban 1808-1817. Ed. by I.J. Rousseau. 1930.
D'Urban was quartermaster-general in the Portuguese army

DYOTT, GENERAL WILLIAM.

1300. Dyott's diary 1781-1845. A selection from the journal
of William Dyott, sometime general in the British army
and aide-de-camp to His Majesty George III. Ed. by
R.W. Jeffery. 2 vols. 1907.

1301. Papers: Stafford C.R.O.

ELERS, GEORGE.

1302. Memoirs of George Elers, Captain in the 12th regiment
of Foot (1777-1842), to which are added correspondence
and other papers with genealogy and notes. Ed. by
Lord Morrison and G. Leveson-Gower. 1903. Regimental
life in early nineteenth century India.

EVANS, GENERAL SIR GEORGE DE LACY.

1303. Wood, Major General G.N. 'Evans in the Crimea: a study of our one competent senior commander'. A.Q. vol. 103 no. 3, April 1972, 344-51. Gives some biographical information. A fuller study of this remarkable soldier and army reformer is required.

EWART, LIEUT. GENERAL J.A.

1304. The story of a soldier's life. 2 vols. 1881. A detailed account of regimental life at home, and in the colonies, in the nineteenth century.

EYRE, MAJOR-GENERAL SIR WILLIAM.

1305. Papers: P.R.O. 30/46. As commander of the 2nd brigade 3rd Division and later of the 3rd Division, both in the Crimea, and as commander-in-chief, Canada, 1856-9.

FRANKLAND, SIR F.W.

1306. Walker, W.J. 'Ensign Frankland'. Blackwood's Mag. no. 1553, March 1945, 161-9. The early career in the Peninsula of Sir Frederick Frankland.

FRASER, MAJOR GENERAL THOMAS.

1307. Recollections and reflections. 1914. Fraser was the leading military engineering theorist of his time.

FRAZER, COL. SIR AUGUSTUS SIMON.

1308. Sabine, Major General Edward. Letters of Col. Sir Augustus Simon Frazer, K.C.B. commanding the Royal Horse Artillery in the army under the duke of Wellington, written during the Peninsula and Waterloo campaigns. 1859.

GATACRE, SIR WILLIAM FORBES.

1309. Gatacre, B.W. General Gatacre: the story of the life and services of Sir William Forbes Gatacre ... 1843-1906. 1910. Mainly on his work in South Africa.

'G.B.'

1310. Narrative of a private soldier in one of His Majesty's regiments of foot written by himself. Detailing many circumstances relative to the Irish rebellion in 1798, the expedition to Holland in 1709, and the expedition to Egypt in 1801 . . . Glasgow. 1819.

GERARD, SIR MONTAGU GILBERT.

1311. Leaves from the diaries of a soldier and sportsman during twenty years' service in India, Afghanistan, Egypt and other countries, 1865-1885. 1903.

GILLESPIE, SIR ROBERT ROLLO.

1312. Wakeham, C.E. The bravest soldier. Sir Rollo
      Gillespie 1766-1814. A historical military sketch.
      Edin. 1937. This biography was responsible for the
      revival of his military reputation, and describes
      well his remarkable career.

1313. ---------- 'Fighting dragoon - Major-General Sir
      Rollo Gillespie'. A.Q. vol. LXXIV no. 2, July 1957,
      228-33.

GLEICHEN, A.E.W., LORD.

1314. A guardsman's memories, a book of recollections by
      Major-General Lord Edward Gleichen. Edin. 1932. Mainly
      concerning the author's life in the Grenadier guards
      from 1881 to 1914, including his experiences in the Boer
      war.

GOMM, SIR WILLIAM MAYNARD.

1315. Letters and journal...from 1799 to Waterloo 1815. Ed.
      by F.C. Carr-Gomm. 1881. The editor's text is
      unfortunately of little value, but some useful original
      papers are printed.

GORDON, SIR CHARLES ARTHUR.

1316. Recollections of thirty-nine years in the army. 1898.
      Gordon served in India, the Gold Coast, and China, and
      was the author of a number of works on military
      medicine.

GORDON, GENERAL CHARLES GEORGE.

1317. Boulger, D.C. Life of Gordon. 1896. The best early
      biography.

1318. Allen, B.M. Gordon and the Sudan. 1931. The author
      wrote three scholarly accounts of the various exploits
      of Gordon, based on unpublished materials.

1319. -------- Gordon in China. 1933.

1320. Wortham, H.E. Gordon: an intimate portrait. 1933.
      A useful study of his character and personality.

1321. Allen, B.M. Gordon. 1935.

1322. Elton, Godfrey, Lord. General Gordon. 1954.

1323. -------- ed. General Gordon's Khartoum journals.
      1961. A scholarly edition of his notes made during the
      siege.

1324. Marlowe, John. Mission to Khartum: the apotheosis of General Gordon. 1969. Valuable, _inter alia_, for its introduction 'the Gordon literature and legend' which assesses some of the more important items among the voluminous, and still rapidly increasing, collection of material on General Gordon.

1325. Papers: B.M. Add. Mss. 34474-34479, 51291-51312, 52386-52408. There are many other smaller collections elsewhere.

GORDON, HUGH.

1326. The journal of Lieutenant Hugh Gordon 1st Foot (Royal Scots) April 26, 1814 - February 20, 1816. Aberdeen.1912.

GORDON, JOHN.

1327. My six years with the Black Watch, 1881-1887. Egyptian campaign, eastern Soudan, Nile expedition, Egyptian frontier field force ... including a study of General Charles G. Gordon. Boston, Mass. 1929.

GORDON, SIR J. WILLOUGHBY.

1328. Ward, S.G.P. 'General Sir Willoughby Gordon'. J.S.A.H.R. vol. XXXI no. 126, summer 1953, 58-63. Gordon was quartermaster-general of the army for almost forty years (1811-1851).

1329. Papers: B.M. Add. Mss. 49471-49517, mainly as military secretary to Frederick, duke of York. His papers when quartermaster-general are at the N.A.M.

GORDON, GENERAL SIR THOMAS EDWARD.

1330. A varied life: a record of military and civil service of sport and travel in India, Central Asis and Persia, 1849-1902. 1906.

GOUGH, HUGH, VISCOUNT.

1331. Old memories. 1897.

1332. Rait, Sir Robert Sangster. The life and campaigns of F.M. Viscount Gough. 2 vols. 1903. The only full length biography.

GOWING, SGT. MAJOR TIMOTHY.

1333. A soldier's experience or a voice from the ranks showing the cost of war in blood and treasure. A personal narrative of the Crimean campaign from the standpoint of the ranks, the Indian mutiny, and some of its atrocities; the Afghan campaign of 1863. Also sketches of the lives and deaths of Sir Henry Havelock and Captain Hedley Vicars. Together with some things not generally known. By one of the Royal Fusiliers. Nottingham. 1905.

GRAHAM, SIR GERALD.

1334. Vetch, R.H. Life, letters and diaries of Lieut.
General Sir Gerald Graham...with portraits, plans
and his principal despatches. Edin. 1901. Graham
served in the Crimea, China, Canada (on the staff
with Wolseley), in Egypt, 1882, and Suakim.

GRANT, COLQUHOUN.

1335. Haswell, Jock. The first respectable spy. The life
and times of Colquhoun Grant, Wellington's head of
intelligence. 1969. The only biography,
it uses all the available material.

GRANT, SIR HOPE.

1336. Knollys, Sir Henry. Life of General Sir Hope Grant.
2 vols. 1894. Useful for the China wars and the
Indian mutiny. Grant was quartermaster-general, 1865-
70.

GRATTAN, WILLIAM.

1337. Adventures with the Connaught Rangers. 1809 to 1814.
2 vols. 1847-53. See also 1902 edn. ed., with an
introduction and notes, by Sir C.W.C. Oman. A well
written and vivid account.

GREEN, JOHN.

1338. The vicissitudes of a soldier's life, or a series of
occurrences from 1806 to 1815, the whole containing
a concise account of the war in the Peninsula. Louth.
1827. Green was in the 68th Durham Light Infantry.

GRENFELL, FRANCIS WALLACE, LORD.

1339. Memoirs of F.M. Lord Grenfell. 1925. He served in
the Zulu and Boer wars, and Egyptian campaign of 1882.

GREY, GENERAL CHARLES, FIRST EARL.

1340. 'The military career of the first Earl Grey'. Edinburgh
Review. vol CXCVI, 1902, 408-35.

1341. Papers: University of Durham. One of the most
important collections of military papers for the earlier
part of the Napoleonic wars.

GRIERSON, SIR JAMES MONCRIEFF.

1342. Macdiarmid, D.S. The life of Lieut. General Sir
James Moncrieff Grierson. 1923. Military life, 1881-
1914, as military attache in Berlin and on the staff
in South Africa.

HAINES, SIR FREDERICK PAUL.

1343. Rait, Sir Robert Sangster. The life of F.M. Sir
Frederick Paul Haines. 1911. The authorised account
of his long military career mainly in India.

HALL, SIR JOHN.

1344. Mitra, S.M. The life and letters of Sir John Hall.
1911. Much original correspondence is printed in the
only full account of the individual who represented
and upheld the official view of army medical services,
and military medicine, during the Crimean period.

1345. Papers: Royal Army Medical College, London, for the
period 1814-1866.

HAMILTON, SIR IAN.

1346. Listening for the drums. 1944. Details of service
in India, and in the Nile expedition, between 1872
and 1898, is recorded here.

1347. Hamilton, I.B.M. The happy warrior. A life of
General Sir Ian Hamilton. 1966.

1348. Papers: Centre for Military Archives, Kings College,
University of London.

HAMLEY, SIR EDWARD BRUCE.

1349. Shand, A.I. The life of General Sir Edward Bruce
Hamley. 2 vols. 1895. Hamley was Commandant of the
Staff College in the 1870's, and an important military
writer.

HARE, EDWARD.

1350. Hare, E.C. Memoirs of Edward Hare, late Inspector
general of hospitals. Bengal. 1900. Useful for
Afghan and Burma wars.

HARLEY, JOHN.

1351. The veteran or forty years in the British service.
2 vols. 1838.

HARNESS, GENERAL SIR HENRY DRURY.

1352. Collinson, General T.B. General Sir Henry Drury
Harness, K.C.B., colonel commandant, royal engineers.
1903. Contains various papers by and about General
Harness.

HARNESS, WILLIAM.

1353. Trusty and well beloved. The letters home of William
Harness, an officer of George III. Ed. by C.M. Duncan-
Jones. 1957. The editing is poor.

HARRIS, JOHN.

1354. Recollections of Rifleman Harris (old 95th) with
    anecdotes of his officers and his comrades, Ed.
    by H. Curling. 1848. The best book of reminiscences
    of the Napoleonic period, as retold to Curling.
    Some of the events have been confused by the passage
    of time.

HARRISON, GENERAL SIR RICHARD.

1355. Recollections of a life in the British army during
    the latter half of the nineteenth century. 1908.
    One of the best autobiographies of the period.

HAVELOCK, MAJOR-GENERAL SIR HENRY.

1356. Cooper, Leonard. Havelock. 1957. A brief popular
    account.

1357. Pollock, John C. Way to glory. The life of Havelock
    of Lucknow. 1957. Based on Havelock's papers.

1358. Papers: North Riding of Yorks. R.O.

HENDERSON, COL. G.F.R.

1359. Smirnoff, Alexander. 'A tribute to the memory of
    Col. G.F.R. Henderson'. A.Q. vol. XVII no. 2, January
    1929, 335-41. One of the outstanding military writers
    of the period.

HENEGAN, SIR RICHARD.

1360. Seven years campaigning in the Peninsula and the
    Netherlands, from 1808 to 1815. 2 vols. 1846.
    Rather confused in places.

HENRY, WALTER.

1361. Surgeon Henry's trifles: events of a military life.
    Ed. with an introduction by P. Hayward. 1970.
    Originally published as Events of a military life.
    1843. Useful for army medical services under Wellington.

HERVEY, ALBERT.

1362. Ten years in India: or, the life of a young officer.
    3 vols. 1850.

HIGGINSON, SIR G.W.A.

1363. Seventy-one years of a guardsman's life. 1916.
    Mainly concerned with the author's experiences during
    the Crimean war.

HILL, ROWLAND, LORD.

1364. Sidney, Edwin. The life of Lord Hill, commander of
the forces. 1845. Only valuable for the many
extracts from Hill's private papers, now in the
British Museum (see below).

1365. Sheppard, E.W. 'Little known soldiers of the past.
III Field Marshal Lord Hill (1777-1842)'. A.Q. vol.
LXXXIV no. 2, July 1962, 190-4. A brief resume of his
career in the Peninsula and at the Horse Guards.

1366. Papers: B.M. Add. Mss. 35059-35067.

HOLDICH, GENERAL E.A.

1367. Cook, H.C.B. 'The diaries of General E.A. Holdich'.
J.S.A.H.R. vol. XLIX no. 200, winter 1971, 212-247;
vol. L no 201, spring 1972, 46-60. Useful for the
second Burmese war, for which first hand accounts are
not numerous.

HOLLOWAY, JAMES.

1368. Thomas, J.H. 'The letters of Private James Holloway'.
A.Q. vol. C no. 2, July 1970, 241-7. Service in
India, 1844-52.

HOME, SURGEON GENERAL SIR A.D.

1369. Service memories. Ed. by Col. C.H. Melville. 1912.

HOPE, LIEUT. JAMES.

1370. The military memoirs of an infantry officer. 1833.

HUMBLEY, CAPT. W.W.W.

1371. The journal of a cavalry officer, including the
memorable Sikh campaign of 1845-1846. 1854.

JACKSON, LIEUT. COL. BASIL.

1372. Notes and reminiscences of a staff officer chiefly
relating to the Waterloo campaign and to St. Helena
during the captivity of Napoleon. Ed. by R.C. Seaton.
1903.

JACKSON, THOMAS.

1373. Narrative of the eventful life of Thomas Jackson,
late Sergeant in the Coldstream Guards, details of his
military career during twelve years of the French war,
describing his perils by sea and land. Birmingham.
1857.

JACOB, GENERAL JOHN.

1374. The views and opinions of Brig. General John Jacob.
      Ed. by L. Pelly. Bombay. 1858.

1375. Shand, A.I. General John Jacob, commandant of the
      Scinde Irregular Horse, and founder of Jacobabad.
      1900.

1376. Lambrick, H.T. John Jacob of Jacobabad. 1960. The
      detailed standard work.

JAMES, JOHN H.

1377. Surgeon James's journal, 1815. Ed. by Jane Vansittart.
      1964.

JELF, W.W.

1378. Hark back! 1935. Includes reminiscences of the Boer
      war.

JERVIS-WALDY, W.T.

1379. From eight to eighty: the life of a Crimean and Indian
      mutiny veteran. 1914.

KINCAID, CAPT. SIR JOHN.

1380. Adventures in the Rifle Brigade, in the Peninsula,
      France, and the Netherlands, from 1809 to 1815. 1830.
      A selective and rather amusing account.

1381. Random shots from a rifleman. 1835. A further volume
      of reminiscences.

KITCHENER, HORATIO HERBERT, EARL.

1382. Arthur, Sir George C.A. Life of Lord Kitchener. 3
      vols. 1920. Much useful detail, from original papers.

1383. De Watteville, H.G. Lord Kitchener. 1939. Popular.

1384. Magnus, Sir Philip. Kitchener: portrait of an
      imperialist. 1958. The best, and a very readable,
      account.

1385. Papers: 1877-1938: PRO 30/57.

LAKE, GERARD, VISCOUNT.

1386. Pearse, Major H.W. Memoir of the life and military
      service of Viscount Lake of Delhi and Laswarce,
      1744-1808. Edin. 1908. The only biography.

LAWRENCE, LIEUT. GENERAL SIR GEORGE ST. PATRICK.

1387. Forty-three years in India ... including the Cabul
      disasters, captivities in Afghanistan and the Punjab,
      and a narrative of the mutinies in Rajputana. Ed.
      by W. Edwards. 1874.

LAWRENCE, WILLIAM.

1388. The autobiography of Sgt. William Lawrence. Ed.
by G.N. Bankes. 1901. The author served in the
Peninsula in the 40th Foot.

LEACH, LIEUT. COLONEL JONATHAN.

1389. Rough sketches of the life of an old soldier, during
his service in the West Indies: at the siege of
Copenhagen, 1807; in the Peninsula and the south of
France in the campaigns from 1808 to 1814 with the
Light Division; in the Netherlands 1815, including
the battle of Quatre Bras and Waterloo. 1831.

1390. Rambles on the banks of the Styx. 1847. Peninsula
reminiscences.

LEFROY, GENERAL SIR JOHN HENRY.

1391. Autobiography of General Sir John Henry Lefroy. Ed.
by Lady Lefroy. 1895.

1392. Papers: In private possession: Guildford, Surrey.
An unpublished H.M.C. report is available at the
N.R.A.

LEITH, LIEUT. GENERAL SIR JAMES.

1393. Papers: John Rylands Library concerning the Peninsula
war. Information on this officer may be found in the
memoirs of his aide-de-camp in the Peninsula: Sir A.
Leith Hay. Narrative of the Peninsula war. 2 vols. 1879.

LE MARCHANT, MAJOR GENERAL SIR JOHN GASPARD.

1394. Le Marchant, Sir Dennis. Memoirs of the late Major
General Le Marchant. 1841. A privately printed limited
edition, now very rare, with selections from his own
correspondence.

1395. Thoumine, R.H. Scientific soldier: a life of General
Le Marchant, 1766-1812. 1968. Based on ms. sources
but should be used with caution, as there are a number
of inaccuracies.

1396. Papers: Royal Military College, Sandhurst; Sir Dennis
Le Marchant, Hungerton Hall, Grantham, Lincs.

LOWE, CAPT. A.C.

1397. Diary of an officer of the 16th (Queen's) Lancers,
1822-1840. 1894.

LUKIN, MAJOR GENERAL SIR HENRY TIMSON.

1398. Johnston, R.E. Ulundi to Delville Wood: the life story
of Major-General Sir Henry Timson Lukin. Capetown. 1930.

LYNEDOCH, THOMAS GRAHAM, LORD.

1399. Delavoye, A.M. Life and letters of Sir Thomas Graham,
Lord Lynedoch. 1868. Contains long extracts from
his unpublished journals.

1400. Oglander, C.F.A. Freshly remembered. The story of
Thomas Graham. 1956.

1401. Brett–James, Antony. General Graham, Lord Lynedoch.
1959. The best modern account, based on the papers
noted immediately below.

1402. Papers: N.L.S.

LYTTLETON, GENERAL SIR NEVILLE G.

1403. Eighty years: soldiering, politics, games. 1927.
Reminiscences of a distinguished career supplemented
by his diary and correspondence.

MACDONALD, GENERAL HECTOR.

1404. Coates, T.F.G. Hector MacDonald or the private who
became a general. 1900.

MACKAY, ARCHIBALD.

1405. Beaufort, B. 'One of Moore's men'. A.Q. vol. LXXIV
no. 2, July 1957, 240–4. Letters (1806–1814) of
Archibald Mackay, sergeant–major, 92nd Highlanders.

MACKENZIE, LIEUT. GENERAL COLIN.

1406. Storms and sunshine of a soldier's life. 2 vols.
Edin. 1884. Vol. 1 is mainly concerned with the
first Afghan war.

MACKINNON, DANIEL HENRY.

1407. Military service and adventures in the far east:
including sketches of the campaigns against the
Afghans in 1839, and the Sikhs in 1845–6, by a cavalry
officer. 2 vols. 1847.

MACMUNN, SIR GEORGE.

1408. Behind the scenes in many wars: being the military
reminiscences of Lieut. General Sir George MacMunn.
1930. The author served in India, during the Boer
war, and at the War Office, but is best known now as
a military historian.

MAINWARING, COL. FRED.

1409. 'An ensign in Wellington's army, 1811–1815'. Ed. by
W.V. Knocker. A.Q. vol. LXXXII no. 1, April 1961,
81–8. A soldier's early career in the Peninsula and
at Waterloo, written in 1844.

MAITLAND, F.H.

1410. Hussar of the line. 1951. Life of a trooper in
    the Hussars immediately before World War I.

MALCOLM, SIR JOHN.

1411. Kaye, Sir John William. The life and correspondence
    of Sir John Malcolm, G.C.B., late envoy to Persia
    and governor of Bombay. 2 vols. 1856. A full and
    definitive biography.

MARLING, COL. SIR PERCIVAL.

1412. Rifleman and hussar. An autobiography. 1931. The
    author served in several campaigns in the late nine-
    teenth century, and won the V.C. in the Sudan in 1884.

MAURICE, SIR JOHN FREDERICK.

1413. Sir Frederick Maurice. A record of his work and
    opinions with eight essays on discipline and national
    efficiency. Ed. by Sir Frederick Maurice. 1913.
    Maurice was a noted military writer and thinker, and
    associate of Wolseley. The work was edited by his son.

MAXWELL, GENERAL EDWARD HERBERT.

1414. With the Connaught Rangers in quarters, camp and on
    leave. 1883. Service in India.

McCALMONT, SIR HUGH.

1415. The memoirs of Major-General Sir Hugh McCalmont.
    Ed. by Sir Charles Edward Callwell. 1924. Details
    of active service between 1870-1890.

McGRIGOR, SIR JAMES.

1416. The autobiography and services of Sir James McGrigor,
    Bart. 1861. McGrigor was chief medical officer under
    Wellington and later the director-general of the army
    medical department.

METCALFE, HENRY.

1417. The chronicle of Private Henry Metcalfe, H.M. 32nd
    Regiment of Foot. Ed. by Lieut. General Sir Francis
    Tuker. 1953. A private soldier's experiences during
    the siege of Lucknow.

MILLER, BENJAMIN.

1418. Dacombe, M.R. and Rowe, B.J.H. 'The adventures of
    Sergeant Benjamin Miller, during his service in the
    4th battalion Royal Artillery, from 1796 to 1815'.
    J.S.A.H.R. vol. VII no. 27, January 1928, 9-51.
    Miller served in Egypt and the Peninsula.

MOLE, EDWIN.

1419. A King's Hussar: being the military memoirs for
twenty-five years of a troop-sergeant-major of the
14th (King's) Hussars. Ed. by Herbert Compton.
1893. Covers the period 1863-88; the author only
saw active service towards the end of the Transvaal
war.

MOORE, LIEUT. GENERAL SIR JOHN.

1420. Moore, James C. The life of Lieutenant-General Sir
John Moore, K.B. 3 vols. 1834.

1421. The diary of Sir John Moore. Ed. by Sir J.F. Maurice.
2 vols. 1904. Moore's journal, with a rather
partisan commentary by the editor.

1422. Brownrigg, Beatrice, Lady. The life and letters of
Sir John Moore. 1923.

1423. Oman, Carola. Sir John Moore. 1953. The standard
work, unlikely to be replaced. There is a valuable
resume of the literature on Moore with the author's
critical remarks. See also H.R. Wright, General Moore
at Shorncliffe, Sandgate, 1965. A short biographical
account.

1424. Official papers: in private possession, London. There
is an unpublished H.M.C. report at the N.R.A. Diaries
and correspondence: B.M. Add. Mss. 57320-57332; 57539-
57554. See also (1650).

MORRIS, THOMAS.

1425. Recollections of military service, in 1813, 1814, and
1815, through Germany, Holland, and France; including
some details of the battles of Quatre Bras and
Waterloo. 1845.

MUNRO, MAJOR GENERAL THOMAS.

1426. Gleig, Rev. George Robert. The life of Major General
Thomas Munro. 3 vols. 1830. Useful for the campaign
against Tippo Sultan, and the second Mahralta war.

MUNRO, GENERAL SIR WILLIAM.

1427. Records of service and campaigning in many lands.
2 vols. 1887. Munro served in the medical corps.

MURRAY, GENERAL SIR GEORGE.

1428. Papers: N.L.S. A major collection, particularly
important for the Peninsula war. See also (110).
Correspondence and memoranda relating to his military
career, and as Secretary for War, and Master General of
the Ordnance: P.R.O. W.O. 80.

NAPIER, SIR CHARLES JAMES.

1429. Napier, William C.E. The life and opinions of
General Sir Charles Napier. 4 vols. 1857. The last
of three separate studies of his brother: all were a
vigorous and partisan defence of his career.

1430. Butler, Sir W.F. Sir Charles Napier. 1890.

1431. Papers: P.R.O. 30/64. B.M. Add. Mss. 40018-40055.

NAPIER, SIR GEORGE THOMAS.

1432. Passages in the early military life of Sir George
Thomas Napier. Ed. by W.C.E. Napier. 1884.

NAPIER, ROBERT, LORD.

1433. Napier, Lieut. Col. H.D. Field Marshal Lord Napier
of Magdala. 1927. Quotes extensively from Napier's
private correspondence. The standard biography.

1434. Papers: India Office Library.

NAPIER, SIR WILLIAM C.E.

1435. Life of General Sir William Napier, author of "History
of the Peninsula war". Ed. by H.A. Bruce. 2 vols. 1864.

1436. Papers: Bodleian Library, Oxford. This includes
material relating to other members of the family. See
also, B.M. Add. Mss. 49086-49172.

NOLAN, LOUIS EDWARD.

1437. Moyse-Bartlett, H. Louis Edward Nolan and his influence
on the British cavalry. 1971. The standard and only
biography of an officer who helped to introduce many
important innovations.

NORMAN, SIR HENRY WYLIE.

1438. Warner, Sir William Lee. Memoirs of F.M. Sir Henry
Wylie Norman. 1908. Mainly on his role in the Indian
mutiny, and in the reorganisation of the Indian army.

NOTT, MAJOR GENERAL SIR WILLIAM.

1439. Stocqueler, J.H. Memoirs and correspondence of Major
General Sir William Nott. 1854.

NUGENT, F.M. SIR GEORGE.

1440. Papers: N.A.M. See also, (105) for details of the
contents of the collection.

O'CALLAGHAN, GENERAL SIR DESMOND.

1441. Guns, gunners and others. 1925. Autobiography of an
artillery officer.

OUTRAM, SIR JAMES.

1442. Goldsmid, Sir Frederic. James Outram. A biography...
2 vols. 1880. The authorised account, with many
extracts from his papers.

1443. Trotter, L.J. The bayard of India. A life of General
Sir James Outram, Bart. 1903. An uncritical survey
based on Goldsmid's work.

PAGET, HON. SIR EDWARD.

1444. Letters and memorials of General the Hon. Sir Edward
Paget. Ed. by H.M. Paget. 1898. Produced by his
family in the absence of enough material for a full
biography.

PAKENHAM, SIR EDWARD.

1445. Pakenham letters 1800 to 1815. 1914. Privately
published. Served in the Peninsula, and was killed
in the campaign for New Orleans, 1815.

PARR, SIR HALLAM.

1446. Fortescue-Brickdale, Sir Charles. Major General Sir
Hallam Parr K.C.B. : recollections and correspondence
with a short account of his sons, Lieutenants A.H.H.
Parr and G.R. Parr. 1917. Parr served in South Africa
in the 1870's and 1880's, in the Egyptian army, and
at the War Office.

PARSONS, R.B.

1447. Reminiscences of a Crimean veteran of the 17th Foot
regiment. Kendal. 1905.

PASLEY, GENERAL SIR CHARLES WILLIAM.

1448. Kealy, P.H. Sir Charles Pasley, 1780 to 1861. n.d.
Pasley was an early army reformer and military writer,
and advocate of military education.

1449. Papers: B.M. Add. Mss. 41961-41995.

PEACOCKE, SIR W. MARMADUKE.

1450. Papers: P.R.O. W.O. 134: as commander at Lisbon, 1809-
1814.

PEARMAN, JOHN.

1451. Sergeant Pearman's memoirs. Being, chiefly, his account
of service with the Third, King's Own, Light Dragoons
in India, from 1845 to 1853, including the first and
second Sikh wars. Ed. by the Marquess of Anglesey.
1968. Throws some light on life in the ranks in India
before the Mutiny and, as the title indicates, on the
first and second Sikh wars.

PICTON, LIEUT. GENERAL SIR THOMAS.

1452. Robinson, H.B. Memoirs of Lieut. General Sir Thomas
Picton. 1836.

1453. Letters, 1800–14: N.L.W.

POLLOCK, FIELD MARSHAL SIR GEORGE.

1454. Low, Charles R. The life of and correspondence of F.M.
Sir George Pollock. 1873.

1455. Papers: Cambridge University library.

POMEROY-COLLEY, GENERAL SIR GEORGE.

1456. Butler, Sir W.F. The life of Sir George Pomeroy-Colley
1835–1881. Including services in Kaffraria – in China –
in Ashanti – in India and in Natal. 1899. A modern
reassessment of Colley is needed.

1457. Papers: are among the Add. Mss. in the British Museum.

PRENDERGAST, SIR HARRY NORTH DALYRMPLE.

1458. Vibart, H.M. The life of General Sir Harry N.D.
Prendergast...(the happy warrior). 1914. Includes
service in central India during the mutiny, the
Abyssinian expedition, and the third Burma war, 1885-6.

RAGLAN, FITZROY SOMERSET, LORD.

1459. Hibbert, Christopher. The destruction of Lord Raglan.
1961. The only modern account, mainly on his command
in the Crimea, but with a useful chapter on his earlier
military career.

1460. Papers: N.A.M. for material relating to Crimean war;
there is an unpublished index available. Private papers:
Cefntilla Court, Usk, Mon.

RAWLINSON, HENRY SEYMOUR, LORD.

1461. Maurice, Sir Frederick. The life of General Lord
Rawlinson of Trent from his journals and letters. 1928.
The best account based on his voluminous private
journals and papers.

REID, SIR CHARLES.

1462. Papers: N.A.M. Includes material relating to the siege
of Delhi and the 1st Sikh war.

RICE, COL. SAMUEL.

1463. Mockler-Ferryman, Lieut. Col. A.F. The life of a
regimental officer during the great war, 1793-1815.
Compiled from the correspondence of Col. Samuel Rice,
C.B., K.H., 51st Light Infantry and from other sources.
Edin. 1913. Rice, who served with the 51st regiment
from 1793 to 1831, the last fourteen years in command,
received his initial training under Sir John Moore.

ROBERTS, FREDERICK, EARL.

1464. Forty-one years in India, from subaltern to commander-
in-chief. 2 vols. 1897. Like his contemporary Wolseley
Roberts did not write an autobiography which covered
his entire service life.

1465. James, David. Lord Roberts. 1954. The standard
biography favourable to its subject.

1466. Hannah, W.H. Bobs, Kipling's general: life of F.M.
Earl Roberts of Kandahar. 1972. A competent summary
based on secondary sources.

1467. Papers: P.R.O. W.O. 105, mainly relating to operations
in South Africa, where Roberts was commander-in-chief;
Army Museums Ogilby Trust, London, S.W.1.

ROBERTSON, CAPTAIN FREDERICK.

1468. Leslie, J.H. 'Reminiscences of a Woolwich cadet of
1802 by the late second captain Frederick Robertson'.
J.S.A.H.R. vol. V no. 19, January-March 1926, 1-16.

ROBERTSON, JAMES PETER.

1469. Personal adventures and anecdotes of an old officer.
1906.

ROBERTSON, SIR WILLIAM.

1470. From private to field marshal. 2 vols. 1906. His
autobiography, with many useful extracts from his
correspondence and papers.

1471. Leask, G.A. Sir William Robertson: the life story
of the Chief of the Imperial General Staff. 1917.

1472. Bonham-Carter, Victor. The life and times of F.M.
Sir William Robertson, Bt., 1860-1933. 1963. The
standard biography.

1473. Papers: Centre for Military Archives, King's College,
University of London.

ROSS-LEWIN, HENRY.

1474. The life of a soldier. A narrative of 27 years service
in various parts of the world. 2 vols. 1834. Published
also in 1904, ed. by J. Wardell.

SCOVELL, GENERAL SIR GEORGE.

1475. Papers: P.R.O. W.O. 37. The collection largely consists of intercepted despatches, reports and maps captured during the Peninsula war, and a diary.

SEATON, JOHN COLBORNE, LORD.

1476. Smith, G.C. Moore. Life of Sir John Colborne, Lord Seaton. 1903. The standard account, with selections from his correspondence.

SEATON, MAJOR GENERAL SIR THOMAS.

1477. From cadet to colonel. The record of a life of active service. 2 vols. 1866. Service in India.

SHIPP, JOHN.

1478. Memoirs of the extraordinary military career of John Shipp, late a lieutenant in his Majesty's 87th regiment. 1843. The author was twice promoted from the ranks to a commission. He also wrote <u>The military bijou, or the contents of a soldier's knapsack, being the gleanings of 33 years' active service.</u> 1831.

SIMMONS, MAJOR GEORGE.

1479. A British rifleman: journals and correspondence of Major George Simmons, Rifle Brigade, during the Peninsula war and the campaign of Waterloo. Ed. by W.W.C. Verner. 1899.

SMET, JOHN FRANCIS.

1480. 'Extracts from journals of John Francis Smet, Surgeon, 8th Hussars, 1815-1824'. <u>J.S.A.H.R.</u> vol. XXIX no. 120, winter 1951, 172-8. Service in Ireland and India.

SMITH, SIR HARRY.

1481. The autobiography of Lieut. General Sir Harry Smith, Baronet of Aliwaland Sutlej, G.C.B. Ed. by G.C. Moore Smith. 1903. The editor added some supplementary chapters on the latter part of Smith's life.

SMITH, MAJOR GENERAL SIR ROBERT MURDOCH.

1482. Dickson, W.K. The life of Major General Sir Robert Murdoch Smith...Royal Engineers. Edin. 1901. An engineers officer perhaps better known as an archaeologist.

SMITH-DORRIEN, GENERAL SIR HORACE.

1483. Memories of forty-eight years' service. 1925. Includes his service in the Zulu war, the Egyptian campaign of 1882, and the Nile expedition to relieve Khartum.

1484. Ballard, Colin. Smith-Dorrien. 1931. A rather formal account, superseded by the work listed below.

1485. Smithers, A.J. The man who disobeyed. Sir Horace Smith-Dorrien and his enemies. 1970. Some useful information, but mainly valuable for Smith-Dorrien's role in World War I.

SMYTH, MAJOR GENERAL SIR JAMES CARMICHAEL.

1486. Papers, official and semi-official correspondence, 1805-1837, 1860: P.R.O. 30/35.

STAVELEY, LIEUT. GENERAL WILLIAM.

1487. Jackson, Sir Louis. One of Wellington's staff officers: Lieut. General William Staveley'. J.S.A.H.R. vol. XIV no. 55, autumn 1935, 155-166.

STEEVENS, LIEUT. COL. CHARLES.

1488. Reminiscences of my military life from 1795 to 1818. Ed. by Lieut. Col. Nathaniel Steevens. Winchester. 1878.

STEPHENSON, SIR FREDERICK.

1489. At home and on the battlefield: letters from the Crimea, China and Egypt, 1854-1888. Together with a short memoir of himself. Ed. by H.A. Pownall. 1915.

STEVENSON, JOHN.

1490. A soldier in time of war. 1841. Details of 21 years service in the Scots guards.

STEWART, SIR DONALD.

1491. F.M. Sir Donald Stewart... An account of his life mainly in his own words. Ed. by G.R. Elsmie. 1903.

STRATHNAIRN, FIELD MARSHAL SIR HUGH HENRY ROSE, LORD.

1492. Papers: B.M. Add. Mss. 42796-42838. A full collection of the correspondence and papers of the soldier who distinguished himself in the Indian mutiny, and later as commander-in-chief in India.

SURTEES, WILLIAM.

1493. Twenty-five years in the Rifle Brigade. 1833. repr. 1973. Includes experiences in the Peninsula, and during the expedition to New Orleans, 1814, as well as a description of his early life and services.

SYDENHAM SIR GEORGE CLARKE, LORD.

494. My working life. 1927. Sydenham was involved in the
planning of changes in army organisation introduced
following the Boer war. His papers are among the Add.
Mss. in the British Museum.

SYLVESTER, JOHN HENRY.

495. Cavalry Surgeon. The recollections of Deputy Surgeon
General John Henry Sylvester, Bombay army. Ed. by
A. McKenzie Annand. 1971. Service during the Indian
mutiny and in the Umbeyla campaign.

TAYLOR, SIR ALEX.

496. Taylor, A.C. General Sir Alex Taylor: his times,
his friends and his work. 2 vols. 1913. Services in
the 1st and 2nd Sikh wars, and the Indian mutiny.

TAYLOR, SIR HERBERT.

497. Taylor, Ernest. The Taylor papers. Being a record of
certain reminiscences, letters, and journals in the
life of Lieut. General Sir Herbert Taylor. 1913.
Taylor was, among other things, military secretary to the
duke of York.

TAYLOR, GENERAL T.W.

498. Carew, Peter. 'A hussar of the hundred days'.
Blackwood's no. 1561, November 1945, 299-305. Selections
from his correspondence.

THACKWELL, SIR JOSEPH.

499. Wylly, H.C. The military memoirs of Lieut. General Sir
Joseph Thackwell. Arranged from his correspondence
and diaries. 1908. Thackwell served in the Peninsula
war, the first Afghan war, and both Sikh wars.

THOMPSON, GENERAL T. PERRONET.

500. Johnson, L.G. General T. Perronet Thompson, 1783-1869
his military, literary and political campaigns. 1957.

THOMSON, COL. JOHN ANSTRUTHER.

501. Eighty years' reminiscences. 1904.

TOMKINSON, LIEUT. COL. WILLIAM.

502. The diary of a cavalry officer in the Peninsula and
Waterloo campaigns, 1809-1815. Ed. by James Tomkinson.
1894. Contains information not easily to be found
elsewhere.

TROYTE, LIEUT. J.E.A.

1503. Through the ranks to a commission. 1881.

TULLOCH, GENERAL SIR ALEXANDER BRUCE.

1504. Recollections of forty years' service, Edin. 1903.
      Active service from the Crimea to Tel-el-Kebir and
      South Africa.

TURNER, SIR A.E.

1505. Sixty years of a soldier's life. 1912.

VERNER, LIEUT. COL. SIR WILLIAM.

1506. Reminiscences of William Verner (1782-1871) 7th Hussars.
      An account of service in the 7th Hussars, including the
      battle of Waterloo, copied from the original notes
      taken by Sir William Verner at the time, by his daughter,
      Emily Verner, at Tunbridge Wells, January 4th, 1853.
      Ed. by Ruth W. Verner. <u>S.A.H.R.</u> Special publication
      no. 9. 1965. Service from 1805, when he joined the
      regiment, to the army of occupation in France.

VIETH, F.H.D.

1507. Recollections of the Crimean campaign and the expedition
      to Kinburn in 1855. Including also sporting and
      dramatic incidents in connection with garrison life in
      the Canadian lower provinces. Montreal. 1907.

VIVIAN, RICHARD HUSSEY, LORD.

1508. Vivian, Hon. Claud. Richard Hussey Vivian, First
      Baron Vivian, a memoir. 1897. Relates to the period
      of war 1793-1815.

WALKER, T.M.

1509. Through the mutiny: reminiscences of thirty years'
      active service and sport in India 1854-1883. 1907.

WATERFIELD, ROBERT.

1510. The memoirs of Private Waterfield, soldier in Her
      Majesty's 32nd Regiment of Foot (Duke of Cornwall's
      Light Infantry) 1842-1857. Ed. by Arthur Swinson and
      D. Scott. 1968. An important contribution to knowledge
      of the British army in India before the mutiny.

WAUCHOPE, MAJOR GENERAL ANDREW GILBERT.

1511. Douglas, Sir George. The life of Major-General
      Wauchope. 1904.

WELLINGTON, SIR ARTHUR WELLESLEY, DUKE OF.

512. The general orders of F.M. the duke of Wellington,
K.G. etc. in Portugal, Spain and France. Ed. by
Lieut. Col. John Gurwood. 1832.

513. The dispatches of F.M. the duke of Wellington during
his various campaigns. Ed. by Lieut. Col. John
Gurwood. 12 vols. 1834-8. An indispensable reference
work which should be used with caution as some of the
material was omitted on the duke's orders and the index
is incomplete and misleading.

514. Maxwell, William Hamilton. Life of Wellington. 2
vols. 1839-41. Still of much value to the specialist.

515. Supplementary despatches, correspondence, and memoranda
of F.M. Arthur, duke of Wellington. Ed. by the duke of
Wellington. 11 vols. 1858-64. The second duke of
Wellington was a much more competent editor than
Gurwood, and these volumes contain a large amount of
private correspondence which had been omitted from
Gurwood's work. See also, Wellington at War, 1794-1815.
A selection of his wartime letters. Ed. by Antony
Brett-James. 1961.

516. Gleig, Rev. George Robert. The life of Arthur, duke
of Wellington. 2 vols. 1862. Partly based on the
work of M. Brialmont whose study of Wellington the
author translated, and who was his principal guide to
the duke as a soldier.

517. Stanhope, Philip, Earl. Notes of conversations with
the duke of Wellington, 1831-1851. 1888.

518. Maxwell, Sir Herbert E. The life of Wellington. The
restoration of the martial power of Great Britain. 2
vols. 1899. Remains a major source.

519. Gleig, Rev. George Robert. Personal reminiscences of
the first duke of Wellington, with sketches of some of
his guests and contemporaries. 1904. A useful source
of anecdotes.

520. Fortescue, Hon. Sir J.W. Wellington. 1925. A brief
popular survey.

521. Sheppard, E.W. 'The first duke of Wellington'. A.Q.
vol. XV no. 2, January 1928, 358-71. Some useful notes.

522. Guedalla, Philip. The duke. 1931. Useful for his
political career and personal life.

523. Wellesley, Muriel. The man Wellington. 1937. One of
the best assessments of his character and personality.

524. Aldington, Richard. The Duke: being an account of the
life and achievements of Arthur Wellesley, 1st duke of
Wellington. 1946. Better as a survey of the duke's personality than as a study of his military achievements.

1525. Davies, Godfrey. 'Wellington the man'. <u>J.S.A.H.R.</u>
vol. XXX no. 123, autumn 1952, 96-112. A useful
discussion of Wellington's character.

1526. Petrie, Sir Charles. Wellington: a reassessment.
1956.

1527. Howard, M.E. 'Wellington and the British army'. In
<u>Wellingtonian Studies</u>. Ed. by M.E. Howard. 1959, 77-91.
An interesting survey of the duke's influence on the
army after the Napoleonic wars. See also the essays
by the Hon. G.R. St. Aubyn 'Wellington the man' and by
Piers Mackesy 'Wellington the general'.

1528. Ward, S.P.G. Wellington. 1963. A simple short
introductory essay on his life, with a concluding chapter on his place in English history.

1529. Glover, Michael. Wellington as military commander.
1968. A thorough analysis of his abilities as a militar
leader.

1530. Longford, Elizabeth, Lady. Wellington: the years of
the sword. 1969. The best modern life.

1531. Bryant, Sir Arthur. The great duke; or, the invincible
general. 1971.

1532. Longford, Elizabeth, Lady. Wellington: pillar of
state. 1972. The second volume of Lady Longford's
fine biography covering the period from 1815.

1533. Weller, Jac. Wellington in India. 1972. Wellington's
nine years in India, and his development as a military
leader. There is a useful, annotated, bibliography.

1534. Papers: Stratfield Saye, Berkshire and Apsley House,
London.

WELSH, COL. JAMES.

1535. Military reminiscences: extracts from a journal of
nearly forty years' active service in the East Indies.
2 vols. 1830.

WHEATLEY, EDMUND.

1536. The Wheatley diary. A journal and sketch book kept
during the Peninsula war and Waterloo campaign. Ed.
by Christopher Hibbert. 1964. Wheatley was an ensign
in the King's German legion.

WHEELER, WILLIAM.

1537. The letters of Private Wheeler, 1809-1828. Ed. by
Capt. Sir B.H. Liddell Hart. 1951.

WHITE, F.M. SIR GEORGE.

1538. Durand, Sir Henry Mortimer. The life of F.M. Sir
George White. 2 vols. Edin. 1915.

WILLCOCKS, SIR JAMES.

1539. From Kabul to Kumassi: twenty-four years of soldiering and sport. 1904.

1540. The romance of soldiering and sport. 1925.

WILSON, MAJOR GENERAL SIR CHARLES WILLIAM.

1541. Watson, Sir Charles M. The life of Major General Sir
Charles William Wilson, Royal Engineers. 1909.

WILSON, SIR HENRY.

1542. Callwell, Sir Charles Edward. Sir Henry Wilson: life
and diaries. 2 vols. 1927.

WILSON, SIR ROBERT T.

1543. Life of General Sir Robert Wilson, from autobiographical
memoirs, journals, manuscripts, correspondence, etc.
Ed. by Herbert Randolph. 2 vols. 1862. Deals with
his early career down to the Peace of Tilsit in 1807.

1544. Costigan, Giovanni. Sir Robert Wilson: a soldier of
fortune in the Napoleonic wars. Madison, Wis. 1932.

1545. General Wilson's journal, 1812-14. Ed. by Antony
Brett-James. An edited edition of Wilson's Private
diary of travels, personal services, and public events,
during mission and employment with the European armies
in the campaigns of 1812, 1813, 1814, from the
invasion of Russia to the capture of Paris. 2 vols.
1861. There is little of direct relevance, but useful
background material.

WOLSELEY, GARNET JOSEPH, VISCOUNT.

1546. The story of a soldier's life. 2 vols. 1903.

1547. The letters of Lord and Lady Wolseley, 1870-1911. Ed.
by Sir George C.A. Arthur. 1922. The editing is not
scholarly.

1548. Maurice, Sir Frederick and Arthur, Sir George C.A.
The life of Lord Wolseley. 1924. A very uncritical
account, favourable to Wolseley. An earlier biography
by Charles R. Low, A memoir of Lieut. General Sir
Garnet J. Wolseley, 2 vols. 1878, is of little value
now.

1549. Lehmann, Joseph H. All Sir Garnet. A life of Field
Marshal Lord Wolseley. 1964. Not entirely satisfactory,
this biography is best on his early life in the army.

1550. Papers: Hove Public Library; P.R.O.; N.A.M.

WOOD, MAJOR-GENERAL SIR ELLIOT.

1551. Life and adventure in peace and war. Campaigns in
Egypt in 1882, Sudan 1884-5, and the Boer war (as
engineer in chief at G.H.Q.).

WOOD, F.M. SIR HENRY EVELYN.

1552. From midshipman to field marshal. 2 vols. 1906.
One of the more notable military reminiscences covering
the period from the Crimean war.

WYATT, HENRY.

1553. Events of a military life. 2 vols. 1843.

YORK, FREDERICK, DUKE OF.

1554. Burne, Alfred H. The noble duke of York: the military
life of Frederick, duke of York and Albany. 1949. A
full and favourable account of his role in the Flanders
campaign, 1793-4 and the Helder expedition, but less
satisfactory in other ways.

1555. Hudleston, F.J. 'Frederick, the soldiers' friend'.
A.Q. vol. IX no. 2, January 1925, 273-86.

YOUNGHUSBAND, SIR GEORGE JOHN.

1556. Forty years a soldier. 1923. The author served in
India, and also wrote The Queen's Commission: how to
prepare for it, how to obtain it, and how to use it,
etc., 1891.

1557. A soldier's memories in peace and war. 1927.

YPRES, SIR JOHN FRENCH, FIRST EARL OF.

1558. French, E.G. The life of F.M. Sir John French, first
earl of Ypres. 1931.

7. MILITARY THOUGHT, TACTICS, DISCIPLINE AND DRILL.

The works by Walton (205) and Lloyd (719) are particularly
valuable on tactics and drill. The items in this section are
listed in chronological order of publication.

559. ALBEMARLE, GEORGE MONCK, DUKE OF. Observations upon
     military and political affairs 1671. Ed. by J. Heath.
     1761.

560. VENN, THOMAS. Military and maritime discipline.Book I.
     Military observations or tactics. Book II. An exact
     method of military architecture. Book III. The compleat
     gunner. 1672.

561. BINNING, CAPT. THOMAS. A light to the art of gunnery.
     Wherein is laid down the true weight of powder both
     for proof and action, of all sorts of great ordnance.
     Also the true ball, and allowance for wind, etc. 1679.

562. ENGLISH MILITARY DISCIPLINE or the way and method of
     exercising horse and foot, according to the practice
     of this present time. With a treatise of all sorts of
     arms and engines of war. 1680.

563. AN ABRIDGEMENT OF THE ENGLISH MILITARY DISCIPLINE.
     Printed by special command for the use of His Majesty's
     Forces. 1686. The best contemporary guide.

564. COMMANDS FOR THE EXERCISE OF FOOT, armed with firelock
     muskets and pikes: with the evolutions... 1690. A
     later edition (Dublin, 1701) included a section on
     'the exercise of the horse, grenadiers of horse, and
     dragoons'.

565. COMPLEAT GENTLEMAN SOLDIER: or a treatise of military
     discipline, fortifications and gunnery. 1702.

566. MILITARY DICTIONARY explaining all the difficult terms
     in martial discipline, fortifications, and gunnery.
     1702.

567. THE DUKE OF MARLBOROUGH'S NEW EXERCISE OF FIRELOCKS AND
     BAYONETS: appointed by His Grace to be used by all the
     British forces... 1712.

1568. BLAND, LIEUT. GENERAL HUMPHREY. A treatise of military discipline, in which is laid down and explained the duty of the officer and soldier, through the several branches of the service. 1727. The most important **work** of its kind produced in the eighteenth century and was reprinted many times during that period. It deals with drill, orders of march, encampments, sieges, etc.

1569. EXERCISE FOR THE HORSE, DRAGOONS AND FOOT FORCES. 1739. The exercise is dated 6th January 1727.

1570. AN INTRODUCTION TO THE ART OF FORTIFICATION containing draughts of all the common works used in military architecture, and of the machines and utensils employed in attacks and defences; with brief references for their explanation. Also, a military dictionary, wherein the said works and machines are not only more fully described, but all the other technical terms and phrases made use of in the science of war, are distinctly explained. 1745.

1571. MULLER, JOHN. The attack and defence of fortified places. 1747. See also, '...the third edn...enlarged, ...also, Bellidor's new method of mining; and Valliese on countermines. 2 pt. 1770.

1572. --------- A treatise containing the elementary part of fortification, regular and irregular, with remarks on the construction of Vauban and Coehorn. 1756.

1573. --------- A treatise of artillery, ... to which is prefixed, an introduction, with a theory of power applied to firearms. The third edition, with additions. 1757. There is an artillery dictionary published as a supplement to the treatise.

1574. A SYSTEM OF CAMP DISCIPLINE, military honours, garrison duty and other regulations for the land forces, collected by a gentleman of the army. In which are included Kane's discipline for a battalion in action. 1757. Includes standing orders, sections on drill, dress, and allowances. There is also a list of military events, 1661-1756.

1575. FAGE, EDWARD. A regular form of discipline for the militia, as it is performed by the West Kent regiment. 1759. Deals with inter alia drill and wheeling.

1576. THE MANUAL EXERCISE as ordered by His Majesty. Together with plans and explanations of the method generally practised at reviews and field days. 1759.

1577. MOLYNEUX, THOMAS M. Conjunct expeditions or, expeditions that have been carried on jointly by the fleet and army, with a commentary on a littoral war. 1759.

1578. ALMON, JOHN. A new military dictionary: or, the field of war. Containing a particular and circumstantial account of the most remarkable battles, sieges, bombardments and expeditions, whether by sea or land, such as related to Great Britain ... to which is added, an essay on fortification: and a table, explaining the military and naval terms of art. 1760.

1579. DALRYMPLE, CAMPBELL. A military essay, containing reflections on the raising, arming, clothing, and discipline of the British infantry and cavalry; with proposals for the improvement of the same. 1761.

1580. AN ESSAY ON THE COMMAND of small detachments. 1766.

1581. ESSAY ON FIELD FORTIFICATION (by an officer of experience in the Prussian service). 1768.

1582. GENERAL WOLFE'S INSTRUCTIONS to young officers: also his orders for a battalion and an army. 1768.

1583. SIMES, THOMAS. The military medley, containing the most necessary rules and directions for attaining a competent knowledge of the art: to which is added an explanation of military terms alphabetically digested. 1768.

1584. --------- The military guide for young officers - containing a system for the art of war. 2 vols. 1776. There is 'a military, historical, and explanatory dictionary' on pp. 385-571.

1585. --------- The military course for the government and conduct of a battalion, designed for their regulations in quarter camp or garrison with useful observations and instructions for their manner of attack and defence. 1777.

1586. THE RUDIMENTS OF WAR: comprising the principles of military duty, in a series of orders issued by commanders in the English army. To which are added some other military regulations, for the sake of connecting the former. 1777.

1587. A MILITARY DICTIONARY, explaining and describing the technical terms, phrases, works and machines, used in the science of war: embellished with copperplates of all the common works used in military architecture: as well as the utensils employed in attacks and defence; with references for their explanation: and an introduction to fortification. 1778.

1588. HINDE, ROBERT. The discipline of the light horse. 1778. Illustrated. A comprehensive manual on drill, training, and the administration of a light cavalry regiment.

1589. SMITH, GEORGE. A universal military dictionary, or a copious explanation of the technical terms, etc. used in the equipment, machinery, movements and military operations of an army. 1779.

1590. ELEMENTS OF MILITARY MANAGEMENT, and of the discipline of war, adapted to the practice of the British infantry. 1780.

1591. SIMES, THOMAS. A treatise on the military science. 1780.

1592. GUIBERT, J.A.H. A general essay on tactics: with an introductory discourse upon the present state of politics and military science in Europe. 2 vols. 1781. A widely used treatise.

1593. LLOYD, MAJOR GENERAL H.E. The history of the late war in Germany between the King of Prussia and the Empress of Germany and her allies. 3 vols. 1781-90. Perhaps the best known military work of the period.

1594. --------- 'Some extracts from a military work of the eighteenth century'. Ed. by Capt. Sir B.H. Liddell-Hart. J.S.A.H.R. vol. XII no. 47, autumn 1933, 138-52.

1595. DUNDAS, SIR DAVID. Principles of military movements, chiefly applied to infantry. Illustrated by manoeuvres of the Prussian troops, and by an outline of the British campaigns in Germany during the war of 1757. 1788.

1596. RULES AND REGULATIONS for the formation, field exercise, and movements of His Majesty's forces, as prescribed by the general order dated June 1, 1792. 1792. Produced by Sir David Dundas.

1597. REIDE, THOMAS. A treatise on the duty of infantry
officers and the present system of British military
discipline. 1795.

1598. LE MARCHANT, MAJOR GENERAL J.G. Rules and regulations
for the sword exercise of the cavalry. 1796. A
training manual which remained in use for many years.

1599. REGULATIONS for the exercise of riflemen and light
infantry. 1798.

1600. JAMES, MAJOR CHARLES. A new and enlarged military
dictionary, or alphabetical explanation of technical
terms: containing ... a succinct account of the different
systems of fortification, tactics, etc: also the various
French phrases and words that have an immediate or
relative connection with the British service. 1802.
A comprehensive small encyclopaedia, which is of much
value still.

1601. RUSSELL, JOHN. Movements and changes of position of a
battalion of infantry, in strict conformity to His
Majesty's orders and regulations. 1802.

1602. JARRY, FRANCIS. Instruction concerning the duties of
light infantry in the field. 1803. A thorough manual,
officially sanctioned, by a chief instructor at the
Royal Military College.

1603. ADYE, RALPH WILLET. The bombardier and pocket gunner.
1804. 4th edn. A comprehensive guide for gunners which
was reprinted a number of times.

1604. JENNINGS, WILLIAM. A general system of attack and
defence with one general rule for erecting fortifications,
without the circuitous aid of trigonometry. 1804.

1605. RUSSELL, JOHN. Remarks on the inutility of the third
rank of firelocks, and the propriety of increasing the
effective force of the country by drawing up the
musquetry two deep, and forming the third rank of pike-
men. 1805.

1606. COOPER, T.H. A practical guide for the light infantry
officer: comprising valuable extracts from all the most
popular works on the subject: with further original information: and illustrated by a set of plates on an entire
new and intelligible plan; which simplify every movement and manoeuvre of light infantry. 1806.

1607. CONGREVE, SIR WILLIAM. A concise account of the origin
and progress of the rocket system. With a view of the
apparent advantages both as to the effect produced, and
the ... saving of expense, arising from the peculiar
facilities of application which it possesses, as well
for naval as military purpose. (Speculation as to the
principles of the flight of rockets). 2 pts. 1807.

1608. ALDINGTON, MAJOR JOHN. A short essay on the construction and advantages of light artillery for acting with
infantry; and a description of the loaded spear
recommended for the use of the rear ranks. Carlisle.
1808.

1609. JAMES, CHARLES. The regimental companion: containing
the pay, allowances and relative duties of every officer
in the British service. 4 vols. 1811-13. A comprehensive guide, with many official forms and documents
reproduced.

1610. THE PRINCIPLES OF WAR, exhibited in the practice of the
camp; and as developed in general orders ... in the
Peninsula with parallel orders of George II, the duke
of Cumberland, the duke of Marlborough, etc... 1815.

1611. TORRENS, MAJOR GENERAL SIR HENRY. Field exercise and
evolutions of the army. 1824. A restatement of
Dundas's principles (1595) in the light of changing
conditions.

1612. TUCKER, J.G.P. Hints to young officers. 1826.

1613. CAMPBELL, E.S.N. A dictionary of the military science:
containing an explanation of the principal terms used
in mathematics, artillery and fortification: and comprising the substance of the latest regulations on court
martials, pay, pensions, allowances, etc. 1830.

1614. MITCHELL, MAJOR-GENERAL JOHN. Thoughts on tactics and
military organisation: together with an enquiry into
the power and position of Russia. 1838. Although this
work gives Mitchell's views on war as a 'scientific
subject' it is mainly valuable for the fundamental
criticisms it makes of the defects of the officer corps
and its unwillingness to study the profession seriously.

1615. SINNOT, LIEUT. JOHN. A military catechism, designed for
the use of n.c.o.'s and others, of the infantry and
adapted to the revised system of the Field Exercise, and
evolutions of the army. Portsmouth. 1841.

1616. JEBB, LIEUT. COL. SIR JOSHUA. Practical treatise on the duties required to be performed by officers and soldiers of the army at a siege with an explanation of the principles on which an attack is conducted and the mode in which the different operations are carried on. 1849. He wrote other works on the same subject.

1617. STOCQUELER, J.H. The military encyclopaedia: a technical, biographical and historical dictionary, referring exclusively to the military sciences, the memoirs of distinguished soldiers, and the narratives of remarkable battles. 1853.

1618. DE ROS, W.L.L.F., LORD. The young officers' companion: or essays on military duties and qualities: with examples and illustrations from history. 1857.

1619. SCOTT, PERCY. A hand-book dictionary for the militia and volunteer services; including an epitome of the duties of all ranks. 1861.

1620. MACDOUGALL, MAJOR GENERAL PATRICK. Modern warfare as influenced by modern artillery. 1864. Analyses the impact of the breech loader on tactics.

1621. SMITH, M.W. A treatise on drill and manoeuvres of cavalry combined with horse artillery. 1865.

1622. HAMLEY, SIR EDWARD BRUCE. The operations of war explained and illustrated. 1866. A textbook of major importance, which explained the main principles of war and which had a profound effect on many English officers.

1623. SMITH, M.W. Modern tactics of the three arms: with reference to recent improvements in the arms of precision. 1869. A long, detailed and technical account.

1624. WOLSELEY, GARNET JOSEPH, VISCOUNT. The soldier's pocket-book for field service. 1869. Concerned with the duties of the soldier in the field, this much reprinted work was the forerunner of the Field service regulations.

1625. MAURICE, SIR JOHN FREDERICK. The system of field manoeuvres best adapted for enabling our troops to meet a continental army. Edin. 1872. Mainly an analysis of Prussian tactics.

1626. HOME, LIEUT. COL. ROBERT. A precis of modern tactics. 1873. An official war office intelligence division publication.

1627. MACDOUGALL, MAJOR GENERAL PATRICK. Modern infantry
    tactics. 1873. Mainly a critique of Prussian tactics,
    and the statement of his own doctrine.

1628. CLERY, LIEUT. COL. SIR C.F. Minor tactics. 1875.
    An important manual. See also, Rishworth, A.H. and
    Sichel,H.D. Notes on Clery's tactics. 1886.

1629. VOYLE,G.E. A military dictionary, comprising terms,
    scientific and otherwise, connected with the science of
    war. 1876.

1630. WALKER, SIR C.P.B. The organisation and tactics of the
    cavalry division. 1876.

1631. GOODENOUGH, O.H. Manual of interior economy: a simple
    explanation of all matters affecting a soldier from
    enlistment to discharge, more especially with regard to
    the Royal Artillery. 1878.

1632. CAMPBELL-COPELAND, T. The colour-sergeant's pocket
    book. 1881.

1633. FARROW, E.S. Military encyclopaedia: a dictionary of
    military knowledge. 3 vols. 1885.

1634. ASPLAND, J.L. English drill: a historical sketch, 1678-
    1884. 1887. The only survey of its kind.

1635. LLOYD, E.W. and HADCOCK, A.G. Artillery: its progress
    and present position. Portsmouth. 1893.

1636. CALLWELL, SIR CHARLES EDWARD. Small wars, their prin-
    ciples and practice. 1896. The most important work
    dealing with the theory of colonial warfare in the nine-
    teenth century.

1637. HENDERSON, COL. G.F.R. Combined training. 1902. A
    standard guide to the tactics of all the arms of the
    service. In 1905 it became Pt. 1 of Field service
    regulations. See also, other official works at this time
    which reflected the lessons of the Boer war: Cavalry
    training, 1904, Infantry training, 1905, The manual of
    engineering, 1905 and Field artillery training, 1907.

1638. MAGUIRE, T. MILLER. The development of tactics since
    1740. 1904. rev. edn. The first edition only covers
    the period from 1866.

1639. HENDERSON, COL. G.F.R. The science of war. 1905. An
    important collection of essays on the theory of war.

1640. WALLIS, CHARLES BRAITHWAITE. West African warfare.
1905. A manual for officers.

1641. JOHNSTON, H.M. A history of tactics. 1906.

1642. HENEKER, W.C.G. Bush warfare. 1907. Problems of
operating in West Africa.

1643. JACKSON, LIEUT. A.V. Machine guns and their tactical
uses with notes on training. 1910. One of the most useful of the professional manuals which takes account of
the profound effect of the machine gun on tactics.

1644. BETHELL, H.A. Modern artillery in the field: a
description of the artillery of the field army, and the
principles and methods of its employment. 1911.

1645. CHILDERS, R.E. German influences on British cavalry.
1911.

1646. RIMINGTON, MAJOR GENERAL M.F. Our cavalry. 1912.
Includes chapters on tactics, equipment and the education
of cavalry officers.

Modern Works

Listed in chronological order of content.

1647. ROGERS, COL. H.C.B. Artillery through the ages. 1972.
A popular guide.

1648. ROBSON, ERIC. 'British light infantry in the mid-
eighteenth century: the effect of American conditions'.
A.Q. vol. LXIII no. 2, January 1952, 209-22.

1649. FULLER, J.F.C. British light infantry in the eighteenth
century. An introduction to 'Sir John Moore's system of
training'. 1925. The best available guide to the
development of light infantry.

1650. ---------- Sir John Moore's system of training. 1925.

1651. SHEPPARD, E.W. 'An old guide to military wisdom'.
A.Q. vol. LXVIII no. 1, April 1954, 93-5. A discussion
of one of the several handbooks for young officers
published in the late eighteenth and nineteenth centuries
entitled <u>Military mentor, comprising a course of elegant
instruction calculated to unite the character and
accomplishments of the gentleman and the soldier</u>. 1809.

1652. LUVAAS, JAY. The education of an army: British military
thought, 1815-1940. 1965. An invaluable scholarly
survey of the evolution of military thought by an
analysis of the theories of a number of major figures,
including Napier, Mitchell, MacDougall and Spencer
Wilkinson. It is the only work of its kind.

1653. PRESTON, A.W. 'British military thought, 1856-1890'.
A.Q. vol. LXXXIX no. 1, October 1964, 57-74. A clear
summary of the main developments.

1654. KING, D.W. 'Military thought 1860' in, The Prince
Consort's library, Aldershot, 1860-1960. 1960.

1655. LUVAAS, JAY. The military legacy of the civil war: the
European inheritance. Chicago. 1959. The impact of
the American civil war on military thought.

1656. BOND, BRIAN. 'Doctrine and training in the British
cavalry, 1870-1914'. In, The theory and practice of
war: essays presented to Captain B.H. Liddell Hart. Ed.
by M.E. Howard. 1965, 95-125.

1657. CLARKE, D.A.V. ed. 'The autumn manoeuvres of 1872'.
J.S.A.H.R. vol. L no. 204, winter 1972, 221-36.

1658. TOWLE, PHILIP. 'The Russo-Japanese war and British
military thought'. J.R.U.S.I. vol. CXVI, December 1971,
64-8.

18.   WEAPONS

1659. BLACKMORE, HOWARD L. British military firearms, 1650-
1850. 1961. A fine account based on, perhaps, the first
thorough examination of the Ordnance office records at
the P.R.O. There is a useful bibliography which includes
articles in scholarly journals.

1660. CARMAN, W.Y. A history of firearms. 1955. An introductory survey.

1661. FFOULKES, CHRISTOPHER. Arms and armament: a historical
survey of the weapons of the British army. 1945.

1662. --------- The gun-founders of England. Camb. 1937.
The definitive account.

1663. --------- 'Notes on service firearms'. J.S.A.H.R.
vol. XIII no. 51, autumn 1934, 128-135.

1664. --------- and HOPKINSON, E.C. Sword, lance and bayonet: a record of arms of the British army and navy. 1938. Arms in use in the army from 1745 to 1914.

1665. --------- 'The swords of the British army'. J.S.A.H.R. vol. XI no. 44, October 1932, 238-47; vol. XII no. 45, spring 1933, 1-8; no. 47, autumn 1933, 152-8; vol. XIII no. 50, summer 1934, 66-70; vol. XV no. 53, spring 1935, 12-16. A good scholarly summary of the state of knowledge on the subject.

1666. GEORGE J.N. English pistols and revolvers ... from the seventeenth century to the present day. Onslau, N.C.1938.

1667. HALFORD, SIR H. St. J. The new service magazine rifle. Aldershot. 1888.

1668. HALL, A.R. Ballistics in the seventeenth century. Camb. 1952.

1669. HELD, ROBERT. The age of firearms: a pictorial history. 1959.

1670. HUGHES, B.R. British smooth-bore artillery: the muzzle-loading artillery of the eighteenth and nineteenth centuries. 1969.

1671. JACKSON, H.J. European hand firearms of the sixteenth, seventeenth and eighteenth centuries, with a treatise on Scottish hand arms ... 1923. Comments upon a series of fine illustrations.

1672. LATHAM, JOHN WILKINSON. British military swords from 1800 to the present day. 1966.

1673. POLLARD, H.B.C. A history of firearms. 1926.

1674. POPE, D. Guns: from the invention of gunpowder to the twentieth century. 1965.

1675. RICKETTS, HOWARD. Firearms. 1962. Valuable, with many illustrations.

1676. ROADS, CHRISTOPHER H. The British soldier's firearm, 1850-1864. 1964. The definitive account of the change from the smooth-bore musket   to the small-bore rifle. Much of the work is purely technical. The bibliographies at the end of each chapter are a useful guide to primary sources.

1677. --------- The history of the introduction of the percussion breech-loading rifle into British military service, 1850-1870. Cambridge University. Unpublished Ph.D. thesis. 1962.

1678. ROGERS, COL. H.C.B. Weapons of the British soldier. 1960. The best introductory guide for the non specialist.

1679. SCURFIELD, R. 'British military smooth-bore firearms'. J.S.A.H.R. vol. XXXIII no. 134, summer 1955, 63-79; no. 135, autumn 1955, 110-113; no. 136, winter 1955, 147-160.

1680. STEVENS, FREDERICK J. Bayonets: an illustrated history and reference guide. 1968. Not confined to England.

1681. WILKINSON, R.J. British military bayonets from 1700 to 1967. A useful guide.

19. MEDALS AND UNIFORMS.

There has been a large number of books and pamphlets on military uniforms published in recent years, most of which are popular and add nothing to current knowledge. Only one or two of the more outstanding examples of this type of publication have been listed here. See also, (52).

1682. ABBOTT, P.E. and TAMPLIN, J.M.A. British gallantry awards. 1971. A scholarly reference work.

1683. ALMACK, E. Regimental badges worn in the British army one hundred years ago. Reproduced in facsimile from the pen and ink drawings in the notebook of a silversmith of that time. The regiments identified, and notes bearing on their history added. 1900.

1684. BARNES, R.M. Military uniforms of Britain and the Empire, 1742 to the present time. 1960. Inferior illustrations, but a useful general introduction to the subject.

1685. CAMPBELL, D. ALISTAIR. The dress of the Royal Artillery. 1971. The first comprehensive account of the dress of the regiment throughout its existence.

1686. CARMAN, W.Y. British military uniforms from contemporary pictures: Henry VII to the present day. 1957.

1687. --------- Headdresses of the British army: Yeomanry. 1970. The only work of its kind.

1688. ---------- Indian army uniforms under the British. 2 vols. 1960-9. Vol. I deals with the cavalry, and vol. II with the artillery, engineers and infantry.

1689. CARTER, THOMAS. Medals of the British army and how they were won. 3 pts. 1860-1.

1690. DAWNAY, N.P. The badges of warrant and non-commissioned rank in the British army. S.A.H.R. special publication no. 6. 1949. A scholarly account of the evolution of the modern badges of rank, with many useful line drawings.

1691. ---------- The distinction of rank of regimental officers, 1684-1855. S.A.H.R. special publication no. 7. 1960. Equivalent to the work listed immediately above, for officers.

1692. ---------- 'The evolution of the badges of commissioned rank of the British army'. J.S.A.H.R. vol. XVI no. 64, winter 1937, 218-34.

1693. DORLING, H.T. Ribbons and medals: naval, military, air force and civil. 1963.

1694. DRESS REGULATIONS, 1846. 1971. Based upon the official 'Dress regulations for officers, 1846', with a commentary by W.Y. Carman. See also, Dress regulations for the army, 1900. rep. 1969. A reprint of the official regulations, with notes by W.Y. Carman, and illustrations.

1695. EDWARDS, T.J. Regimental badges. 1951. 4th revised edn., 1966. An illustrated record of the cap badges of the regiments and corps of the British army in use today, with notes on their origin.

1696. GORDON, LAWRENCE L. British battles and medals. A description of every campaign medal awarded from the Armada, 1588, to the India service medal 1946, together with the names of all the regiments, ships and squadrons of the Royal Air Force entitled to them. Aldershot. 1947. 4th rev. edn. The best general work available on the subject.

1697. HASTINGS-IRWIN, D. 'Notes on the evolution of uniform, 1660-1822'. J.R.U.S.I. vol. LX August 1915, 63-88. Extracts from ms. records, mainly at the P.R.O.

1698. INDEX TO MILITARY COSTUME PRINTS, 1500-1914. 1972. An important contribution to the study of British military uniforms consisting of detailed lists of nearly a thousand series of prints followed by some 1500 individual prints not at present known to have formed part of any series.

1699. KIPLING, A.L. and KING, H.L. Headdress badges of the
British army. 1973. The standard authority on the
subject: nearly 2000 badges are illustrated, and a
larger number are described in detail.

1700. LAFFIN, JOHN. British campaign medals. 1964. A
simple introductory guide covering the period from the
siege of Gibraltar, 1779-1783.

1701. LAVER, JAMES. British military uniforms. 1948. A
work in the now rare 'King Penguin' series, by a
specialist in the history of costume.

1702. LAWSON, C.C.P. A history of the uniforms of the
British army, from its beginnings to 1760. 5 vols.
1940-67. An authoritative record based on official
warrants with numerous illustrations.

1703. LUARD, JOHN. A history of the dress of the British
soldier. 1852. A pioneering work, organised by reigns.

1704. MACDONALD, R.J. The history of the dress of the Royal
Regiment of Artillery, 1625-1897. 1899. The definitive
work, it is also useful for the interesting chapter
entitled 'military reminiscences of the latter end of
18th and beginning of the 19th centuries'.

1705. MAY, W.E., CARMAN, W.Y. and TANNER, JOHN. Badges of
insignia of the British armed services. 1974. See the
section on the army by W.Y. Carman.

1706. MAYO, J.H. Medals and decorations of the British army
and navy. 2 vols. 1897. A detailed record of all
British and Indian medals and decorations issued up to
the date of publication. Includes selections from
relevant official documents.

1707. MILNE, S.N. The standards and colours of the army from
the Restoration. Leeds. 1893. A useful reference work.

1708. NEVILL, RALPH. British military prints. 1909. A large
number of prints are reproduced, with a commentary on
various regiments, and their uniforms and equipment.

1709. PARKYN, H.G. 'Buttons of the British regular army'.
J.S.A.H.R. vol. XIII no. 51, autumn 1934, 159-169.

1710. ---------- 'The earlier buttons of the British army'.
Connoisseur, vol. LXVII 1923, 133-42.

1711. ---------- 'English militia regiments, 1757-1935; their
badges and buttons'. J.S.A.H.R. vol. XV no. 60, winter
1936, 216-248.

1712. --------- 'The later buttons of the British army'.
Connoisseur vol. LXVIII, 1924, 17-23.

1713. --------- Shoulder-belt plates and buttons. Aldershot.
1956. The standard reference guide.

1714. PARRY, D.H. Britain's roll of glory: or, the Victoria
cross, its heroes and their valour. From personal
accounts, official records, and regimental tradition.
1906.

1715. PAYNE, A.A. A handbook of British and foreign orders,
war medals and decorations awarded to the army and navy.
1911.

1716. PERRY, O.L. Rank and badges, precedence, salutes,
colours and small arms, in Her Majesty's army and navy
and auxiliary forces. 1887. Based on official
regulations, it was designed as a practical guide.

1717. SMITHERMAN, PHILIP HENRY. Cavalry uniforms of the
British army. 1962.

1718. --------- Infantry uniforms of the British army. 3
pts. 1965-70. Includes a number of fine illustrations.
The other volumes in the series are of a similar
standard.

1719. --------- Uniforms of the Royal Artillery, 1716 - 1966.
1966.

1720. --------- Uniforms of the Scottish regiments. 1963.

1721. --------- Uniforms of the Yeomanry regiments. 1967.

1722. SMYTH, SIR JOHN. The story of the George Cross. 1968.

1723. --------- The story of the Victoria Cross, 1856-1963.
1963. The best general history of the award.

1724. STRACHAN, HEW. British military uniforms, 1768-1796.
The dress of the British army from official sources.
1975. Consists of a collection of mainly original contemporary sources, including warrants, inspection returns,
manuals, and a number of illustrations. A valuable
reference work.

1725. SUMNER, REV. PERCY. 'Notes on regimental uniforms
from the Irish treasury papers, 1713 to 1782'. J.S.A.H.R.
vol. XIV no. 56, winter 1935, 206-20.

1726. ---------- 'Uniforms and equipment of cavalry regiments, from 1685 to 1881'. _Ibid_. vol. XIII no. 50, summer 1934, 82-106; vol. XIV no. 54, summer 1935, 82-101; no. 55, autumn 1935, 125-142. Extracts from the War Office and other records at the Public Record Office. See other important articles by Sumner on uniforms in _Ibid_.

1727. TYLDEN, GEOFFREY. 'The accoutrements of the British infantryman, 1640 to 1940'. _Ibid_. vol. XLVII no. 189, spring 1969, 4-22.

1728. ---------- Horses and saddlery: an account of the animals used by the British and Commonwealth armies from the seventeenth century to the present day, with a description of their equipment. 1965. A detailed illustrated guide, with a good bibliography.

1729. UNIFORMS OF THE SCOTTISH INFANTRY 1740 to 1900. 1970. Produced by the Scottish United Services museum, it is based on contemporary sources in its possession, with accompanying notes.

1730. WILKINS, P.A. The history of the Victoria Cross, being an account of the 520 acts of bravery for which the decoration has been awarded. 1904.

1731. WILKINSON, F.J. Badges of the British army, 1820-1960. 1969. A booklet of little value.

1732. WILSON, SIR A.T. and McEWEN, J.H.F. Gallantry. Its public recognition and reward in peace and in war at home and abroad. Oxf. 1939.

20.   GENERAL

     This highly select list excludes, with the exception of
one or two standard reference works, general histories of the
art of war. The best general studies of the campaigns of the
army are to be found in the general histories of the army
listed above in section 8.

1733. ADAMS, W.H.D.   Memorable battles in English history
      1066-1857 with lives of the commanders. 2 vols. 1879.
      See also by the same author, England at war: the story
      of the great campaigns of the British army, including
      a historical sketch of the rise and growth of the
      military establishment in England. 2 vols. 1886.

1734. ANDERSON, J.H.   Precis of great campaigns, 1796-1817.
      1907.

1735. ATKINSON, C.T.   'Gleanings from the Cathcart mss.
      Part I - Marlborough's wars (general). Pt. II -
      Marlborough's campaigns of 1707-8. Pt. III - Marlborough's
      campaigns of 1709-12. Pt. IV - the Netherlands, 1794-
      1795. Pt. V - the younger Pitt's last venture : the
      expedition to Hanover, 1805-6. Pt. VI - the "conjoint"
      expedition to Copenhagen 1807.' J.S.A.H.R. vol. XXIX
      no. 117, spring 1951, 20-5; no 118, summer 1951, 64-8;
      no. 119, autumn 1951, 97-103; no. 120, winter 1951, 144-
      157; vol. XXX no 121, spring 1952, 22-9; no. 122, summer
      1952, 80-7. Extracts from, and commentary on, the very
      important military papers of the Cathcart family which
      shed light on a number of campaigns of the army.

1736. BARRETT, C.R.B.   Battles and battlefields of England.
      1896.

1737. BLACKWOOD, R.M.   The battles of the British army: being
      a popular account of all the principal engagements during
      the last hundred years. 1905.

1738. BURNE, ALFRED H.   The battlefields of England. 1950.
      repr. 1973. There is a chapter on the battle of Sedgemoor
      and a detailed bibliography which includes a number of
      references to relevant mss.

1739. CHANDLER, DAVID.   A traveller's guide to the battlefields
      of Europe. 2 vols. 1965. A handbook of the geography
      of European battles.

1740. COLE, D.H. and PRIESTLEY, E.C. An outline of British
military history. 1936. A widely used concise
standard textbook.

1741. CREASEY, SIR EDWARD. The fifteen decisive battles of
the world: from Marathon to Waterloo. 1864. A
classic work, which includes accounts of Blenheim and
Waterloo.

1742. DELAVOYE, A.M. British minor expeditions, 1746 to 1814.
1884. An officially published summary, which adds little
of value to existing knowledge.

1743. EGGENBERGER, DAVID. A dictionary of battles. N.Y. 1968.
A standard reference work.

1744. FIELD, COL. CYRIL. Echoes of old wars. Personal and
unofficial letters and accounts of bygone battles by land
and sea. A martial anthology. 1934. A collection of
interesting letters and accounts mostly of the eighteenth
and early nineteenth centuries.

1745. THE FIELD OF MARS: being an alphabetical digestion of
the principal naval and military engagements in Europe,
Asia, Africa and, America, particularly of Great Britain
and her allies, from the ninth century to the peace of
1801. 2 vols. 1801.

1746. FRONTIER AND OVERSEAS EXPEDITIONS FROM INDIA. 8 vols.
Calcutta and Simla. 1907-11. The official history of
Indian army campaigns throughout the nineteenth century,
which includes campaigns in Asia and Africa in which
Indian soldiers were involved.

1747. GLEIG, REV. GEORGE ROBERT. A sketch of the military
history of Great Britain. 1845.

1748. THE GREAT BATTLES OF THE BRITISH ARMY. 1856.

1749. HAYES-McCOY, G.A. Irish battles: a military history of
Ireland. 1969. A scholarly account, particularly useful
for William III's campaigns in Ireland.

1750. MACDONALD, ROGER. The British martial register:
comprehending a complete chronological history of all the
most celebrated land battles by which the English
standard has been distinguished in the field of Mars, fro
the earliest period to the present time. 4 vols. 1806.

1751. MACMUNN, SIR GEORGE. Always into battle: some forgotten
army sagas. Aldershot. 1952. An uneven collection, whi
includes essays on the Abyssinian campaign of 1867, the
exploits of the British Legion in Spain in 1837, and the
Oudh Irregular Force.

1752. MAGUIRE, T. MILLER. The British army on the continent
of Europe 1701-1855. 1897. Campaigns of the army from
Marlborough to the Crimea.

1753. MIDDLETON, O.R. Outlines of military history: or, a
concise account of the principal campaigns in Europe
between the years 1740 and 1870, being those generally
referred to in our military textbooks. 1885.

1754. NORMAN, C.B. Battle honours of the British army. 1911.
A standard reference work, detailing the battle honours
of the army from Tangiers to the Boer war.

1755. SEYMOUR, WILLIAM W. On active service. 1939.
Descriptions of several campaigns, 1661-1885, based on
accounts of participants.

1756. SOLDIERS' BATTLE TALES from Blackwood's. 1968.

1757. WOOD, SIR HENRY EVELYN. ed. British battles on land and
sea. 2 vols. 1915.

21.   1660 - 1714

In chronological order of content.

1758. LEACH, D.E. Arms for empire: a military history of the
British colonies in North America, 1607-1763. 1973.
A valuable survey of the role of the British army in
America from earliest times to the end of the seven years
war.

1759. HARGREAVES, REGINALD. The bloodybacks; the British
serviceman in North America and the Caribbean 1655-1783.
1968. The best general survey of the British military
role in the continent and which includes details of army
life.

1760. ATKINSON, C.T. 'Charles II's regiments in France, 1672-78'
J.S.A.H.R. vol. XXIV no. 98, summer 1946. 53-65;
no. 99, autumn 1946, 129-36; no. 100, winter 1946, 161-72.

1761. McCANCE, H.M. ed. 'Tangier - 1680. The diary of Sir
James Halkett' S.A.H.R. Special publication, December 1922.
Diary of the C.O. of the Royal Scots on active service in
Tangier. Useful bibliography of works relating to
Britain's short possession of Tangier.

1762. PARKER, ROBERT. Memoirs of military transactions, 1683-
1718, in Ireland and Flanders. Dublin. 1746. Very
similar to the work by Kane listed below (1769).

1763. McGUFFIE, T.H. 'The last battle on English soil: Sedgemoor, 1865'. History Today, vol. V, January 1955, 54-60. Based on ms. diaries.

1764. CAMBRIDGE, MARQUESS OF. 'The march of William of Orange from Torbay to London - 1688'. J.S.A.H.R. vol. XLIV no. 179, September 1966, 152-174.

1765. BOULGER, D.C. The battle of the Boyne: together with an account based on French and other unpublished records of the war in Ireland 1688-1691 and of the formation of the Irish brigade in the service of France. 1911. Scholarly.

1766. PECKHAM, HOWARD H. The colonial wars 1689-1762. Chicago. 1964. One of the most useful introductory surveys of Britain's military role in America.

1767. WADDELL, L.M. The administration of the English army in Flanders and Brabant from 1689 to 1697. University of North Carolina. Unpublished Ph.D. thesis. 1971.

1768. WEBB, S.S. Officers and governors: the role of the British army in imperial politics and the administration of the American colonies 1689-1722. Madison, Wisonsin. 1965.

1769. KANE, MAJOR GENERAL RICHARD. Campaigns of King William and Queen Anne: from 1689 to 1712, also, a new system of military discipline, for a battalion of foot on action; with the most essential exercise of the cavalry...1745. See Hook, D.F. 'The memoirs of General Kane, 1689-1712' A.Q. vol. XIV no. 1, April 1927, 146-155. Perhaps the most important contemporary review of the wars.

1770. JOHNSTON, S.H.F. ed. 'A scots chaplain in Flanders, 1691-7'. J.S.A.H.R. vol. XXVII, no. 109, spring 1949, 3-10. Letters of Alexander Shields, chaplain to the Earl of Angus's regiment among the Laing mss. in Edinburg University Library.

1771. WADDELL, L.M. 'The paymaster accounts of Richard Hill at Allingham Park'. Ibid. vol. XLVIII, no. 193, spring 1970, 50-9. Account books of Richard Hill, Deputy Paymaster to the forces, 1691-1699. Information is provided about the army that was maintained in the low countries during the nine years' war.

1772. D'AUVERGNE, E. A relation of the most remarkable transactions of the last campaigns...in the Spanish Netherlands, 1692-7. 6 pts. 1693-8. The author, a Chaplain in the Scots guards, gives a great deal of valuable detail on the life of a soldier, lists of regiments, and other relevant information.

War of Spanish Succession

The best account of the war is probably still that in
Churchill (1169).

1773. DEVIZE, M.   The history of the siege of Toulon.   1708.

1774. BRODRICK, THOMAS A.   A compleat history of the late
war in the Netherlands, together with an abstract of
the treaty of Utrecht.   2 vols.   1713.

1775. IMPARTIAL ENQUIRY into the Duke of Ormonde's conduct
in the campaign of 1712.   1715.

1776. BANKS, J.   The history of the Duke of Marlborough,
including...a methodical narrative of the late war
upon the Danube.   1755.

1777. STANHOPE, PHILIP, EARL OF.   History of the war of the
succession in Spain.   2 pts.   1832-3.   Largely superseded
by Parnell (1779).

1778. DEANE, J.M.   A journal of the campaign in Flanders
A.D. MDCCVIII, including the battle of Oudenarde and the
siege of Lille.   1846.   The author was a sergeant in the
Grenadier guards.

1779. PARNELL, HON. ARTHUR.   The war of succession in Spain
during the reign of Queen Anne.   1888.   Critical of
Lord Peterborough, but a well documented account.

1780. PARKMAN, FRANCIS.   A half century of conflict.   France
and England in North America.   2 vols.   Boston.   1892.
A detailed account of the period from 1702 to 1750.

1781. CRASTER, H.H.E.   ed.   'Letters of the first Earl of Orkney
during Marlborough's campaigns'.   E.H.R. vol. 19,
April 1904, 307-21.   Contains accounts of Blenheim,
Ramilies, and Malplaquet.

1782. ATKINSON, C.T.   'The war of the Spanish succession'.
In The Cambridge modern history.   1908. vol. v, 401-36.
A good short account, with a full bibliography.

1783. MAYCOCK, F.W.O.   An outline of Marlborough's campaigns.
1913.

1784. TAYLOR, FRANK.   The wars of Marlborough 1702-1709.
Ed. by G.W. Taylor. 2 vols. Oxf. 1921.   A fine
posthumously published, unfinished work.

1785. KEARSEY, A.H.C.   Marlborough and his campaigns, 1702-
1709 with the battles described in conjunction with
Field Service regulations.   2 vols.   Aldershot. 1929-31.

1786. BELLOC, HILAIRE. The tactics and strategy of ...
Marlborough. Bristol. 1933. A very clear brief
account of the main operations.

1787. ATKINSON, C.T. 'Marlborough's sieges'. <u>J.S.A.H.R.</u>
vol. XIII. no. 52, winter 1934, 195-205. A full list
of sieges is provided.

1788. ----------- 'Marlborough's orders of battle'. <u>Ibid,</u>
vol. XV no 58, summer 1936, 107-113.

1789. ----------- ed. A royal dragoon in the Spanish
succession war. A contemporary narrative. <u>S.A.H.R.</u>
Special publication no. 5,1938. This account by an
unknown soldier, written in 1760, is a useful addition
to the small number of extant narratives by soldiers
of this period.

1790. ----------- 'The Peninsular "second front" in the
Spanish succession war'. <u>J.S.A.H.R.</u> vol. XXII no. 90,
summer 1944, 223-33. A resume of Peterborough's
campaigns in Spain.

1791. ----------- 'Queen Anne's war in the West Indies'.
2 pts. <u>Ibid,</u> vol. XXIV no. 99, autumn 1946, 100-110;
no. 100, winter, 1946, 183-97. Pt. I deals with
Jamaica, and Pt. II with the Windward sphere.

1792. ----------- 'Marlborough's sieges. Further evidence'.
<u>Ibid,</u> vol. XXIV. no. 98, summer 1946, 83-7. Adds to
his earlier article on the same subject (1787).

1793. SUMNER, PERCY. 'The battle of Almanza. An eye-witness's
account by General Hawley'. <u>Ibid,</u> vol. XXV. no. 101,
spring 1947, 27-31. Extracts from the voluminous papers
of Lieut. General Henry Hawley (1679?-1759) at Windsor
Castle.

1794. ATKINSON, C.T. 'More light on Almanza from the Hawley
papers'. <u>Ibid,</u> vol. XXV. no. 104, winter, 1947, 144-
161.

1795. ----------- 'Sidelight on a "side show". Spain and
Portugal in the Spanish succession war'. <u>Ibid,</u> vol. XXV,
no. 101, spring, 1947, 11-21.

1796. BURTON, I.F. 'The supply of infantry for the war in
the Peninsula, 1703-1707'. <u>Bull. Institute for Historical
Research</u>, vol. 28. no. 77, 1955, 35-62. Troops for the
campaign in Spain.

1797. DICKINSON, H.T. 'Peterborough and the capture of
Barcelona, 1705'. <u>History Today.</u> vol. XIV, October, 1964
705-15.

798. ------- 'The Earl of Peterborough's campaign
in Valencia, 1706'. J.S.A.H.R. vol. XLV no. 181,
spring 1967, 35-52.

799. SCOULLER, MAJOR R.E. 'Marlborough's administration in
the field'. 2 pts. A.Q. vol. LXXXXV no. 2, January
1968, 197-208; vol. LXXXXVI no. 1, April 1968, 102-113.
Mainly on organization, supplies and the discipline of
officers and men.

800. BELFIELD, E.M.G. Oudenarde, 1708. 1972. Popular.

801. FRANCIS, DAVID. 'Marlborough's march to the Danube'.
J.S.A.H.R. vol. L. no. 202, winter 1972, 78-100.

802. GREEN, DAVID. Blenhaim. 1974. A useful concise study.

22.   1714 - 1793

803. CUST, GENERAL THE HON. SIR EDWARD. Annals of the wars
of the eighteenth century, compiled from the most
authentic histories of the period. 5 vols. 1862-9.

804. TAYLER, ALISTAIR and HENRIETTA. 1715; the story of the
rising. 1936. The best single account.

805. BAYNES, JOHN. The Jacobite rising of 1715. 1970. A
balanced account, which covers more than merely the
military aspects. There is a useful appendix 'table of
main figures connected with the rising'.

806. AN IMPARTIAL ACCOUNT of the late famour siege of Gibraltar.
1728.

807. HANNAY, R.K. ed. 'Gibraltar in 1727: with extracts from
the 'Journal of a voyage from Leith to Barcelona, etc.
in 1726-27' by Edward Bond. S.H.R. vol. XVI, 1919,
325-34. Documents relating to the siege.

808. LESLIE, J.H. 'The siege of Gibraltar by the Spaniards -
1727'. J.S.A.H.R. vol. III no. 13, July 1924, 111-45.
Long extracts from two ms. books.

809. BEATSON, ROBERT. Naval and military memoirs of Great
Britain 1727-1783. 3 vols. Edin. 1790. Useful particularly for the American campaigns of the army.

810. ATKINSON, C.T. 'Jenkin's ear, the Austrian succession
war and the forty-five. Gleanings from sources in the
Public Record Office'. J.S.A.H.R. vol. XXII no. 91,
autumn 1944, 280-98.

The War of the Austrian Succession

1811. OPERATIONS OF THE BRITISH and the allied armies during
the campaigns of 1743 and 1744. 1744.

1812. BRINDLEY, J. The theatre of the present war in the
Netherlands and upon the Rhine... Also a military
dictionary more copious than has hitherto appeared,
explaining all the technical terms in the science of
war. 1745.

1813. ROLT, RICHARD. An impartial representation of the conduc
of the several powers of Europe, engaged in the late
general war, including a particular account of all the
military and naval operations from 1739 to 1748. 4 vols
1749-50.

1814. TOWNSHEND, GEORGE. A brief narrative of the late campai
in Germany and Flanders. 1751.

1815. BIGGS, W. The military history of Europe, etc., from
the commencement of the war with Spain in 1739 to 1748.
1755.

1816. REMARKS ON THE MILITARY OPERATIONS of the English and
French armies in 1747. 1760.

1817. SKRINE, F.H.B. Fontenoy and Great Britain's share in the
war of the Austrian succession, 1741-48. 1906. Perhaps
the most useful account, although the duke of Cumberland'
biography also provides a competent survey (1119-20).

1818. BURNE, ALFRED H. '"Butcher" Cumberland versus Marshal
Saxe. Fontenoy 11th of June 1745'. _A.Q._ vol. XXXVII
no. 1, October 1938, 138-49.

1819. ATKINSON, C.T. 'A Flanders sideshow: Hulst 1747'.
_J.S.A.H.R._ vol. XXII no. 89, spring 1944, 205-12.

1820. ----------- 'Fontenoy and other letters from the mss.
of the Earl of Harrowby'. _Ibid._ vol. XXVII, no 112,
winter 1949, 160-70.

1821. PARKER W.M. 'Wade's campaign in Flanders'. _A.Q._ vol.
LXXXVI. no. 1, April 1963, 106-14. A useful article on
Wade's operation in 1744.

The Forty-Five

1822. HOME, JOHN. The history of the rebellion in the year
1745. 1802.

1823. TERRY, C.S. The rising of 1745. 1903. new edn.
Contains a useful bibliography.

824. PETRIE, SIR CHARLES. The 'forty-five'. New English Rev. vol. XI. no. 2, June 1945, 141-47

825. ATKINSON, C.T. 'Some letters about the "forty-five"'. J.S.A.H.R. vol. XXXVII no. 151, September 1959, 112-126. Letters from the Hannoverian side, mainly from the pen of Sir Everard Fawkener, secretary to the Duke of Cumberland.

826. THOMASON, K. and BUIST, F. Battles of the '45. 1962. A good concise account of the military operations.

---

827. CARMICHAEL-SMYTH, SIR JAMES. Precis of the wars in Canada, from 1755 to the treaty of Ghent in 1814, with military and political reflections. 1862. Originally produced in 1826 as a confidential paper for the Duke of Wellington.

The Seven Years War in Europe and North America.

828. LIVINGSTON, WILLIAM. A review of military operations in North America, 1753-1756. 1757.

829. JOURNAL OF THE CAMPAIGN on the coast of France, 1758. 1758. A rather formal record of the expedition.

830. ENTICK, JOHN. The general history of the late war: containing its rise, progress, and event, in Europe, Asia, Africa, and America. 5 vols. 1763-4.

831. THE OPERATIONS OF THE ALLIED ARMY under Ferdinand, Duke of Brunswick during the greatest part of six campaigns, 1757-62. 1764.

832. MANTE, THOMAS. The history of the late war in North America and the islands of the West Indies, including the campaigns of 1763 and 1764 against His Majesty's Indian enemies. 1772. The best early history of the war.

833. SARGENT, WINTHROP. ed. The history of an expedition against Fort Du Quesne in 1755. Philadelphia. 1855.

834. ROGERS, ROBERT. Journals of Major Robert Rogers containing an account of the several excursions he made under the generals who commanded upon the continent of North America during the late war, etc. Ed. by F.B. Gough. Albany. 1883. Active service in 1765.

835. PARKMAN, FRANCIS. Montcalm and Wolfe. 2 vols. Boston 1884. Perhaps the finest volume of his monumental work on Canada.

1836. WADDINGTON, RICHARD. La guerre de sept ans: histoire
diplomatique et militaire. 5 vols. Paris. 1899-1914.
Remains the standard history.

1837. BRADLEY, A.G. The fight with France for North America.
1900.

1838. DOUGHTY, A.G. and PARMELEE, G.W. The siege of Quebec
and the battle of the plains of Abraham. 6 vols.
Quebec. 1901. Includes extracts from numerous journals
accounts, letters.

1839. KIMBALL, G.S. ed. Correspondence of William Pitt, wher
Secretary of State, with colonial governors and military
and naval commanders in America. 2 vols. N.Y. 1906.
Many major documents printed.

1840. CORBETT, SIR JULIAN S. England in the Seven Years' War:
a study in combined strategy. 2 vols. 1907. Still the
best English account of British strategy and is based
on thorough research.

1841. KNOWLES, SIR LEES. Minden and the Seven Years' War.
1914. A review of the battle of Minden from a British
viewpoint, with a short examination of the background to
the conflict, and its consequences.

1842. KNOX, JOHN. Historical journal of the campaigns in
North America for the years, 1757, 1758, 1759 and 1760.
Ed. by A.G. Doughty. 3 vols. Toronto. 1914. The
most extensive contemporary account.

1843. WRONG, GEORGE McKINNON. The fall of Canada, a chapter
in the history of the Seven Years' War. Oxf. 1914.
A scholarly study of France's defeat.

1844. FYERS, E.W.H. 'The loss and recapture of St. John's,
Newfoundland in 1762'. J.S.A.H.R. vol. XI. no. 44,
October, 1932, 179-215.

1845. PARGELLIS, STANLEY. Lord Loudoun in North America.
New Haven. 1933. A scholarly study of his command,
based on ms. sources.

1846. ATKINSON, C.T. 'British strategy and battles in the
Westphalian campaigns 1758-62'. J.R.U.S.I. vol. LXXIX.
no. 516, November 1934, 733-40.

1847. BASS, BENJAMIN and DOOR, MOSES. 'Fort Frontenac and For
Stanwix. A journal of the expedition against Fort Front
nac in 1758 by Lieut. Benjamin Bass. Also, a journal by
Ensign Moses Door from May 25 to October 28, 1758, inclu
ing an account of the erection of Fort Stanwix'. New Yo
History vol. XVI. no. 4, October 1935, 449-64

184

848. PARGELLIS, STANLEY. ed. Military affairs in North America, 1748-1756: selected documents from the Cumberland papers in Windsor Castle. 1936. Mainly for the period after 1754, when Cumberland was captain general.

849. ALEXANDER, R.O. ed. 'The capture of Quebec. A manuscript journal relating to the operations before Quebec from 8th May 1759, to 17th May, 1760. Kept by Col. Malcolm Fraser, then lieutenant in the 78th foot (Fraser's Highlanders)'. J.S.A.H.R. vol. XVIII. no. 7, autumn 1939, 135-68.

850. ATKINSON, C.T. 'The Highlanders in Westphalia, 1760-62, and the development of light infantry'. Ibid. vol. XX no. 80, winter 1941, 208-23.

851. McGUFFIE, T.H. 'Some fresh light on the siege of Minorca, 1756'. Ibid. vol. XXIX, no. 119, autumn 1951, 111-15.

852. ATKINSON C.T. 'A soldier's diary of the seven years' war' Ibid. 118-27, no. 120, winter 1951, 158-69. A short discussion of other diaries written at the time is included.

853. HIBBERT, CHRISTOPHER. Wolfe at Quebec. 1959. Has some rather critical observations on Wolfe.

854. STACEY, C.P. Quebec, 1759. The siege and the battle. 1959. The best modern account, which corrects and supplements that of Parkman listed above.

855. LLOYD, CHRISTOPHER. The capture of Quebec. 1959. Another account produced for the bicentenary, and which adds little new.

856. SAVORY, SIR REGINALD. His Britannic Majesty's army in Germany during the seven years' war. Oxf. 1966. The definitive account of this aspect of the war.

857. BROWNING, REED. 'The Duke of Newcastle and the financial management of the seven years' war in Germany'. J.S.A.H.R. vol. XLIX. no. 197, spring 1971, 20-35.

858. FURNEAUX, RUPERT. The seven years' war. 1973. A short popular account, with many valuable illustrations.

859. SHY, JOHN. Toward Lexington - the role of the British army in the coming of the American revelution. Princeton, 1965. A detailed study of the army in America, and its organisation, from the seven years' war to the War of Independence.

The American War of Independence

1860. BURGOYNE, JOHN. A statement of the expedition from
Canada, as laid before the House of Commons by Lieut.
General Burgoyne...with a collection of authentic
documents, and an addition of many circumstances which
were prevented from appearing before the House by the
prorogation of Parliament. 1780.

1861. HOWE, WILLIAM, VISCOUNT. The narrative of Lieut. Genera
Sir William Howe, in a committee of the House of Commons
on the 29th April, 1779, relative to his conduct, during
his late command of the King's troops in North America.
1780. See also his Orderly book ed. by Benjamin F.
Stevens. 1890, for detailed information about regimental
life in America at this time.

1862. TARLETON, SIR BANASTRE. A history of the campaigns of
1780 and 1781 in the southern provinces of North America
1787.

1863. RAMSEY, DAVID. Military memoirs of Great Britain or a
history of the war, 1775-1783. Edin. 1779.

1864. STEDMAN, CHARLES. The history of the origin, progress,
and termination of the American war by Charles Stedman,
who served under Sir W. Howe, Sir H. Clinton, and the
Marquis Cornwallis. 2 vols. 1794. Perhaps the best
account written during the eighteenth century.

1865. JAMES, MAJOR CHARLES. A new and enlarged account of the
military occurrences of the late war between Great Brita
and the United States of America. 2 vols. 1818.

1866. SARGENT, WINTHROP. Life and career of Major John Andre,
adjutant-general of the British army in America. Boston
1861.

1867. CARRINGTON, H.B. Battles of the American revolution,
1775-1781. Historical and military criticism, with
topographical illustration. N.Y. 1876.

1868. JOHNSTON, HENRY. The Yorktown campaign and the surrende
of Cornwallis, 1781. N.Y. 1881.

1869. STEVENS, BENJAMIN F. The Clinton-Cornwallis controversy
2 vols. 1888. Six pamphlets on the Yorktown campaign
are reprinted, with notes etc.

1870. HADDEN, JAMES MURRAY. Hadden's journal and orderly book
A journal kept in Canada and upon Burgoyne's campaign in
1776 and 1777. Ed. by H. Rogers. Albany. 1884. Hadde
was an artillery officer in Burgoyne's army.

1871. KEMBLE, STEPHEN. The Kemble papers. 2 vols. N.Y. 1884-5. Contains the journals of Stephen Kemble, deputy adjutant-general between 1772-9.

1872. ANDRE, MAJOR JOHN. Andre's journal: an authentic record of the movements and engagements of the British army in America from June, 1777 to November, 1778 as recorded from day to day by Major John Andre. Ed. by H.C. Lodge. 2 vols. Boston, Mass. 1903.

1873. FISHER, SIDNEY GEORGE. The struggle for American Independence. 2 vols. 1908. A standard guide.

1874. BELCHER, HENRY. The first American civil war: first period, 1775-1778, with chapters on the continental or revolutionary army and on the forces of the crown. 2 vols. 1911. Of most value for its discussion of the organisation and social composition of the army at the time of the war of independence.

1875. ANBUREY, THOMAS. Travels through the interior parts of America by Thomas Anburey, lieutenant in the army of General Burgoyne. Boston, Mass. 1923.

1876. BARKER, JOHN. The British in Boston: being the diary of Lieutenant John Barker of the King's Own Regiment from November 15, 1774 to May 31, 1776. Ed. by E.E. Dana. Camb., Mass. 1924.

1877. FYERS, E.W.H. 'General Sir William Howe's operations in Pennsylvania, 1777. The battle on the Brandywine Creek-11 September - and the action at Germantown - 4 October'. J.S.A.H.R. vol. VIII no. 34, October 1929, 228-241; vol IX no. 35, January, 1930, 27-42.

1878. MACKENZIE, FREDERICK. Diary of Frederick Mackenzie, giving a daily narrative of his military service as an officer of the regiment of Royal Welsh Fusiliers during the years 1775-1781 in Massachusetts, Rhode Island, and New York. Camb., Mass. 2 vols. 1930.

1879. STACKE, H.F. 'Princeton' J.S.A.H.R. vol. XIII no. 52, winter 1934, 214-28.

880. ANDERSON, T.S. The command of the Howe brothers during the American revelution. Oxf. 1936. A critical scholarly review of Sir William Howe's role in America.

881. FRENCH, ALLEN. 'The British expedition to Concord, Massachusetts in 1775'. J.S.A.H.R. vol. XV no. 57, spring 1936, 17-31.

882. HARGREAVES, REGINALD. 'Cavalry in the American war of Independence'. Cavalry Jour. vol.XXVII, Oct.1937, 555-63.

1883. BURNE, ALFRED H. 'Cornwallis at Yorktown'. J.S.A.H.R. vol. XVII no. 66, summer 1938, 71-6.

1884. MACMUNN, SIR GEORGE. The American war of independence in perspective. 1939. Not the best work in this series: it is not always a very objective account.

1885. ATKINSON, C.T. 'British forces in North America, 1774-1781: their distribution and strength'. J.S.A.H.R. vol. XVI no. 61, spring 1937, 3-23; vol. XIX no. 75, autumn 1940, 163-6; vol. XX no. 80, winter 1941, 190-2.

1886. ROBSON, ERIC. 'The raising of a regiment in the war of American independence with especial reference to 80th and 94th regiments'. Ibid. vol. XXVII no. 111, autumn 1949, 107-115.

1887. PECKHAM, HOWARD H. The war for independence, a military history. Chicago. 1950. A competent survey.

1888. ROBSON, ERIC. ed. Letters from America, 1773-1780. Manchester.1951. Letters of Sir James Pulteney-Murray.

1889. WILLCOX, W.B. ed. The American rebellion: Sir Henry Clinton's narrative of his campaigns, 1775-1782. 1954. The only principal on either side who told his story himself.

1890. HELGESEN, M.P. 'The British army in Boston - June 1774 to March 1776'. A.Q. vol. LXXVIII no. 1, April, 1959, 99-113.

1891. BIRD, HARRISON. March to Saratoga: General Burgoyne and the American campaign. Oxf. 1963. An excellent account.

1892. MACKESY, PIERS. The war for America 1775-1783. 1964. A study of British leadership and strategy. Probably the best British work on the war in recent years.

1893. VIVIAN, FRANCES ST. CLAIR. 'A defence of Sir William Howe with a new interpretation of his action in New Jersey, June 1777'. J.S.A.H.R. vol. XLIV no. 178, June 1966, 69-83.

1894. SMITH, SAMUEL S. The battle of Princeton. N.J. 1967. A good account using contemporary documents, and fine illustrations.

1895. FURNEAUX, RUPERT. Saratoga the decisive battle. 1971. Burgoyne's disastrous defeat is objectively retold and assessed.

1896. DRINKWATER, JOHN. A history of the late siege of
      Gibraltar with a description and account of that
      garrison from the earliest period. 1786. The fullest
      contemporary account.

1897. ANCELL, SAMUEL. A circumstantial journal of the long
      and tedious blockade and siege of Gibraltar, from the
      twelth of September 1779 to the third of February 1783,
      in a series of letters from the author to his brother.
      By Samuel Ancell of the 58th regiment. Liverpool. 1785.

1898. HERRIOT, JOHN. A historical sketch of Gibraltar, with
      an account of the siege which that fortress stood against
      the combined forces of France and Spain. 1792.

1899. SPILSBURY, JOHN. A journal of the siege of Gibraltar,
      1779-1783. Ed. by B.H.T. Frere. Gibraltar, 1908.

1900. McGUFFIE, T.H. The siege of Gibraltar, 1779-1783. 1965.
      The standard account, which places the siege clearly in
      the context of the wider conflict.

1901. SMITHERS, A.J. The Kaffir wars 1779-1877. 1973. An
      account of the nine wars fought by the English and Dutch
      against the indigenous population, between 1779 and 1887.

23.   1793-1815

1902. EPOSITO, V.J. and ELTING, J.R. A military history and atlas
      of the Napoleonic wars. 1964. A useful work of reference.

1903. FRISCHAUER, P. England's years of danger, a new history
      of the world war, 1792-1815. Oxf. 1938. One of the
      most useful general summaries of the entire conflict.

1904. EVANS, MAURICE. The aegis of England: or, the triumphs
      of the late war as they appear in the thanks of
      parliament, progressively voted to the navy and army:
      and the communications either oral or written on the
      subject. Chronologically arranged, with notices,
      biographical and military. 1817.

1905. LE MARCHANT, MAJOR GENERAL J.G. 'New light on the
      Flanders campaign of 1793. Contemporary letters of
      Captain J.G. Le Marchant'. Ed. by Alfred H. Burne.
      J.S.A.H.R. vol. XXX no. 123, autumn 1952, 116-21

1906. LESLIE, J.H. ed. 'Campaigning in 1793 - Flanders'.
      Ibid. vol. VIII no. 31, January 1929, 2-32. Extracts
      from the letters of Major Jesse Wright, and the diary of
      Lieut. Howard Fenwick, both of the R.A., during service
      in the low countries under the Duke of York.

1907. BRYANT, SIR ARTHUR. The years of endurance, 1793-1802. 1942. The first of three volumes (1924) of a standard guide to Britain and her involvement in the Napoleonic wars.

1908. JONES, CAPT. L.T. A historical journal of the British campaign on the continent in the year 1794, with the retreat through Holland, in the year 1795. 1797. Perhaps the most important contemporary published accoun by a participant.

1909. ANGLESEY, MARQUESS OF. ed. 'Two brothers in the Netherlands, 1794-1795. Part of the Duke of York's campaign as seen through the eyes of two young commanding officers, based upon hitherto unpublished letters in the "Plas Newydd papers"'. J.S.A.H.R. vol. XXXIII no. 130, summer 1954, 74-82; no. 131, autumn 1954, 96-106. Henry William, Lord Paget and his brother Edward.

1910. ST. GEORGE, THOMAS BALDWIN. 'The St. George diary. A junior regimental officer in the low countries, 1794-95' Ed. by Col. H.C.B. Cook. Ibid. vol. XLVII no. 192, winter 1969, 233-250. Diary of an officer in the R.A.

1911. BELLOC, HILAIRE. Tourcoing. 1931. Published the same year in his, Six British battles Crecy, Poitiers, Blenheim, Malplaquet, Tourcoing, Waterloo.

1912. BROWN, ROBERT. An impartial journal of a detachment fror the brigade of Foot Guards, commencing 25th February 179_ and ending 9th May 1795, by Robert Brown, Corporal in the Coldstream Guards. 1795.

1913. STEWART, CHARLES. 'The campaign in Flanders of 1793-179_ Journal of Lieutenant Charles Stewart, 28th Foot'. Ed. by R.M. Grazebrook. J.S.A.H.R. vol. XXIX no. 117, spri_ 1951, 2-17.

1914. GUPPY, H.B. ed. 'Letters of an officer in the Duke of York's campaigns in Holland in 1793-5 and 1799'. U.S.M. vol. CLXXIII, 1916, 299-305.

1915. REYNARDSON, H.B. 'South Africa, 1795-1921'. A.Q. vol. IV no. 1, April 1922, 9-13. A short review of the British Army in South Africa.

1916. MAXWELL, WILLIAM HAMILTON. The victories of the British armies 1797-1815, with anecdotes illustrative of modern warfare. 2 vols. 1839.

1917. MACKESY, PIERS. The strategy of overthrow 1798-1799. Statesmen at war. 1974. Particularly useful for analysi_ of the Helder expedition 1799, based on original sources.

918. RODGER, A.B. The war of the second coalition, 1798-
1801: a strategic commentary. Oxf. 1964. Includes
expeditions to Egypt and North Holland, and is a
valuable survey of series of complex events.

919. BURGOYNE, SIR J.M. A short history of the naval and
military operations in Egypt from 1798 to 1802. 1885.

920. BURNE, ALFRED H. 'An amphibious campaign - North
Holland, 1799'. A.Q. vol. XXXIX no. 1, October 1939,
103-123. The best available account with a map.

921. BUNBURY, SIR HENRY. Narratives of some passages in the
great war with France 1799-1810. 1854. Later edn. ed.
by the Hon. Sir J.W. Fortescue. 1927. Perhaps the finest
record by a soldier, who records his experiences during
the Helder expedition, and later in the Mediterranean and
elsewhere. There are some useful introductory remarks on
the condition and services of the army between 1793-99.

922. TYLDEN, GEOFFREY. 'The third Kaffir war, 1799-1802'.
J.S.A.H.R. vol. XXXVII no. 150, June 1959, 72-82. The
first campaign by the British army against Bantu tribes
with a short annotated bibliography.

923. ANDERSON, A.E. A journal of the forces which sailed April
1800 under Lieut. General Pigot, and all the subsequent
transactions of the army under General Sir Ralph Abercromby in Egypt, and the latter operations under Lieut. General Lord Hutchinson to the surrender of Alexandria. 1802.

924. BRYANT, SIR ARTHUR. Years of victory, 1802-1812. 1944.
The concluding part of the trilogy was entitled, The age
of elegance, 1812-1822. 1950.

925. MACKESY, PIERS. The war in the Mediterranean, 1803-1810.
1957. Deals with combined operations.

926. BIRD, SIR W.D. 'British strategy in Europe, 1803-1814'.
A.Q. vol. XL no. 2, July, 1940, 299-308.

927. BUTLER, LEWIS. 'Minor expeditions of the British army
from 1803-1815'. U.S.M. vol. XXX (N.s.) no. CMXIV.
January 1905, 388-403; no. CMXV, February 1905, 509-17;
no. CMXVI, March 1905, 589-99; vol. XXXI (N.s.) no. CMXVII,
April 1905, 87-98; no. CMXVIII, May 1905, 176-80;
no. CMXIX, June 1905, 277-87; no. CMXX, July 1905, 384-94;
no. CMXXI, August 1905, 499-513; no. CMXXII, September
1905, 614-23; vol. XXXII no. CMXXIV, November 1905, 200-7;
no. CMXXV, December 1905, 295-302; no. CMXXVI, January
1906, 429-442; no. CMXXVII, February 1906, 538-43;
no. CMXXVIII, March 1906, 647-58; vol. XXXIII (N.s.)
no. CMXXIX, April 1906, 65-78; no. CMXXX, May 1906,
160-73. The only scholarly survey of its kind.

1928. POWELL, G.S. The Kandyan wars. The British army in
      Ceylon 1803-1818. 1973. The only work of its kind on
      the costly conquest of Ceylon.

1929. LESLIE, J.H. 'The diary of 1st Lieutenant William
      Swabey, R.A. 28 July to 31 October 1807'. J.R.U.S.I.
      vol. LXI no. 441, February 1916, 63-90. A journal of
      the expedition to Copenhagen.

1930. A SHORT NARRATIVE of the late campaign in Zealand of the
      British army, under the orders of the Rt. Hon. the Earl
      of Chatham. 1810.

The Peninsular War

1931. MOORE, JAMES C. A narrative of the campaigns of the
      British army in Spain, commanded by his excellency Sir
      John Moore. 1809. The author was Sir John Moore's
      brother.

1932. GLEIG, REV. GEORGE ROBERT. The subaltern. 1825. Repr.
      many times including 1969, with the sub-title a chronicl
      of the Peninsula war. Based on the author's personal
      experiences.

1933. JONES, MAJOR GENERAL SIR J.T. Journals of the sieges
      carried on by the army under the Duke of Wellington in
      Spain 1811-14. 2 vols. 1827. A detailed specialised
      account by a distinguished officer of the Engineers. Se
      also Military autobiography of Major General Sir J.T.
      Jones 1853, of which only twelve copies were printed.

1934. SOUTHEY, ROBERT. History of the Peninsula war. 3 vols.
      1832. His literary reputation did not ensure the succes
      of this work which lacked the quality of Napier's, or
      even Londonderry's histories.

1935. LONDONDERRY, CHARLES STEWART, MARQUESS OF. Narrative of
      the Peninsula war 1808-1813. 2 vols. 1829. Based as
      much on his own experiences as on any serious research.

1936. NAPIER, SIR WILLIAM F. A history of the war in the
      peninsula and in the south of France, 1807 to the year
      1814 giving references to English and French sources wit
      a wealth of factual detail. 5 vols. 1832-3. Napier's
      history has become a classic work of literature, as well
      as remaining a standard source. Inevitably much of the
      work has been superseded by later research, and he does
      not always give a balanced judgement. Undoubtedly one
      of the finest works of military history ever published
      in England. Many subsequent nineteenth century studies
      were based excessively on Napier.

1937. MAXWELL, WILLIAM HAMILTON. ed. Peninsula sketches,
by actors on the scene. 2 vols. 1845. A collection of
anonymous accounts of campaigning in the Peninsula.

1938. LARPENT, FRANCIS SEYMOUR. The private journal of F.S.
Larpent, judge-advocate general of the British forces in
the Peninsula attached to the headquarters of Lord
Wellington during the Peninsula war from 1812 to its
close. Ed. by Sir G. Larpent. 2 vols. 1853.

1939. ATKINSON, C.T. 'The composition and organisation of the
British forces in the Peninsula 1808-14'. E.H.R. vol.
XVII, 1902, 110-33. A standard reference guide.

1940. OMAN, SIR C.W.C. A history of the Peninsula war. 5 vols.
Oxf. 1902-30. The definitive modern history, and one of
the finest examples of military history produced in
England since Napier's classic study which this work
aimed to correct and supplement. See also (459).

1941. BUTLER, LEWIS. Wellington's operations in the Peninsula,
1808-1814. 2 vols. 1904. Useful factual account.

1942. KNOWLES, ROBERT. The war in the Peninsula: some letters
of Lieut. Robert Knowles, a Bolton Officer. Ed. by Sir
Lees Knowles. Bolton. 1909.

1943. WARRE, LIEUT. GENERAL SIR WILLIAM. Letters from the
Peninsula 1808-1812. Ed. by Edmund Warre. 1909. A
graphic description of the life of a staff officer.

1944. GORDON, ALEX. A cavalry captain in the Corunna campaign
1808-1809. Ed. by H.C. Wylly. 1913.

1945. MADDEN, C.D. 'The diary of Charles Dudley Madden,
lieutenant 4th Dragoons, Peninsula war 1809-11. A
journal of events which took place from the day I marched
from Chichester to embark'. J.R.U.S.I. vol. LVIII March
1914, 334-58; April 1914, 501-26. A diary with many full
entries and a number of powerful descriptions.

1946. SMITH, WILLIAM. 'Journal of Captain William Smith of the
11th Light Dragoons during the Peninsula war, May 1811-
November 1812'. Ibid. vol. LX, 1915, 165-76. Extracts
from a ms. then in the possession of the RUSI, but which
appears to contribute little new.

1947. YOUNG, K.E. 'Some Peninsular letters'. U.S.M. vol. LXII
(N.s.), Feb. 1916, 508-17. Written by an Irish officer
of the 38th regiment, an ensign when the letters begin.

1948. HOUGH, HENRY. 'Journal kept by Lieut. Hough from 22 March
1812 to 13 May 1813'. J.R.U.S.I. vol. LXI no. 443, August
1916, 840-80.

1949. WHEATLEY, MAJOR-GENERAL WILLIAM. 'Letters from the front 1812'. Ed. by G.E. Hubbard. U.S.M. vol. LVIII (n.s.), March 1919, 435-52. The author of these letters was in the first division in the Peninsula.

1950. DOWNMAN, THOMAS. 'Diary of Major Thomas Downman, Royal Horse Artillery, in the Peninsula'. J.S.A.H.R. vol. V no. 22, October-Devember, 1926, 178-86. Although it is stated at the end of the article that it was "to be continued", no further extracts were published.

1951. DALLAS, A.R.C. 'Experiences of a British commissariat officer in the Peninsular war'. Ed. by H.A. Dallas. A.Q. vol. XIII no. 1, October 1926, 127-37; no. 2, January 1927, 360-7; vol. XV no. 1, October 1927, 78-90. Extracts from his autobiography.

1952. GARRETT, LIEUT. GENERAL ROBERT. 'A subaltern in the Peninsular war. Letters of Lieutenant Robert Garrett, 1811-1813'. Ed. by A.S. White. J.S.A.H.R. vol. XIII no. 49, spring 1934, 3-22. Letters to his fiancee, while serving as an ensign in the 2nd Queen's Royal Regiment and later as a lieutenant in the Royal Fusiliers.

1953. CARNOCK, MAJOR LORD. ed. Cavalry in the Corunna campaign (as told in the diary of the adjutant of the 15th Hussars S.A.H.R. Special publication no. 4, 1936. Mainly written by Lieut. C. Jones for the period of the Corunna campaign to which these extracts relate.

1954. BELL, D.H. Wellington's officers. 1938. Biographical sketches of, and general observations on, officers and men in the Peninsula.

1955. WARD. S.P.G. 'The quartermaster general's department in the Peninsula, 1809-1814'. J.S.A.H.R. vol. XXIII no. 96, winter 1945, 133-54.

1956. CARSS, JOHN. 'The 2nd/53rd in the Peninsula war. Contemporary letters from an officer of the regiment'. Ed. by S.H.F. Johnson. Ibid. vol. XXVI no. 105, spring 1948, 2-17. His letters as Adjutant of the 2nd/53rd, one of which gives new information on the battle of Talavera

1957. BINGHAM, SIR GEORGE R. 'The Bingham manuscripts. 2nd/ 53rd in the Peninsular war, 1809-10 and 1812-13'. Ed. by T.H. McGuffie. Ibid. vol. XXVI no. 107, autumn 1948, 106-11. Extracts in the editor's text from papers of a lieutenant-colonel of the 53rd Foot in the Peninsula.

1958. DALLAS, R.W. 'A subaltern of the 9th in the Peninsula and at Walcheren'. Ed. by C.T. Atkinson. Ibid. vol. XXVIII no. 114, summer 1950, 59-67. Extracts from the papers of Ensign Dallas.

1959. WARD, S.P.G. 'Some fresh light on the Corunna campaign'. Ibid. vol. XXVIII no. 115, autumn 1950, 107-126. Based upon the papers of General Sir George Murray.

1960. SCARFE, NORMAN. ed. Letters from the Peninsula. 1953. Correspondence between William and Edward Freer of 1/43rd Foot, their uncle, Daniel Gardner, of the same regiment, and their parents.

1961. DAVIES, GODFREY. Wellington and his army. Oxf. 1954. Wellington as a general, and his relationship with his officers and men. There are also chapters on 'amusements and recreation' and 'wives and children'.

1962. MACFARLANE, JOHN. 'Peninsular private'. Ed. by Eric Robson. J.S.A.H.R. vol. XXXII no. 129, spring 1954, 4-14. His notebooks while serving with 1st battalion, 71st Highland regiment.

1963. ROBINSON, F.P. 'A Peninsular brigadier. Letters of Major General Sir F.P. Robinson, K.C.B. dealing with the campaign of 1813'. Ed. by C.T. Atkinson. Ibid. vol. XXXIV no. 140, December 1956, 153-70.

1964. WARD, S.P.G. Wellington's headquarters. A study of the administrative problems in the Peninsula, 1809-1814. Oxf. 1957. A scholarly survey based in part on General Sir George Murray's papers in the N.L.S. There is a chapter of more general relevance entitled 'the administration of the army in peace and war'.

1965. BADCOCK, LOVELL. 'A light dragoon in the Peninsula. Extracts from the letters of Capt. Lovell Badcock, 14th Light Dragoons 1809-1814'. Ed. by C.T. Atkinson. J.S.A.H.R. vol. XXXIV no. 138, June 1958, 70-9. These letters to his family give much useful information on conditions of service, the ideas of the troops and the behaviour of the enemy.

1966. HIBBERT, CHRISTOPHER. Corunna. 1961. A competent survey based on secondary sources.

1967. WELLER, J. Wellington in the Peninsula 1808-1814. 1962. Serves as one of the best concise guides to military operations in Spain and Portugal with a valuable assessment of Wellington's contribution to ultimate victory.

1968. DOUGLAS, NEIL. 'The diary of Captain Neil Douglas, 79th Foot, 1809-1810'. Ed. by Antony Brett-James. J.S.A.H.R. vol. XLI no. 166, June 1963, 101-7. Extracts relating to service in the Peninsula.

1969. GLOVER, MICHAEL. Wellington's Peninsular victories.
Busaco, Salamanca, Vittoria, and Nivella. 1963. Focuses
on Wellington's four greatest triumphs.

1970. HORWARD, D.D. The battle of Busaco: Massena vs.
Wellington. 1965.

1971. HOWSON, J.M. 'The administration of Wellington's army
in the Peninsula 1809-1814'. A.Q. vol. LXXXX no. 2,
July 1965, 168-72.

1972. FITZGERALD, EDWARD FOX. 'With the tenth Hussars in Spain
Letters of Edward Fox Fitzgerald'. Ed. by D.J. Haggard.
J.S.A.H.R. vol. XLIV no. 178, June 1966, 88-113.

1973. BARNARD, SIR ANDREW. 'Letters of a Peninsula war
commanding officer. The letters of Lieut. General Sir
Andrew Barnard, G.C.B.'. Ed. by M.C. Spurrier. Ibid.
vol. XLVII no. 191, autumn 1969, 131-48.

1974. GLOVER, MICHAEL. Britannia sickens: Sir Arthur Wellesley
and the convention of Cintra. 1970.

1975. GUNN, JAMES. 'The memoirs of Private James Gunn'. Ed.
by R.H. Roy. J.S.A.H.R. vol. LXIX no. 198, summer 1971
90-120. A soldier in the 42nd regiment.

1976. BRETT-JAMES, ANTONY. Life in Wellington's army. 1972. A
detailed reconstruction of day to day existence in the
Peninsula which draws upon a number of unpublished
diaries and letters. There is a useful bibliography.

1977. NIGHTINGALL, MILES. 'The Nightingall letters. Letters
from Major General Miles Nightingall in Portugal,
February to June, 1811'. J.S.A.H.R. vol. LI no. 207,
autumn 1973, 129-54.

1978. YOUNG, PETER and LAWFORD, J.P. Wellington's masterpiece
The battle and campaign of Salamanca. 1973.

1979. GLOVER, MICHAEL. The Peninsular war 1807-1814. A concise military history. Newton Abbott. 1974. A thorough
survey of the military campaign based on wide research.
There is little material on the political or diplomatic
background.

1980. AUCHINLECK, G. A history of the war between Great Britain
and the United States of America during the years, 1812,
1813, and 1814. 1856. The most valuable early account.

1981. LUCAS, C.P. The Canadian war of 1812. Oxf. 1906.

1982. COMMINS, JAMES. 'The war on the Canadian frontier
1812-14. Letters written by Sergeant James Commins,
8th. Foot'. Ed. by N.C. Lord. J.S.A.H.R. Vol. XVIII
no. 72, winter 1939, 199-211.

1983. STANLEY, G.F.G. 'British operations in the American
north-west, 1812-15'. Ibid. vol. XXII no. 87, autumn
1943, 91-106.

1984. ADAMS, HENRY. The war of 1812. Ed. by H.A. De Weerd.
Washington, D.C. 1944. Taken from his monumental
History of the United States during the administration
of Jefferson and Madison. 9 vols. N.Y. 1889-91.

1985. HITSMAN, J. MACKAY. The incredible war of 1812 : a military history. Toronto. 1966. Emphasises Canadian aspects
of the war excessively, but has a good bibliography.

1986. HORSMAN, REGINALD. The war of 1812. 1969. A good
scholarly summary.

1987. SPERLING, JOHN. Letters of an officer of the Corps of
Royal Engineers from the British army in Holland, Belgium
and France to his father : from the latter end of 1813
to 1816. 1872.

1988. MAYCOCK, F.W.O. The invasion of France, 1814. 1914.

1989. LESLIE, J.H. 'Artillery services in North America in
1814 and 1815, being extracts from the journal of Col.
Sir Alexander Dickson, K.C.B., commanding Royal Artillery'.
J.S.A.H.R. vol. VIII no. 32, April 1929, 79-113; no. 33,
July 1929, 147-78; no. 34, October 1929, 213-27. Extracts
from his journal giving a full account of the artillery
services in the operations against New Orleans and Mobile
in 1814-15. See also, (1291).

1990. THORN, WILLIAM. Memoir of the conquest of Java with the
subsequent operations of the British forces in the Orient.
1815.

1991. RAINBOW, S.G. 'English expeditions to the Dutch East
Indies during the revolutionary and Napoleonic wars'.
Bull. of the Institute of Historical Research, vol. XI
no. 33, February 1934, 192-5.

Waterloo

There is an enormous volume of books and other writings
on this subject alone. There is a useful select guide to the
literature in Weller (2007).

1992. BATTY, ROBERT. A sketch of the late campaign in the
Netherlands. 1815.

1993. CURLING, J. Observations on the campaign in the
       Netherlands terminated by the battle of Waterloo.
       1858.

1994. JAMES, W.H. The campaign of 1815, chiefly in Flanders.
       1908.

1995. COTTON, EDWARD. A voice from Waterloo : a history of
       the battle fought on the 18th. June, 1815, with a
       selection from the Wellington despatches, general
       orders and letters relating to the battle. 1849.
       Cotton was a sergeant-major in the 7th. Hussars, and
       participated in the battle.

1996. SIBORNE, MAJOR GENERAL H.T. Waterloo letters. A
       selection from original and hitherto unpublished letters
       bearing on the 16th, 17th and 18th June, by officers who
       served in the campaign. 1891. Selections from the
       letters collected by his father, Captain William Siborne
       for his book listed immediately below.

1997. SIBORNE, CAPTAIN WILLIAM. The Waterloo campaign. 1894.
       Partly based on letters he solicited from all surviving
       Waterloo officers some years later.

1998. CHESNEY, COL. C.C. Waterloo lectures : a study of the
       campaign of 1815. 1907.

1999. MERCER, GENERAL CAVALIE. Journal of the Waterloo cam-
       paign kept through the campaign of 1815. 1927. Probably
       the best narrative of Waterloo by a participant.

2000. EDMONDS, SIR JAMES. 'Wellington's staff at Waterloo'.
       J.S.A.H.R. vol. XII no. 48, winter 1933, 239-47. List
       and brief biographies of Wellington's staff.

2001. MACKWORTH, SIR DIGBY. 'The Waterloo diary of Sir Digby
       Mackworth'. A.Q. vol. XXXV no. 1, October, 1937, 123-31;
       no. 2, January 1938, 320-7.

2002. KELLY, EDWARD. 'Kelly at Waterloo'. Ed. by T.H.
       McGuffie. J.S.A.H.R. vol XXXIII no. 135, autumn 1955,
       97-109. Letters of a captain in the first Life
       Guards to his wife.

2003. JOHNSTON, SGT. 'A Waterloo Journal'. Ed. by C.T.
       Atkinson. Ibid. vol. XXXVIII no. 154, March 1960, 29-42.
       The journal of a soldier about whom very little is known,
       who served in the Royal Scots Greys. The article include
       a few bibliographical comments on other personal
       reminiscences.

2004. NAYLOR, JOHN. Waterloo. 1960. A good concise account.

2005. McGUFFIE, T.H. 'The British soldier at Waterloo'.
History Today, vol. XV, July 1965, 373-80.

2006. SUTHERLAND, JOHN. Men of Waterloo. 1967. A popular
account which gives information on the immediate background to the battle, and on the participating armies
and soldiers.

2007. WELLER, JAC. Wellington at Waterloo. 1967. The
narrative is confined to the battle as Wellington
actually fought it. One of the best available accounts.

2008. PERICOLI, UGO. 1815 : the armies at Waterloo. 1973.
Supplementary text by Michael Glover. The best work on
the uniforms of the period with fine illustrations,
although other aspects are fully covered.

24. <u>1815 - 1914</u>

2009. CUST, GENERAL THE HON. SIR EDWARD. Annals of the wars of
the nineteenth century, compiled from the most authentic
histories of the period. 4 vols. 1862-3.

2010. BRUCE, GEORGE. The Burma wars, 1824-1886. 1973. A
popular account, which also gives a brief survey of the
second and third Burma wars.

2011. SNODGRASS, MAJOR J.J. Narrative of the Burmese war,
detailing the operations of Major General Sir A.Campbell's
army from its landing at Rangoon in May 1824, to the
conclusion of a treaty of peace at Yandaboo, in Feb. 1826.
1827. Snodgrass was military secretary to the commander-
in-chief.

2012. DOVETON, CAPT. FREDERICK B. Reminiscences of the
Burmese war in 1824-5-6. 1852.

2013. WILSON, HORACE H. Narrative of the Burmese war in 1824-
26, as originally compiled from official documents. 1852.
He also wrote, <u>Documents illustrative of the Burmese
war</u>, Calcutta, 1827.

2014. DE RHE-PHILLIPE, G.W. A narrative of the first Burmese
war, 1824-26: with the various official reports and
despatches describing the operations of the naval and
military forces employed, and other documents bearing
upon the origin, progress, and conclusion of the contest.
1905. The most detailed account available.

2015. PEARN, B.R. 'A forgotten campaign, Arakan 1824-25'.
J.S.A.H.R. vol. XXIV no. 99, autumn 1946, 115-24.

2016. PEARSALL, R.J. 'The Burmese war of 1824-26. A nineteenth century Vietnam?' A.Q. vol. C no. 2, July 1970,
233-40.

2017. RICKETTS, H.I. Narrative of the Ashanti war. 1831. On
the war, 1824-31.

2018. LLOYD, ALAN. The drums of Kumasi. The story of the
Ashanti wars. 1964. A good popular summary of the
Ashanti wars, and the political background down to 1901.

2019. ARMYTAGE, HON. MRS. FENELLA FITZHARDINGE. Wars of Queen
Victoria's reign, 1837 to 1887. 1887.

2020. BOND, BRIAN. ed. Victorian military campaigns. 1967.
Includes essays by various authors on the Sikh wars,
1845-9; the third China war, 1860; the expedition to
Abyssinia, 1867-8; the Ashanti campaign, 1873-4; the
South African war, 1880-1; the Egyptian campaign, 1882;
the reconquest of the Sudan, 1896-9.

2021. FAREWELL, BYRON. Queen Victoria's little wars. 1973.
The best modern summary of its kind. One of the
appendices contains a full, if not comprehensive, list of
the 'little wars'.

2022. FEATHERSTONE, DONALD. Colonial small wars. 1837-1900.
1973. A short illustrated work on minor Victorian
campaigns which adds nothing new to the subject.

2023. JUDD, DENIS. Someone has blundered. Calamities of the
British army in the Victorian age. 1973. A rather
superficial account of six wars, from the invasion of
Afghanistan 1838-42 to the Boer war, and the reasons for
the military failures which occurred.

2024. FORBES, ARCHIBALD. The Afghan wars 1839-42 and 1878-80.
1892.

2025. EYRE, MAJOR GENERAL SIR VINCENT. The military operations
at Cabul which ended in the retreat and destruction of the
British army, January 1842. With a journal of imprison-
ment in Afghanistan.1843. An important account by a
participant.

2026. SALE, FLORENTIA, LADY. A journal of the disasters in
Afghanistan 1841-2. 1843. rep. 1969. The journal
starts in September, 1841 and continues for a year when
she is rescued by her husband after nine month's imprison
ment in Afghan hands.

2027. KAYE, SIR JOHN WILLIAM. History of the war in
Afghanistan from the unpublished letters and journals
of political and military officers employed in
Afghanistan throughout the entire period of British
connection with that country. 2 vols. 1851. The
definitive account.

2028. DURAND, SIR HENRY MARION. The first Afghan war and
its causes. Ed. with a memoir of the author by General
Sir Henry Mortimer Durand. 1879.

2029. MACORY, PATRICK. Signal catastrophe. The story of the
disastrous retreat from Kabul, 1842. 1966. One of the
greatest defeats of the army in Asia is well described
in a work owing much to Kaye.

2030. NORRIS, J.A. The first Afghan war 1838-1842. Camb.
1967. A scholarly account which is critical of Kaye.

2031. JOCELYN, ROBERT, VISCOUNT. Six months with the Chinese
expedition or leaves from a soldier's notebook. 1841.

2032. OUCHTERLONY, JOHN. The Chinese war: an account of the
operations of the British forces from the commencement
to the treaty of Nanking. 1844.

2033. HOLT, EDGAR. The opium wars in China. 1964. A useful
recent work on the wars of Britain and China 1839-1860.
A list of eye witness accounts is given on pp. 285-6.

2034. SELBY, JOHN. The paper dragon: an account of Britain's
wars against and relations with China in the nineteenth
century. 1968. Popular.

2035. ALEXANDER, J.E. Bush fighting: illustrated by remarkable
actions and incidents of the Maori wars in New Zealand.
1873.

2036. HARROP, A.J. England and the Maori wars. 1937. A
scholarly study of British policy towards New Zealand
based on ms. sources.

2037. COWAN, JAMES. The New Zealand wars. A history of the
Maori campaigns and the pioneering period. 2 vols.
Wellington, New Zealand. 1955. Valuable for its detailed
accounts of the operations.

2038. HOLT, EDGAR. The strangest war: the story of the Maori
wars in New Zealand, 1843-1872. 1962. Perhaps the best
recent work, with a full bibliography.

2039. GIBSON, T.A. The Maori wars. The British army in New
Zealand 1840-1872. 1974. Contributes little further to
an understanding of the subject.

2040. STACEY, C.P. Canada and the British army, 1846-1871.
A study in the practice of responsible government. 1936.

2041. KING, W.R. Campaigning in Kaffirland, 1851-2. 1853.
A useful contemporary account of the Kaffir war 1850-3.

2042. LAURIE, WILLIAM, F.B. The second Burmese war. A
narrative of the operations at Rangoon in 1852. 1853.

The Crimean War

There is a valuable bibliography, which includes several
French works, in B.D. Gooch. The new Bonapartist generals in
the Crimean War. Distrust and decision-making in the Anglo-
French Alliance. The Hague. 1959.

2043. DUBERLY, FRANCES ISABELLA. A journal kept during the
Russian war. 1855. The wife of a British officer who
accompanied the expedition to the Crimea.

2044. PEARD, G.S. Narrative of a campaign in the Crimea:
including an account of the battles of Alma, Balaclava
and Inkerman. 1855.

2045. RUSSELL, SIR W.H. The war from the landing at Gallipolli
to the death of Lord Raglan. 2 vols. 1855. His
despatches to the Times. See also, his later work: The
great war with Russia. The invasion of the Crimea. A
personal retrospect of the battles of the Alma, Balaclava
and Inkerman and of the winter of 1854-55 etc. 1895.

2046. RYAN, GEORGE. Our heroes of the Crimea. 1855.
Biographical sketches of the British commanders.

2047. BRACKENBURY, GEORGE. The campaign in the Crimea. 2 vols.
1855-6. Mainly valuable for the reproductions of 110
drawings made in the Crimea during the war.

2048. CALTHORPE, HON. S.J.G. Letters from headquarters: or
the realities of the war in the Crimea. 2 vols. 1856.
A valuable and detailed source by a member of Raglan's
staff.

2049. CARDIGAN, JAMES THOMAS BRUDENELL, EARL OF. Eight months
on active service : or a diary of a general officer of
cavalry in 1854. 1856.

2050. PORTER, MAJOR GENERAL WHITWORTH. Life in the trenches
before Sebastopol. 1856.

2051. NOLAN, EDWARD HENRY. The history of the war against
Russia. 2 vols. 1857. A fully detailed, but not always
very accurate, account.

2052. RANKEN, MAJOR GEORGE. Six months at Sebastopol: being
      selections from the journal and correspondence of the
      late Major George Ranken, by...W.B. Ranken. 1857. See
      also, Canada and the Crimea or sketches of a soldier's
      life from the journals and correspondence of the late
      Major Ranken. Ed. by W.B. Ranken. 1862.

2053. ADYE, GENERAL SIR JOHN MILLER. A review of the Crimean
      war to the winter of 1854-5. 1860.

2054. KINGLAKE, A.W. The invasion of the Crimea: its origin
      and an account of its progress down to the death of
      Lord Raglan. 8 vols. 1863-7. A monumental work which
      had a profound influence on later writings on the subject,
      but which is neither very objective nor a complete study
      of the war as it ends with the death of Lord Raglan.

2055. PACK, COL. R. Sebastopol trenches, and five months in
      them. 1878.

2056. PAGET, GEORGE A.F., LORD. The light cavalry brigade in
      the Crimea. 1881. See also his Extracts from the
      letters and journal of General Lord George Paget during
      the Crimean war. 1881.

2057. HAMLEY, GENERAL SIR EDWARD BRUCE. The war in the Crimea.
      1891. He also published, The story of the campaign of
      Sebastopol written in the camp. 1855. The history
      published by Hamley in 1891 is one of the best accounts
      of the war.

2058. CAMPBELL, COLIN F., BARON. Letters from camp to his
      relatives during the siege of Sebastopol. 1894. Critical
      of Raglan, and the military authorities.

2059. HUME, JOHN R. Reminiscences of the Crimean campaign with
      the 55th Regiment. 1894.

2060. LYSONS, GENERAL DAVID. The Crimean war from first to
      last. 1895. An account of active service as a junior
      regimental officer.

2061. WOOD, SIR HENRY EVELYN. The Crimea in 1854, and 1894.
      1895.

2062. WINDHAM, SIR C.A. The Crimean diary and letters of
      Lieut. General Sir Charles Ashe Windham with observation
      upon his services during the Indian mutiny, and an
      introduction by Sir W.H. Russell. Ed. by Major H.W.
      Pearse. 1897.

2063. KELLY, SIR RICHARD. An officer's letters to his wife
      during the Crimean war. 1902.

2064. REID, DOUGLAS ARTHUR. Memories of the Crimean war, January, 1855 to June, 1856. 1911. A surgeon's letters.

2065. JOCELYN, HON. STRANGE. With the Guards we shall go: a guardsman's letters in the Crimea, 1854-1855. Ed. by the Countess of Airlie. 1933.

2066. MACMUNN, SIR GEORGE. The Crimea in perspective. 1935. A rather uncritical account, favourable to Lord Raglan.

2067. VULLIAMY, C.E. Crimea. The camp of 1854-6, with an outline of politics and a study of the royal quartet. 1939. A well documented study.

2068. PARKER, SERGEANT WILLIAM. 'The Crimea in 1855 and 1856. A contemporary account by Sergeant William Parker, R.A.'. Ed. by Major Geoffrey Tylden. J.S.A.H.R. vol. XXV no. 101, spring 1947, 23-6. Parker served as Pay Sergeant in the Ball Cartridge Brigade attached to the Light Division.

2069. WOODHAM-SMITH, CECIL. The reason why. 1953. A highly critical account of senior army officers, but rather superficial, and there is a very selective use of original sources.

2070. ROBBINS, M. 'The Balaclava railway'. Journal of Transport History. vol. 1, 1953, 28-43.

2071. EVELYN, GEORGE PALMER. A diary of the Crimea by George Palmer Evelyn. Ed. by Cyril Falls. 1954.

2072. GERNSHEIM, H. and A. Roger Fenton, photographer of the Crimean war. 1955.

2073. CLIFFORD, HENRY. His letters and sketches from the Crimea. Ed. by C. Fitzherbert. 1956. Clifford, who won the V.C., was ADC to Buller.

2074. CHESNEY, KELLOW. Crimean war reader. 1961. A useful collection of documents and contemporary evidence, largely from predictable sources.

2075. GIBBS, PETER. The battle of the Alma. 1963. A full discussion of the battle, the events preceding it, and its place in European history. He also produced, Crimean blunder. The story of war with Russia a hundred years ago. 1960.

2076. PEMBERTON, W. BARING. Battles of the Crimean war. 1962. A concise account of the military operations.

2077. HALL, SIR JOHN. 'The diaries of John Hall, principal medical officer in the Crimea, 1854-56'. Ed. by Major General R.E. Barnsley. J.S.A.H.R. vol. XLI no. 165, March 1963, 3-18. Previously unpublished extracts relating to the Crimean war from the same collection used by S.M. Mitra in his biography of Sir John Hall. (1344)

2078. MORGAN, ANTHONY. 'Accounts of the war in the Crimea written on the battlefield. By Lieut. Anthony Morgan of the 95th Foot'. Ed. by John Selby. J.S.A.H.R. vol. XLIV no 177, March 1966, 44-9.

2079. BARKER, A.J. The vainglorious war 1854-6. 1970. One of the better recent accounts, which does not deal only with the British side of the conflict. A useful list of published personal accounts is included.

2080. COMPTON, PIERS. Colonel's lady and camp follower. The story of women in the Crimean war. 1970. The Crimean war was the last occasion on which women went to the battlefields with their husbands on a large and organised scale.

2081. HAWLE, R.B. The Hawley letters. The letters of Capt. R.B. Hawley, 89th regiment, from the Crimea, December,1854 to August, 1856. S.A.H.R. Special publication no. 10. 1970. A collection of vivid and accurate letters.

2082. LAWSON, GEORGE. Surgeon in the Crimea: the experiences of George Lawson recorded in letters to his family, 1854-1855. Ed. by Victor Bonham-Carter. 1970.

2083. SELBY, JOHN. The thin red line. 1970. A popular account concentrating on the battle of Balaclava.

2084. BLAKE, R.L.V.F. The Crimean war. 1971. An outline of the main events of the war, which adds little new. Useful annotated bibliography.

2085. HODGE, EDWARD. 'Little Hodge' being extracts from the diaries and letters of Colonel Edward Cooper Hodge written during the Crimean war, 1854-1856. Ed. by the Marquess of Anglesey. 1971. Hodge commanded the 4th Dragoon Guards during the war, and his papers cover the entire duration of the conflict.

2086. WARNER, PHILIP. The Crimean war. A reappraisal. 1972. Attempts to identify the positive achievements of the war.

2087. HARRIS, JOHN. The gallant six hundred. A tragedy of obsessions. 1973. A rather unnecessary addition to the voluminous literature on the Crimean war.

2088. COOKE, G.W. China: being The Times special correspondence from China in the years 1857-8. 1858.

2089. SWINHOE, ROBERT. Narrative of the North China campaign of 1860. 1861.

2090. WOLSELEY, GARNET JOSEPH, VISCOUNT. Narrative of the war with China in 1860: to which is added the account of a short residence with the Tai-ping rebels at Nankin and a voyage from thence to Hankow. 1862. Based on his journal and letters.

2091. RENNIE, D.F. The British arms in North China and Japan. 1864.

2092. FISHER, ARTHUR A'COURT. Personal narrative of three years' service in China, 1857-1860. 1863.

2093. GRANT, GENERAL SIR HOPE. Incidents in the China war of 1860. Compiled from the private journals of General Sir Hope Grant. Ed. by Sir Henry Knollys. 1875. Grant's campaign in China, edited by his biographer.

2094. ALLGOOD, GEORGE. China war 1860. Letters and journals. 1901.

2095. LEAVENWORTH, C.S. The Arrow war with China. 1901. A fine account.

2096. HURD, DOUGLAS. The Arrow war. 1958.

2097. BIDDULPH, BRIGADIER GENERAL H. ed. 'The Umbeyla campaign of 1863 and the Bhutan expedition of 1865-66. Contemporary letters of Col. John Miller Adye'. J.S.A.H.R. vol. XIX no. 73, spring 1940, 34-47.

2098. SCOTT, W.W. Letters from Abyssinia during the campaign of 1868. 1868.

2099. HOZIER, H.M. The British expedition to Abyssinia. 1869. A short critical account.

2100. PHAYRE, SIR ROBERT. Abyssinian expedition: official journal of the reconnoitring party of the British force in Abyssinia. 1869.

2101. HOLLAND, T.J. and HOZIER, H.M. Record of the expedition to Abyssinia compiled by the order of the Secretary of State for War. 2 vols. 1870.

2102. MOOREHEAD, ALAN. The blue Nile. 1962. An account of the Abyssinian expedition, 1867-8 is contained in this work.

2103. STANLEY, HENRY M. Coomassie and Magdala. The story of two British campaigns in Africa. N.Y. 1874.

2104. MYATT, FREDERICK. The march to Magdala. The Abyssinian war of 1868. 1970. The only full length modern study, it is a comprehensive survey.

2105. HUYSHE, G.L. The Red river expedition. 1871.

2106. BRACKENBURY, GENERAL SIR HENRY. The Ashanti war. A narrative prepared from the official documents. 2 vols. 1874. Probably still the best account, by Lord Wolseley's military secretary.

2107. BOYLE, FREDERICK. Through Fanteeland to Coomassie. A diary of the Ashantee expedition. 1874.

2108. HENTY, G.A. The march to Coomassie. 1874. A detailed account by a journalist.

2109. MAURICE, SIR JOHN FREDERICK. The Ashantee war: a popular narrative. 1874. Wolseley's private secretary, who contributed to the Daily News during the conflict.

2110. READE, WILLIAM WINWOOD. The story of the Ashanti campaign. 1874. Not entirely favourable to Wolseley.

2111. TYLDEN, GEOFFREY. 'The British army and the Transvaal, 1875 to 1885'. J.S.A.H.R. vol. XXX no. 124, winter 1952, 159-171.

2112. GRANT, JAMES. Recent British battles on land and sea 1875 to 1885. 1885. The author was perhaps best known for his novels based on army life.

2113. PRESTON, A.W. 'Sir Garnet Wolseley and the Cyprus expedition, 1878'. J.S.A.H.R. vol. XLV no. 181, spring 1967, 4-16. Extracts from Wolseley's unpublished, and incomplete, campaign journal.

2114. HENSMAN, HOWARD. The Afghan war of 1879-1880. 1882.

2115. HANNA, H.B. The second Afghan war, 1878-1880: its causes, its conduct and its consequences. 3 vols. 1899-1910. A controversial study still of much value.

2116. THE SECOND AFGHAN WAR, 1878-80. Abridged official
account produced in the Intelligence Branch, Army
Headquarters, India. Simla. 1908.

2117. DURAND, SIR HENRY MORTIMER. 'Reminiscences of the
Kabul campaign of 1879-1880'. Blackwood's Mag.
vol. CCI 1917, 521-37; 781-99. A short account by an
eye witness.

2118. ASHE, W. and WYATT-EDGELL, HON. E.V. The story of the
Zulu campaign. 1880.

2119. MONTAGUE, W.E. Campaigning in South Africa. Reminiscences of an officer in 1879. 1880.

2120. TYLDEN, GEOFFREY. 'Some aspects of the Zulu wars
J.S.A.H.R. vol. XVII no. 67, autumn 1938, 127-32.

2121. FRENCH, HON. GERALD. Lord Chelmsford and the Zulu war.
1939. Full account and strong defence of his command.
Also includes details of his subsequent military career.

2122. COUPLAND, SIR REGINALD. Zulu battle piece: Isandlhwana.
1948. An account of the defeat of the British, and the
subsequent action of Rorke's Drift, rather than a full
account of the war.

2123. FURNEAUX, RUPERT. The Zulu war: Isandlhwana and Rorke's
Drift. 1963.

2124. JACKSON, F.W.D. 'Isandlhwana, 1879 - the sources re-
examined'. J.S.A.H.R. vol. XLIII no. 173, March 1965,
30-43; no. 176, December 1965, 169-83. A scholarly
reassessment.

2125. CLAMMER, DAVID. The Zulu war. Newton Abbott. 1973.
Contains little new.

2126. LLOYD, ALAN. The Zulu war, 1879. 1973. A brief competent popular survey based on selected secondary sources.

2127. TYLDEN, GEOFFREY. 'The Basutoland rebellion of 1880-
1881'. J.S.A.H.R. vol. XV no. 58, summer 1936, 98-107.

2128. RANSFORD, OLIVER. The battle of Majuba hill: the first
Boer war. 1967. A popular account of one of the biggest
defeats of the Victorian army.

2129. LEHMANN, JOSEPH H. The first Boer war. 1972. The
standard account, based on research among official
records in England and South Africa.

2130. MACMUNN, SIR GEORGE. 'The story of the British in Egypt and the Sudan'. **A.Q.** vol. LXIII no. 2, January 1952, 150-2. The outlines of the army's involvement in Egypt.

2131. CORBAN, L. Experiences of an army surgeon during the Egyptian expedition of 1882. 1882.

2132. MAURICE, SIR JOHN FREDERICK. Military history of the campaign of 1882 in Egypt. 1887. The official account, and therefore has limitations as source material.

2133. BOND, BRIAN. 'Mr. Gladstone's invasions of Egypt (1881) - a revelation of military weakness'. **A.Q.** vol. LXXXI no. 1, October 1960, 87-92.

2134. GREEN, W.H. 'Tel-el-Kebir, 1882'. **Ibid.** vol. LXXXVIII, no. 2, July 1964, 221-9.

2135. WARD, S.P.G. ed. 'The Scots Guards in Egypt, 1882. The letters of Lieut. C.B. Balfour'. **J.S.A.H.R.** vol. LI, no. 206, summer 1973, 80-104.

2136. ARCHER, THOMAS. The war in Egypt and the Sudan. An episode in the history of the British Empire, being a descriptive account of the scenes and events of that great drama and sketches of the principal characters in it. 4 vols. 1886. A useful very detailed source.

2137. ROYLE, CHARLES. The Egyptian campaigns, 1882 to 1885. 1900.

2138. TYLDEN, GEOFFREY. 'The British army in Zululand, 1883 to 1888'. **J.S.A.H.R.** vol. XXIX no. 118, summer 1951, 48-51.

2139. CROSTHWAITE, SIR CHARLES. The pacification of Burma. 1912. The best account of the third Burmese war about which little has been written.

2140. BRACKENBURY, GENERAL SIR HENRY. The river column: a narrative of the advance of the river column of the Nile expeditionary force and its return down the rapids. 1885. This, and the accounts below by Wilson and Butler are among the most important sources for the study of this campaign.

2141. WILSON, SIR CHARLES W. From Konti to Khartoum. 1885.

2142. BUTLER, SIR WILLIAM. The campaign of the cataracts, being a personal narrative of the great Nile expedition of 1884-5 . . . 1887.

2143. COLVILE, MAJOR GENERAL SIR H.E. Official history
of the Sudan campaign. 2 vols. 1889. An inadequate
account, heavily criticised on publication.

2144. SYMONS, JULIAN. England's pride. The story of the
Gordon relief expedition. 1965. The best account of
the campaign as a whole.

2145. PRESTON, A.W. ed. In relief of Gordon: Lord Wolseley's
campaign journal of the Khartoum relief expedition
1884-85. 1967. Some of Wolseley's unequivocal comments
on his contemporaries are recorded in this journal,
transcribed from papers in the P.R.O.

2146. COMPTON, PIERS. The last days of General Gordon. 1974.
Popular study which concentrates on conditions in
Khartoum immediately before Gordon's death.

2147. BADEN-POWELL, GENERAL ROBERT S.S., LORD. Matabeleland
campaign. 1897.

2148. --------------- Downfall of Prempah. A diary of life
with the native levy in Ashanti, 1895-96. 1896. A diary
of the campaign in Ashanti.

2149. STEEVENS, GEORGE WARRINGTON. With Kitchener to Khartoum.
Edin. 1898. A graphic account by a noted journalist
of the period.

2150. CHURCHILL, SIR WINSTON S. The river war. An historical
account of the reconquest of the Soudan. 2 vols. 1899.
Remains the best narrative.

2151. SUDAN CAMPAIGN, 1896-99. By 'an officer'. 1899.

2152. ZIEGLER, PHILIP. Omdurman. 1973. A good account of
Kitchener's victory based partly on a number of eye-
witness accounts.

Boer War

2153. AMERY, LEO. ed. The Times history of the war in South
Africa. 7 vols. 1899-1902. A fine work still of much
value, particularly for its descriptions of the military
operations.

2154. ATKINS, J.B. The relief of Ladysmith. 1900.

2155. WILKINSON, HENRY SPENCER. Lessons of the war. Being
comments from week to week, to the relief of Ladysmith.
1900. His contributions to the Morning Post republished
in book form.

2156. MAURICE, SIR JOHN FREDERICK. History of the war in South Africa, 1899-1902. Compiled by the direction of His Majesty's government. 4 vols. 1906-10. The content was constrained by the requirements of government, and is little more than a chronicle of military operations with little analysis and interpretation.

2157. ALTHAM, SIR E.A. 'Sir George White at Ladysmith'. A.Q. vol. VIII no. 1, April 1924, 21-30.

2158. 'THE RELIEF OF MAFEKING: a personal narrative'. A.Q. vol. XI no. 2, January 1926, 354-68.

2159. DALY, F.A.B. Boer war memories. Personal experience. Melbourne. 1936.

2160. FULLER, J.F.C. The last of the gentleman's wars. A subaltern's journal of the war in South Africa, 1899 - 1902. 1937. Fuller's early experiences in the army during the conflict he aptly named. See also, the early chapters of The army in my time. 1935.

2161. HOLT, EDGAR. The Boer war. 1958. A competent summary of the military operations.

2162. KRUGER, RAYNE. Good-bye Dolly Gray: the story of the Boer war. 1959.

2163. HOWE, ARTHUR. 'The relief of Ladysmith'. A.Q. vol. LXXXI no. 1, October 1960, 70-3.

2164. SYMONS, JULIAN. Buller's campaign. 1963. A sympathetic reassessment of a rather enigmatic personality.

2165. PEMBERTON, W. BARING. Battles of the Boer war. 1964. Concentrates on the early stages of the war.

2166. GARDNER, BRIAN. Mafeking: a Victorian legend. 1966.

2167. RANSFORD, OLIVER. The battle of Spion Kop. 1969. The story of the major battle of Buller's campaign to relieve Ladysmith.

2168. SELBY, JOHN. The Boer war. A study in cowardice and courage. 1969. Based on archive material in South Africa and England.

2169. GRIFFITH, KENNETH. Thank god we kept the flag flying: the siege and relief of Ladysmith, 1899-1900. 1974. A vivid picture of the siege, but the author does not give balanced judgements on the leading figures involved.

2170. ARMITAGE, C.H. and MONTANARO, A.F.   The Ashanti campaign of 1900.   1901.

2171. MYATT, FREDERICK. The golden stool: an account of the Ashanti war of 1900. 1966. The best modern account of the operations around Kumasi.

2172. FLEMING, PETER. The siege at Peking. 1959.

2173. OFFICIAL HISTORY of the operations in Somaliland 1901-4, 2 vols. 1907. Produced by the general staff.

2174. FLEMING, PETER. Bayonets to Lhasa: the first full account of the British invasion of Tibet in 1904. 1961.

2175. STUART, CAPT. JAMES. History of the Zulu rebellion. 1913.

25.   INDIA

    See Cockle (19)   Other material is listed under the appropriate subject headings.

The army in India

2176. THE ARMY IN INDIA 1850-1914: a photographic record. Ed. by P. Russell-Jones. 1968. The only survey of its kind.

2177. THE ARMY IN INDIA and its evolution. Calcutta. 1924.

2178. BARAT, AMIYA. The Bengal native infantry : its organisation and discipline 1796-1852. Calcutta. 1962.

2179. BOWLING, A.H. Indian cavalry regiments, 1880-1914. 1971. Details of uniforms are included.

2180. BROOME, ARTHUR. History of the rise and progress of the Bengal army. 1850.

2181. CADELL, SIR PATRICK. 'Commanders-in-chief of the Indian army'. J.S.A.H.R. vol. XXII no. 90, summer 1944, 220-2. A list of office holders.

2182. --------- History of the Bombay army. 1938.

2183. CALLAHAN, RAYMOND. The East India company and army reform. 1973. Attempts by the British government to incorporate the company's army into the national army.

2184. CAMBRIDGE, MARQUESS OF. 'Notes on the armies of India'.
J.S.A.H.R. vol. XLVII no. 189, spring 1969, 23-32;
no. 190, summer 1969, 149-56; no. 192, winter 1969,
194-210; vol. XLVIII no. 193, spring 1970, 35-45; no.
194, summer 1970, 105-8; no. 195, autumn 1970, 167-181.
Details of the regiments of the army.

2185. HEATHCOTE, T.A. The Indian army. The garrison of
British Imperial India, 1822-1922. 1972. Concentrates
on the organisation and personnel of the army with
interesting observations on the social composition and
life of officers and men. Perhaps the best modern work
of its kind.

2186. HUGHES, B.P. The Bengal horse artillery. 1800-1861.
The 'red men' - a nineteenth century corps d'elite. 1971.
A narrative of their campaigns.

2187. MACMUNN, SIR GEORGE. The armies of India. 1911.
Limited edition produced with fine illustrations.

2188. MAJUMDAR, B.M. 'Development of the transport system in
the Indian army from 1760 to 1914'. A.Q. vol. LXXVII
no. 2, January 1959, 250-60.

2189. MASON, PHILIP. A matter of honour. An account of the
Indian army its officers and men. 1974. The only
comprehensive survey of its kind, unlikely to be
superseded until a history equivalent to that of
Fortescue is produced.

2190. PALIT, D.K. History of the regiment of artillery
Indian army. 1972. See the first two chapters for the
period before 1935, after which date being the main
focus of the book, which was produced under official
Indian auspices.

2191. RAFTER, GEORGE. Our Indian army. 1856.

2192. SANDES, E.W.C. The military engineers in India.
Chatham. 1933. Definitive.

2193. STUBBS, FRANCIS W. History of the organisation, equipment and war services of the regiment of Bengal artillery
compiled from published works, official records, and
various private sources. 3 vols. 1877-95. The final
chapters of vol. III are on organisation and equipment,
the bulk of the work being on campaigns.

2194. WATSON, WILLIAM ARTHUR. King George's own (King George
V's own) Central India Horse. The story of a local corps
...with a chapter relative to the second Afghan war by
Col. Sir Neville Chamberlain. 2 vols. 1930-50.

2195. WILLIAMS, CAPT. JOHN. An historical account of the
    rise and progress of the Bengal native infantry, from
    its first formation in 1757 to 1796, when the present
    regulations took place. Together with a detail of the
    services on which the several battalions have been
    employed during that period. 1817. A classic early
    account.

2196. WILSON, W.J. History of the Madras army. Madras.
    5 vols. 1882-9. A detailed official account.

Campaigns in India

2197. MALLESON, G.B. The decisive battles of India, 1746-
    1849. 1883. Accounts of fourteen major battles in-
    cluding Plassey and Assaye. Some of the author's state-
    ments of fact and interpretation should not be accepted
    without reservation.

2198. ORME, ROBERT. A history of the military transactions of
    the British nation in Indostan from the year 1745. 2
    vols. 1763-78. Remains an important source for the
    Coromandel and Bengal wars.

2199. CAMBRIDGE, RICHARD OWEN. An account of the wars in
    India between the English and French, on the coast of
    Coromandel, from ... 1750 to 1760. 1761.

2200. EDWARDES, MICHAEL. The battle of Plassey and the con-
    quest of Bengal. 1963. Little space is devoted to the
    battle itself.

2201. MOODIE, JOHN. Remarks on the most important military
    operations of the English forces, on the west side of
    the peninsula of Hindoostan in 1783 and in 1784. 1788.

2202. RENNELL, JAMES. Marches of the British armies in the
    peninsula of India during the campaign of 1790 and 1791.
    1892.

2203. MAULE, GEORGE. 'An engineer in the Mysore war of 1791 -
    1792'. Ed. by E.J. Martin. J.S.A.H.R. vol. XXII no.
    92, winter 1944, 324-339.

2204. CORMACK, A.A. ed. The Mahratta wars, 1797-1805. Letters
    from the front by three brothers, Nicholas, George and
    Thomas Carnegie of Charleton, Montrose. Banff. 1971.

2205. BEATSON, ALEXANDER. View of the origin and conduct of
    the war with Tippo Sultaun comprising a narrative of the
    operations of the army of Lieutenant General Harris and
    of the siege of Seringapatam. 1800.

2206. BURTON, R.G. Wellington's campaigns in India.
Calcutta. 1908. Produced by the Chief of the Staff
Intelligence branch. See also Weller (1533) for a
recent scholarly analysis.

2207. THORN, WILLIAM. Memoirs of the war in India, conducted
by General Lord Lake, Commander-in-chief, and Major
General Sir Arthur Wellesley, duke of Wellington from
its commencement in 1803 to its termination in 1806, on
the banks of the Hyphasis. 1818.

2208. BLACKER, V. Memoir of the operations of the British
army in India during the Mahratta war of 1817, 1818 and
1819. 1821.

2209. BURTON, R.G. The Mahratta and Pindari war. 1910.

2210. BIDDULPH, BRIG. GEN. H. 'Mahratta and Pindari wars
1817-19'. J.S.A.H.R. vol. XXII no. 87, autumn 1943,
120-22.

2211. NEVILL, H.L. Campaigns on the North-west frontier. 1912.
A comprehensive survey from before the Mutiny until 1908.

2212. ELLIOT, J.G. The frontier 1839-1947: the story of the
North-west Frontier of India. 1968.

2213. COLEY, JAMES. Journal of the Sutlej campaign 1845-6.
1856.

2214. LESLIE, J.H. ed. 'The first Sikh war 1845-6. The
battle of Ferozeshah - 21 December, 1845. The battle of
Sobraon - 10 February, 1846'. J.S.A.H.R. vol. XI no. 42,
April 1932, 65-76. Two long letters.

2215. FEATHERSTONE, DONALD. At them with the bayonet! The
first Sikh war. 1968. Popular.

2216. SETHI, R.R. 'The revolt in Kashmir - 1846'. J.S.A.H.R.
vol. XI no. 43, July 1932, 158-67.

2217. GOUGH, SIR CHARLES and INNES, A.D. The Sikhs and the
Sikh wars. 1897.

2218. BURTON, R.G. The first and second Sikh wars. 1911.

2219. GRANT, I.F. 'Every day letters written during the first
and second Sikh wars'. A.Q. vol. X no. 2, July 1925,
337-52. Letters of Major, later Sir, Patrick Grant, on
the staff of General Sir Hugh Gough, and his wife.

2220. BRUCE, GEORGE. Six battles for India. The Anglo-Sikh
wars, 1845-6, 1848-9. 1969. A simple introduction.

2221. EDWARDES, SIR HERBERT.   The Punjab Frontier in 1848-
49.   2 vols.   1851.

2222. THACKWELL, E.J.   Narrative of the second Sikh war.
1851.

2223. BACE, G.A.   'The second Sikh war. The journal of
Lieutenant G.A. Bace, H.M's 61st regiment'.   J.S.A.H.R.
vol. XXX no. 122, summer 1952, 48-67.

Indian Mutiny

2224. KAYE, SIR JOHN WILLIAM.   History of the Sepoy war in
India, 1857-1858.   3 vols.   1865.   A distinguished
history, more objective than might be expected, and
still of much value for the military operations.

2225. MALLESON, G.B.   History of the Indian mutiny.   3 vols.
1878.   A continuation of Kaye, although his first volume
is largely a rewriting of Kaye's third because of
disagreements of fact and interpretation.

2226. HOLMES, T.R.E.   A history of the Indian mutiny and of
the disturbances which accompanied it among the civil
population.   1898.   A favourable account of the British
role.

2227. FORREST, G.W.   A history of the Indian mutiny reviewed
and illustrated from original documents.   2 vols.   1904.

2228. LANG, ARTHUR MOFFATT.   'The diary and letters of Arthur
Moffatt Lang, 1st Lieutenant, Bengal Engineers.   India
1857 to 1859'.   Ed. by J.H. Leslie and Col. F.C.
Molesworth.   J.S.A.H.R.   vol. IX no. 35, January 1930,
1-26; no. 36, April 1930, 72-97; no. 38, October 1930,
189-213, vol. X no. 39a, April 1931, 69-108; no. 39b,
July 1931, 129-142; no. 40, October 1931, 195-206; vol.
XI no. 41, January 1932, 1-25.   Long extracts from an
engineer officer's diary relating to Meean Meer, Delhi
and the relief and capture of Lucknow.

2229. MACMUNN, SIR GEORGE.   The Indian mutiny in perspective.
1931.   A good summary.

2230. ANDERSON, THOMAS.   'Memoirs of a fighting man during the
Indian mutiny, being extracts from the diary of the
late Sergeant Thomas Anderson, E. Troop, Royal Horse
Artillery'.   Ed. by H. Waine.   A.Q.   vol. XXXII no. 2,
July 1936, 314-319, vol. XXXIII no. 1, October 1936,
129-37.

2231. HILTON, RICHARD.   The Indian mutiny: a centenary history
1957.

2232. RUSSELL, SIR W.H. My Indian mutiny diary. Ed. by Michael Edwardes. 1957. Originally published in 1860.

2233. SEN, S.N. Eighteen fifty-seven. Delhi. 1857. The best modern Indian account of all aspects of the rebellion.

2234. WICKINS, CHARLES. 'The Indian mutiny journal of Private Charles Wickins of the 90th Light Infantry'. J.S.A.H.R. vol. XXXV no. 143, September 1957, 96-108; no. 144, December 1957, 170-4.

2235. COLLIER, RICHARD. The sound of fury. An account of the Indian mutiny. 1963. There is a full bibliography, which includes a long list of privately owned ms. diaries and letters.

2236. EDWARDES, MICHAEL. Battles of the Indian mutiny. 1963. The best short guide to the purely military aspects of the revolt.

2237. HARGOOD, WILLIAM. 'Indian mutiny letters of Lieut. William Hargood, 1st Madras Fusiliers'. Ed. by A. Annand. J.S.A.H.R. vol. XLIII no. 176, December 1965, 190-215.

2238. HEWITT, J. ed. Eye-witnesses to the Indian mutiny. 1972.

2239. HARRIS, JOHN. The Indian mutiny. 1973. A short popular account with good illustrations.

2240. LINDSAY, ALEXANDER HADDEN. 'The Indian mutiny letters of Alexander Hadden Lindsay, Bengal Horse Artillery. J.S.A.H.R. vol. L no. 204, winter 1972, 200-20.

2241. EDWARDES, MICHAEL. Red year: the Indian rebellion of 1857. 1973. A valuable reassessment of the mutiny, and of British attitudes to it. He has also produced a useful account of one episode of the rebellion, A season in hell. The defence of the Lucknow residency. 1973.

2242. ROBERTSON, W.R. An official account of the Chitral expedition 1895. Calcutta. 1898.

2243. JAMES, LIONEL. The Indian frontier war being an account of the Mohmund and Tirah expeditions 1897. 1898.

2244. CHURCHILL, SIR WINSTON S. The story of the Malakand field force; an episode of frontier war. 1898. A vivid picture of the conflict.

2245. CALLWELL, SIR CHARLES EDWARD.   Tirah 1897.   1911.   A
      good readable account in the 'Campaigns and their
      lessòns' series.

2246. YOUNGHUSBAND, SIR G.J.   Indian frontier warfare.   1898.
      Tactics, discipline and the effects of frontier war-
      fare in India on the various branches of the army.

The numbers here refer to the individual items listed in
the text, and not to the pagination.

Anderson, A.E., 1923
Anderson, J.H., 1737
Anderson, Joseph, 1211
Anderson, Olive, 568
Anderson, Thomas, 2230
Anderson, T.S., 1880
Anderson, Sir W.H., 158, 811
Andre, John, 219, 1872
Anglesey, G.C.H.V. Paget, Marquess of, 714, 1212, 1451,
  1909, 2085
Anglesey, Henry William Paget, Marquess of, 958, 984, 1212,
  1909
Annand, A. McKenzie, 1495
Annual Bulletin of Historical Literature, 10
Annual Register, 524
Anton, James, 1213
Archer, Thomas, 2136
Archives, 80
Ardagh, Sir John, 1214-5
Armitage, C.H., and Montanaro, A.F., 2170
Army and Navy Gazette, 525
Army and Navy Magazine, 526
Army and Navy Register and Woolwich Gazette, 527
Army in India, 2176
Army in India and its Evolution, 2177
Army List, 874-5, 921
Army Quarterly, 528
Army Review, 529
Armytage, Hon. Mrs. Fenella Fitzhardinge, 2019
Arnold-Forster, H.O., 994-5
Arnold-Forster, M., 994
Arthur, Sir George C.A., 790, 1216, 1382, 1547
Artillery, 693-706, 1559, 1561, 1565, 1573, 1603, 1608, 1635
  1644, 1647
Artillery, regiment of, Indian army, 2190
Ascoli, David, 923
Ashanti wars, 2017-8, 2020, 2103, 2106-2110, 2148, 2170-1
Ashe, W., and Wyatt-Edgehill, Hon, E.V., 2118
Ashley, Maurice, 954
Aspland, J.L., 1634
Atholl mss., 463
Atkins, J.B., 1068, 2154
Atkinson, C.T., 209, 216, 457-8, 662, 840, 845, 848, 850,
  1091, 1167, 1735, 1760, 1782, 1787-92, 1794-5, 1810, 1819-20,
  1825, 1846, 1850, 1852, 1885, 1939, 1958, 1963, 1965, 2003
Atkinson, John, 159
Atlay, J.B., 1033
Aubry-Fletcher, H.L., 826
Auchinleck, G., 1980
Austin H.H., 1217
Austin, Thomas, 1217
Austrian succession war, 1810, 1811-21
Auxiliary services, 750-62

Aytoun, James, 1088

Bace, G.A., 2223
Bacon, Anthony, 1218
Badcock, Lovell, 1965
Baden-Powell, Robert, Lord, 1219-21, 2147-8
Badges, 1683, 1690-2, 1695, 1699, 1711, 1716, 1731
Bagot, J.F., mss., 464
Bagshawe, Samuel, 103
Baird, Sir David, 958, 964, 1222-3
Baker, H.T., 1026
Baker, Norman, 569-70
Baker, Valentine, 708
Baldry, W.Y., 11, 754, 924
Baldry, W.Y., and White, A.S., 663
Ballard, Colin, 1187, 1484
Bamfield, Veronica, 876
Bankes, G.N., 1388
Banks, J., 1776
Banks, Marjorie, 160
Bannatyne, Neil, 815
Barat, Amiya, 2178
Barcelona, battle of, 1797
Barker, A.J. 2079
Barker, Sir Ernest, 213
Barker, Sir George Digby, 1224
Barker, John, 1876
Barker, Lady K.W., 1224
Barnard, Sir Andrew, 1973
Barnes, R.M., 161, 252, 664, 1684
Barnes, R.M., and Allen, C.K., 665
Barnett, Corelli, 162, 634, 1175
Barnsley, R.E., 1142
Barracks, 399, 944, 951
Barrett, C.R.B., 793, 802, 1736
Barrington, M.J., 1128
Barrington, Shute, 996
Barrington, William Wildman, Viscount, 996
Barry, Dr. James, 13
Bartlett, C.J., 1045
Barwick, G.B., 64
Bass, Benjamin, and Dorr, Moses, 1847
Basutoland rebellion, 2127
Bath mss., 465
Bathurst mss., 466
Battle honours, 1754
Batty, Robert, 1992
Bayly, Richard, 1225
Baynes, John, 1805
Bayonets, 1664, 1680-1
Beamish, N. Ludlow, 763
Beatson, Alexander, 2205

Beatson, Robert, 1809
Beauchamp-Walker, Sir C.P., 1226
Beaufort, B., 1405
Beaufort mss., 467
Belcher, Henry, 1874
Belfield, E.M.G., 1800
Bell, D.H., 1954
Bell, Sir George, 1227
Bell, H.C.F., 1060
Bell, William, 1228
Belloc, Hilaire, 1786, 1911
Bellot, H.H., 12
Bengal army, 2180; horse artillery, 2186; native
  infantry, 2178, 2195
Bennett, R.W., 606
Benson, R.H.R., 635
Beresford, Robert Ballard Long, Lord, 958, 984, 1229
Bernardi, John, 1089
Besterman, Theodore, 1
Bethell, H.A., 1644
Bevan, Henry, 1230
Bevan, Margaret, 13
Bhutan expedition, 2097
<u>Bibliographic Index</u>, 2
Biddulph, H., 877, 2097, 2210
Biddulph, John, 780, 1154
Biddulph, Sir Robert, 240
Biggs, W., 1815
Bingham, Sir George, 1957
Binning, Thomas, 1561
Bird, Harrison, 1891
Bird, Sir W.D., 1926
Bishop, Matthew, 1090-1
Bishop, W.J., and Goldie, S., 1054
Blackader, John, 1092
Blacker, V., 2208
Blackmore, H.L., 1659
Blackwood, R.M., 1737
Blake, R.L.V.F., 2084
Blake, Robert, 232
Blakeney, Robert, 1231
Blakiston, John, 1232
Blanco, Richard L., 226, 925-6
Bland, Humphrey, 1568
Blathwayt, William, 997-8
Blenheim, battle of, 1781, 1802
Boehm, E., and Adolphus, L., 141
Boer wars, 2128-9, 2153-69
Boger, A.J., 1218
Bolingbroke, Henry St. John, Viscount, 999-1000
Bolitho, Hector, 865
Bond, Brian, 234, 241, 244, 246-7, 636, 927, 1030,
  1261, 1656, 2020, 2133

Bond, Edward, 1807
Bond, M., 122
Bonham-Carter, Victor, 1472, 2082
Boston, British army in, 1876, 1890
Boughey, John, 571
Boulger, D.C., 1317, 1765
Bowling, A.H., 2179
Bowyer-Bower, T.A., 637
Boyle, Frederick, 2107
Brackenbury, G., 2047
Brackenbury, Henry, 1223-4, 2106, 2140
Braddock, Edward, 1093-4
Bradley, A.G., 1837
Bragge, William, 1235
Brander, Michael, 666
Brandywine creek, battle of, 1877
Braybrooke mss., 468
Brett-James, Antony, 1401, 1515, 1545, 1968, 1976
Brindley, J., 1812
British army, the, 163, 638
British Humanities Index, 142
British Military Library, 531
British Museum, 66-9, 98-100
British National Bibliography, 14
British Union Catalogue of Periodicals, 143
Broad Arrow, 530
Broadfoot, George, 1236
Broadfoot, William, 1236
Brock, Sir Isaac, 1237
Brocklesby, Richard, 724
Brodigan, Francis, 770
Brodrick, T., 1774
Broome, Arthur, 2180
Broomfield, J.H., 572
Brown, A. Gordon, 1205
Brown, David, 1238
Brown, Sir George, 109, 1239
Brown, Robert, 1912
Browne, D.G., 928
Browne, J.A., 695
Browne, Sir James, 1240
Browne, J.G., and Bridges, E.J., 782
Browne, Philip, 1095
Browning, Reed, 1857
Brownrigg, Beatrice, Lady, 1422
Brownrigg, Sir Robert, 1241
Bruce, Alexander, 607
Bruce, A.P.C., 878
Bruce, C.D., 827
Bruce, George, 2010, 2220
Bruce, H.A., 1435
Bryant, Sir Arthur, 872, 1531, 1907, 1924
Buccleuch mss., 469-70

Buchan, John, 823
Buchanan-Dunlop, H.D. 639
Buckinghamshire mss., 471
Buller, Sir Redvers, 976, 1242-6, 2164
Bulletin of the Institute of Historical Research, 532
Bulletin of the Military Historical Society, 533
Bulloch, J.M., 15-16, 800
Bullock, H., 608
Bunbury, Sir Henry, 1921
Burgoyne, J.M., 1919
Burgoyne, John, 1096-8, 1860
Burgoyne, Sir John Fox, 1247-9
Burke, Peter, 609
Burmese wars, 2010-16, 2042, 2139
Burn, W.L., 1099
Burnaby, Frederick, 1250
Burne, Alfred H., 879, 1554, 1738, 1818, 1883, 1920
Burns, P.L., 741
Burrard, Sir Harry, 966
Burton, I.F., 573-4, 1172, 1796
Burton, R.G., 2206, 2209, 2218
Busaco, battle of, 1969-70
Bush, E.W., 164
Butler, Eileen, 1251
Butler, Lewis, 801, 1243, 1927, 1941
Butler, Sir W.F., 1251-2, 1430, 1456, 2142
Buxton, J.W., 575

Cabinet ministers, private papers of, 82-3
Cadell, Charles, 765
Cadell, Sir Patrick, 1179, 2181-2
Caillard, Maurice, 576
Calcraft, John, 1001
Call, George, 104
Calladine, George, 1253
Callahan, Ray, 2183
Calwell, Sir Charles Edward, 577, 1254, 1415, 1542
  1636, 2245
Callwell, Sir Charles Edward, and Headlam, Sir John, 701
Calthorpe, Hon. S.J.G., 2048
Calvert, E.M., and Calvert, R.T.C., 1151
Calvert, Sir Harry, 1255-7
Cambridge, George, Duke of, 1258-63
Cambridge, George Francis Hugh, Marquess of, 1764, 2184
Cambridge, Richard Owen, 2199
Cambridge University Library, 101
Campbell, Sir A., 2011
Campbell, Colin F., Baron, 2058
Campbell, D. Alistair, 1685
Campbell, E.S.N., 1613
Campbell, Sir H. Hume, mss., 472

Campbell, Hon. Sir James, 1099
Campbell-Bannerman, Sir Henry, 1002-4
Campbell-Copeland, T., 1632
Canada, the British army in, 1827, 1835, 1837-8, 1842-5,
  1848-9, 1853-5, 1980-6, 2040, 2105
Canada, Public Archives of, 117
<u>Canadian Historical Review</u>, 534
Cannon, Richard, 667
Cape, J.R., 816
Cardigan, James Thomas Brudenell, Earl of, 1264-5, 2049
Cardwell, Edward, Viscount, 240, 1005-6
Carew, Peter, 1498
Carew, Tim, 668
Carey, A.D.L., and McCance, S., 812
Carleton, George, 1100
Carleton, Sir Guy, 990, 1101
Carman, W.Y., 1660, 1686-8, 1694
Carmichael-Smyth, Sir James, 1827
Carnegie, George and Thomas, 2204
Carnock, Lord, 1953
Carr-Gomm, F.C., 1315
Carrington, H.B., 1867
Carss, John, 1956
Carter, C.E., 1130
Carter, M.E., 1220
Carter, Thomas, 1689
Cassells, S.A.C., 1235
<u>Catalogue of British regimental histories</u>, 17
Cavalry, 704-14, 1564, 1588, 1598, 1645, 1646, 1656, 1728,
  1882, 2179
Central India Horse, 2194
Ceylon, 1928
Chamberlain, Sir Neville, 1266
Chambers, R., 955
Chandler, David, 1173, 1739
Chandos, James Brydges, Duke of, 115, 1007
Chaplains, military, 721-2
Chaplin, H.D., 860
Chapman-Huston, W.W.D.M., and Rutter, Owen, 1284
Charlemont mss., 473
Charteris, Hon. Evan, 1119-20
Chatham, William Pitt, Earl of, 1008-9, 1839
Chelmsford, Frederick Augustus Thesiger, Lord, 1267, 2121
Chesney, C.C., 956, 1998
Chesney, Kellow, 2074
Chichester, H.M., and Burges-Short, George, 669
Childers, E.S.E., 1010
Childers, H.C.E., 1010-11
Childers, R.E., 1645
Childs, Sir Windham, 1268
Chilston, Lord, 1070
China, 2020, 2031-4, 2088-96, 2172
Churchill, Sir Winston S., 1169, 2150, 2244

Dalhousie, Fox Maule, Baron Panmure, Earl of, 1016-7
Dallas, A.R.C., 1951
Dallas, H.A., 1951
Dallas, R.W., 1958
Dalton, Charles, 880-85
D'Alton, John, 886
Dalrymple, Campbell, 1579
Daly, F.A.B., 2159
Dana, E.E., 1876
Daniel, William Henry, 167
Daniell, David Scott, 851, 861
Dartmouth mss., 476
D'Auvergne, E., 1772
Davenport, Richard, 1122
Davies, A.M., 1106
Davies, Christian, 1123
Davies, F.J., 930
Davies, Godfrey, 207, 210-11, 931, 1525, 1961
Davies, Godfrey, and Keeler, M.F., 21
Davies, John, 771
Dawnay, N.P., 1690-2
Deane, J.M., 1778
Defence, Ministry of, Library, 72. See also, War Office
 Library.
De Fonblanque, Edward Barrington, 168, 1096
Delacherois, Nicholas, 1124
Delavoye, A.M., 1399, 1742
De la Warr mss., 477
Denbigh mss., 478
Denholm, Anthony, 1066
Denison, George, 709
Dent, William, 1290
De Rhe-Phillipe, G.W., 2014
De Ros, W.L.L.F., Lord, 640, 1618
Des Cognets, Louis, 1086
Descriptions of courts-martial, 612
Devize, M., 1773
Devonshire, Spencer Compton Cavendish, Marquess of
 Hartington, and Duke of, 1018
De Watteville, H.G., 228, 579, 932-3, 1383
De Weerd, H.A., 1984
Dickinson, H.T., 999, 1188, 1797-8
Dickinson, R.J., 670, 887
Dickson, Sir Alexander, 1291
Dickson, W.K., 1482
Dictionaries, 1566, 1570, 1573, 1578, 1587, 1589, 1600,
 1613, 1617, 1619, 1630, 1633, 1812
Dictionary of National Biography, 960-1
Dillon, Hon. H.A., 169
Dobie, M.R., 109-10
Dodwell, Edward, and Miles, J.S., 888
D'Ombrain, Nicholas, 580
Don, Sir George 1292

Don, W.G., 934
Donaldson, Joseph, 1293-4
Donoughmore mss., 480
Dorling, H.T., 1693
Doughty, A.G., 1842
Doughty, A.G., and Parmelee, G.W., 1838
Douglas, Sir George, 1511
Douglas, Sir George and Ramsay, Sir George, 1016
Douglas, Sir Howard, 1295
Douglas, Neil, 1968
Doveton, F.B., 2012
Dow, A.C., 721
Downman, Thomas, 1950
Downshire mss., 481
Dress regulations (1864), 1694 : (1900), 1694
Drew, Sir Robert, 889
Drill, 1563-5, 1567-9, 1576, 1585, 1611, 1621, 1634,
Drinkwater, John, 109, 1896
Duberly, F.I., 2043
Du Cane mss., 482
Dudley, G.A., 1000
Duncan, Francis, 697
Dundas, Sir David, 1296, 1595-6
Dundee, John Graham of Claverhouse, Viscount of, 959,
  1125-9
Dundonald, D.M.B.H. Cochrane, Earl of, 1297
Dunfermline, James Abercromby, Lord, 1201
Dunlop, J.K., 248
Dupin, F.P.C., Baron, 170
Durand, Sir Henry Marion, 1298, 2028
Durand, Sir Henry Mortimer, 1298, 1538, 2028, 2117
D'Urban, Sir Benjamin, 1299
Dutch East Indies, 1990-1
Dyott, William, 1300-1

E and EO., 581
East India Company, 2183
Eayrs, H.J., 1237
Economist, 535
Edmonds, Sir James, 2000
Edmonds, R.F., 890
Education, military, 403-4, 418, 422, 446, 634-59
Edwardes, Sir H.B., 964, 972, 2221
Edwardes, Michael, 2200, 2236, 2241
Edwards, Francis, 22
Edwards, T.J., 171, 671-2, 891-2, 935, 1695
Edwards, W., 1387
Eggenberger, David, 1743
Egmont mss., 483
Egypt, campaigns in, 1923, 2020-21, 2130-7
Ehrman, John, 582

Ferrar, M.L., 720, 795, 1253
Ffoulkes, Christopher, 737, 1661-3
Ffoulkes, Christopher and Hopkinson, E.C., 1664-5
Field, Cyril, 819, 1744
Field of mars, 1745
Fife, J.G., 1161
Fighting Forces, 537
Finch, A.G., mss., 485
Findlay, J.T., 1197
Finlason, W.F., 613
Firearms, 1659-63, 1666-71, 1673-79
Firebrace, C.W., 893
Firth, Sir C.H., 25
Firth, Sir C.H. and Davies, Godfrey, 675
Fisher, Arthur A'Court, 2092
Fisher, Sidney George, 1873
Fitchett, W.H., 963
Fitzgerald, E.F., 1972
Fitzgerald, Lucas, 641
Fitzherbert, C., 2073
Fitzherbert, Sir W., mss., 486
Flanders, 1735, 1762, 1767, 1770-2, 1774, 1814, 1819,
    1821, 1905-6, 1908-14
Fleetwood-Weston-Underwood mss., 487
Fleming, Peter, 2172, 2174
Fontenoy, battle of, 1817-8, 1820
Forbes, Archibald, 779, 2024
Forbes, Arthur, 745
Ford, Arthur, 614
Ford, P, and G., 124-7
Forrest, G.W., 964, 1105, 1266, 2227
Fortescue, J.B., mss., 488
Fortescue, Hon. Sir J.W., 174-5, 218, 221, 224, 230,
    746, 777, 937, 965-8, 1123, 1168, 1520
Fortescue-Brickdale, Sir Charles, 1446
France, British army in, 1760
Francis, David, 1801
Frankland, Sir F.W., 1306
Frankland-Russell-Astley mss., 489
Fraser, Thomas, 1307
Frazer, Sir Augustus Simon, 694, 1308
Frearson, C.W., 1122
Frederick, J.M.B., 671
Freemantle, Alan, 1009
Freer, Edward, 1960
Freer, William, 1960
Freind, J., 1183
French, Allen, 1881
French, Hon. Gerald, 2121
Frere, B.H.T., 1899
Frewer, L.B., 26
Frischauer, P., 1903
Frontier and Overseas expeditions from India, 1746

Fuller, J.F.C., 1158, 1649-50, 2160
Fullom, S.W., 1295
Furber, Holden, 1048
Furneaux, Rupert, 1069, 1858, 1895, 2123
Fyers, E.W.H., 1844, 1877
Fyler, A.E., 778

Gage, Hon. Thomas, 1130-2
Gardner, Brian, 2166
Gardner, Daniel, 1960
Gardyne, C. Greenhill, 781
Garrett, Robert, 1952
Garrison, F.W., 730
Gatacre, B.W., 1309
Gatacre, Sir William Forbes, 1309
Gathorne-Hardy, Hon. A.E., 1014
Gatliffe, H.E., 1133
Gatliffe, James, 1133
'G.B.', 1310
General Wolfe's instruction to young officers, 1582
Gentleman's Magazine, 538
Geoghegan, S., 794
George, J.N., 1666
Gerard, Sir Montagu Gilbert, 1311
Germain, George Sackville, Lord, 121, 1134-8
Germany, 1856-7
Gernsheim, H. and A., 2072
Gibbs, Peter, 2075
Gibraltar, 1806-8, 1827, 1896-1900
Gibson, T.A., 2039
Gilby, Thomas, 176
Gillespie, Robert Rollo, 966, 1312-3
Gladstone, W.E., 1022
Gleichen, A.E.W., Lord, 1314
Gleig, Rev. G.R., 969, 1426, 1516, 1519, 1747, 1932
Glover, Michael, 894, 1529, 1969, 1974, 1979
Glover, Richard, 223
Goldsmid, Sir Frederic, 1442
Gomm, Sir William Maynard, 1315
Gooch, B.D., 27
Gooch, John, 584
Goodenough, O.H., 1631
Goodenough, W.H., and Dalton, J.C., 177
Goodwin-Austen, A.R., 642
Gordon, Alex, 1944
Gordon, C.A., 1316
Gordon, Charles George, 956, 983, 1317-25, 1327, 2144-6
Gordon, Hampden, 585
Gordon, Hugh, 1326
Gordon, John, 1327
Gordon, Sir J. Willoughby, 1328-9

Gordon, Lawrence, L., 178, 1696
Gordon, T.C., 1203
Gordon, Sir Thomas Edward, 1330
Gordon, Sir William, 956
Gore, A.A., 729
Gorham, C.A., 615
Gough, Sir Charles, and Innes, A.D., 2217
Gough, F.B., 1834
Gough, Hugh, Viscount, 967, 993, 1331-2, 2219
Gowing, Timothy, 1333
Graham, Sir F., mss., 490
Graham, Sir Gerald, 1334
Graham, Henry, 798
Graham, James John, 1139
Graham, J.M., 1191
Graham, R., mss., 491
Graham, Samuel, 1139
Granby, John Manners, Marquess of, 1140
Grant, A.M., 1141
Grant, Colquhoun, 1335
Grant, Sir Hope, 1336, 2093
Grant, I.F., 2219
Grant, James, 1141
Grant, James, 2112
Grant, Sir Patrick, 2219
Granville, Castalla, 1024
Granville, George Leveson Gower, Earl, 1023-4
Grattan, William, 1337
Grazebrook, R.M., 1913
Great battles of the British army, 1748
Green, David, 1802
Green, John, 1338
Green, W.H., 2134
Greenleaf, W.H., 586
Grenadier Guards orderly room, catalogue of manuscripts,
 books, 70
Grenfell, Francis Wallace, Lord, 1339
Grenfell, Russell, 895
Gretton, G. Le M., 794
Grey, Charles, first Earl, 1340-1
Grey, Charles, second Earl, 1025
Grierson, Sir James Moncrieff, 1342
Griffith, Kenneth, 2169
Griffiths, A.G.F., 179
Griffiths, Arthur, 677
Grinnell-Milne, Duncan, 1200
Grose, C.L., 28
Grose, Francis, 180, 896
Groves, Percy, 784
Guards, 685, 764, 766, 768, 783, 826, 832, 842
Guedalla, Philip, 1114, 1522
Guggisberg, F.G., 1900
Guibert, J.A.H., 1592

Gunn, James, 1975
Gunner, 539
Gunter, Edward, 616
Guppy, H.B., 1914
Gurney, Russell, 843
Gurwood, John, 1512-3

Hadden, James M., 1870
Haggard, D.J., 1972
Haines, Sir Frederick Paul, 1343
Haldane, Richard Burdon, Viscount, 1026-32
Halevy, Elie, 225
Halford, Sir H. St. J., 1667
Haliburton, Arthur Lawrence, Lord, 587, 1033
Halkett, Sir James, 1761
Halkett, S., and Laing, J., 29
Hall, A.C.S., 455
Hall, A.R., 1668
Hall, Sir John, 1344-5, 2077
Hamer, P.M., 113
Hamer, W.S., 588
Hamilton, Sir F.W., 768
Hamilton, H.B., 782
Hamilton, Sir Ian, 1346-8
Hamilton, I.B.M., 1347
Hamilton, R., 1142
Hamley, Sir Edward Bruce, 1349, 1622, 2057
Hanham, H.J., 236
Hanna, H.B., 2115
Hannah, W.H., 1466
Hannay, R.K., 1807
Hanover, expedition to, 1735
Hardinge, Charles, 1034
Hardinge, Sir Henry, Lord, 1034-5
Hardwicke, Philip Yorke, Earl of, 1036
Hare, Edward, 1350
Hare, T.J., mss., 492
Hargreaves, Reginald, 938, 1759, 1882
Harley, John, 1351
Harness, Sir Henry Drury, 1352
Harness, William, 1353
Harris, Sir Charles, 1027
Harris, George, Lord, 990, 1143
Harris, John, 1354, 2087, 2239
Harris, P.V., 181
Harrison, Sir Richard, 1355
Harrop, A.J., 2036
Hart, Sir B.H. Liddell, 1537, 1594, 1656
Hartmann, C.H., 1100
Harvey, A.J.W., 644
Harvey, C. Cleland, 206

Hastings, Francis Rawdon, Marquess of, 990, 1145
Hastings, R. Rawdon, mss., 493
Hastings-Irwin, D., 1697
Haswell, Jock, 1335
Havelock, Sir Henry, 1356-8
Hawkes, C.P., 970
Hawley, Henry, 1793-4
Hawley, R.B., 2081
Hay, Sir Andrew Leith, 1393
Hay, G.J., 751
Hay, Ian, 182, 733
Hayes, James, 103, 217, 897-8, 971
Hayes-McCoy, G.A., 1749
Hayward, P., 1361
Head, Sir Francis B., 696
Heathcote, T.A., 2185
Heathfield, George Augustus Elliott, Lord, 992
Held, Robert, 1669
Helder expedition, 1920
Helgesen, M.P., 1890
Henderson, G.F.R., 1359, 1637, 1639
Henecker, W.C.G., 1642
Henegan, Sir Richard, 1360
Hennell, Sir Reginald, 785
Henry, Walter, 1361
Hensman, Howard, 2114
Henty, G.A., 2108
Herbert, Sidney, Lord, 1037-8
Herries, J.C., 1039
Herriot, John, 1898
Hervey, Albert, 1362
Hervey, S.H.A., 1144
Hervey, Hon. William, 1144
Hewitt, J., 2238
Hibbert, Christopher, 1459, 1536, 1853, 1966
Higgins, R.T., 767
Higginson, Sir G.W.A., 1363
Higham, Robin, 30
Hill, Rowland, Lord, 958, 984, 1364-6
Hills, R.J.T., 839
Hilton, Richard, 2231
Hime, H.W.L., 699
Hinde, Robert, 1588
Historical Journal, 540
Historical Manuscripts Commission, Indexes to reports, 453-5
History, 541
History Today, 542
Hitsman, J. Mackay, 1985
Hobday, E.A.P., 703
Hodge, Edward, 2085
Hodgkin, J.E., mss., 494
Hogg, O.F.G., 589, 706, 748
Holdich, E.A., 1367

Jones, R.J., 859
Jones, W.D., 645
Jourdain, H.F.N., and Fraser, Edward, 820
Journal of British Studies, 545
Journal of the campaign on the coast of France, 1829
Judd, Denis, 2023

Kaffir wars, 1901, 1922, 2041
Kane, John, 693
Kane, Richard, 1769
Kashmir, 2216
Kaye, Sir John William, 1411, 2027, 2224
Kealy, P.H., 1448
Kearsey, A.H.C., 1785
Keith, Sir Robert Murray, 1149
Kellaway, William, 31
Kelly, Edward, 2002
Kelly, Sir Richard, 2063
Kemble, Stephen, 1871
Kendall, J.M., 939
Kendrick, N.C.E., 866
Kenyon mss., 496
Ketton, R.W., mss., 497
Kier, David, 593
Kimball, G.S., 1839
Kincaid, Sir John, 1380-1
King, C.C., 184
King, D.W., 1654
King, G.J.S., 974
King, W.R., 2041
Kinglake, A.W., 2054
Kingsford, C.L., 813
Kipling, A.L., and King, H.L., 1699
Kirk, Percy, 1150
Kitchener, Horatio Herbert, Earl, 965, 976, 1382-5
Knight, C.R.B., 786
Knight, H.R., 786
Knight, John, 1151
Knocker, W.V., 1409
Knollys, Sir H., 1336, 2093
Knowles, Sir Lees, 1841, 1942
Knowles, Robert, 1942
Knox, Capt. H.V., mss., 498
Knox, John, 1842
Koss, S.E., 1031
Kruger, Rayne, 2162

Laffin, John, 678, 734, 940, 1700
Laing mss., 499

Lake, Gerald, Viscount, 966, 1386
Lamb, Roger, 1152-3
Lambert, J.M., 646
Lambert, Sheila, 134
Lambrick, H.T., 1376
Lancaster, J.C., 32
Lancers, 711
Lang, Arthur Moffat, 2228
Lansdowne, H.C.K. Petty-Fitzmaurice, Marquis of, 1040-1
Larpent, Francis Seymour, 1938
Larpent, Sir George, 1938
Latham, John Wilkinson, 1672
Lathbury, D.C., 620
Laurie, G.B., 803
Laurie, W.F.B., 2042
Laver, James, 1701
Lawrence, Sir George St. Patrick, 1387
Lawrence, Stringer, 1154
Lawrence, William, 1388
Laws, M.E.S., 702, 704, 1148
Lawson, C.C.P., 1702
Lawson, George, 2082
Leach, D.E., 1758
Leach, Jonathan, 1389-90
Leask, G.A., 1471
Leask, J.C., and McCance, H.M., 806
Leavenworth, C.S., 2095
Lediard, Thomas, 1162
Lee, Albert, 796, 814
Lees-Smith, H.B., 135
Le Fleming mss., 500
Lefroy, Sir J.H., 33, 1391-2
Lehmann, Joseph H., 1549, 2129
Leith, Sir James, 1393
Le Marchant, Sir Denis, 1394
Le Marchant, Sir John Gaspard, 958, 1394-6, 1598, 1905
Leslie, J.H., 34-5, 594, 901, 1177, 1291, 1468, 1808, 1906,
    1929, 1989, 2214
Leslie, J.H., and Smith, David, 36
Leslie, N.B., 902
Lewis, Sir George Cornwall, 1042
Leyborne-Popham, F.W., mss., 501
Liddell, R.S., 773
Ligonier, John Louis, Lord, 1155-6
Lille, siege of, 1778
Lindsay, A.H., 2240
Lineham, D., 106
Ling, Peter, 185
Lister, Jeremy, 1157
List of bibliographical works, 6
Liverpool, Charles Jenkinson, Earl of, 1043
Livingston, William, 1828
Lloyd, Alan, 2018, 2126

Lloyd, Christopher, 1855
Lloyd, E.M., 719
Lloyd, E.W., and Hadcock, A.G., 1635
Lloyd, Henry, 1158, 1593-4
Lochee, Louis, 647
Lodge, H.C., 1872
Londonderry, Charles Stewart, Marquess of, 1935
Londonderry, Robert Stewart, Viscount Castlereagh, Marquis
  of, 1044-6
Long, J.C., 1084
Longford, Elizabeth, Lady, 1530, 1532
Lonsdale mss., 502
Lord, N.C., 1982
Lords, house of, mss., 503
Lothian mss., 504
Loudoun, John Campbell, Earl of, 114, 116, 1159
Lovegrove, Peter, 732
Low, Charles R., 975-6, 1454, 1548
Lowe, A.G., 1397
Luard, John, 1703
Lucas, C.P., 1981
Lukin, Sir Henry Timson, 1398
Lumley, L.R., 844
Lushington, S.R., 1143
Luvaas, Jay, 1652, 1655
Lydenberg, H.M., 1189
Lynedoch, Thomas Graham, Lord, 958, 984, 1399-1402
Lysons, David, 2060
Lyttleton, Sir Neville, G., 1403

McAnally, Sir Henry, 107, 757
McArthur, John, 622
Macaulay, Thomas Babbington, Lord, 1047
McCalmont, Sir Hugh, 1415
McCance, H.M., 1761
McCance, S., 828
Maccardell, Lee, 1093
McCourt, Edward, 1252
Macdiarmid, D.S., 1342
Macdonald, Hector, 976, 1404
Macdonald, R.J., 1704
Macdonald, Roger, 1750
Macdougall, Patrick, 1620, 1627, 1652
Macfarlane, John, 1962
McGrigor, Sir James, 1416
McGuffie, T.H., 104-5, 222, 760, 856, 862, 869, 944-6, 1229,
  1763, 1851, 1900, 1957, 2002, 2005
Mackay, Archibald, 1405
Mackay, Hugh, 1160
Mackay, John, 1160

Mackenzie, Colin, 1406
Mackenzie, Frederick, 1878
Mackesy, Piers, 1892, 1917, 1925
Mackinnon, David, 766
Mackinnon, D.H., 1407
Mackintosh, J.P., 595
Mackworth, Sir Digby, 2001
Maclachlen, A.N.C., 1118
Maclennan, John, 679
Macleod, Donald, 1161
MacMunn, Sir George, 1408, 1751, 1884, 2066, 2130, 2187, 2229
Macory, Patrick, 2029
Macpherson, Allan, 977
Macpherson, John, 977
Macpherson, W.C., 977
Madden, C.D., 1945
Madras army, 2196
Mafeking, 2158
Magnus, Sir Philip, 1384
Maguire, T. Miller, 648, 1638, 1752
Mahon, R.H., 1180
Mahratta wars, 2204-5, 2209-10
Mainwairing, Frederick, 1409
Maitland, F.H., 1410
Majuba Hill, battle of, 2128
Majumdar, B.M., 2188
Malcolm, Sir John, 1104, 1411
Malleson, G.B., 2197, 2225
Malmesbury, Susan Harris, Countess of, 1214
Malplaquet, battle of, 1781
Manners, W.E., 1140
Manoeuvres, 1675
Mante, Thomas, 1832
Manual exercise, 1576
Manual of military law, 621
Maori wars, 2035-9
Mar and Kellie mss., 504
Marlborough, John Churchill, Duke of, 953, 968-9, 978-9
  992-3, 1162-76, 1783-89, 1792, 1799-1800
Marling, Sir Perceval, 1412
Marlow, Louis, 1135
Marlowe, John, 1324
Marshall, Henry, 186, 941-3
Martin, E.J., 2203
Martineau, G.D., 855
Martineau, John, 1052
Mason, Philip, 2189
Matabele campaign, 2147
Matthews, William, 37-8
Maule, George, 2203
Maurice, Sir Frederick, 836, 842, 1028, 1413, 1461
Maurice, Sir Frederick, and Arthur, Sir George, 1548

Moyse-Bartlett, H., 42, 231, 1437
Muir, Augustus, 863
Muller, C.F.J., Jaarsveld, F.A. van, and Wijk, Theo van, 43
Muller, John, 1571-3
Mullins, E.C.L., 147-8
Munro, D.J., 44
Munro, Thomas, 964, 1426
Munro, Sir William, 1427
Murray, A.K., 681
Murray, Sir George, 110, 1164, 1428, 1959, 1964
Murray, Hon. James, 1180
Murray, R.H., 829
Music, military, 735-43
Mutiny act, 431, 626
Myatt, Frederick, 187, 2104, 2171
Mysore war, 2202-3

Napier, Sir Charles James, 953, 964, 967, 972, 993,
  1429-31
Napier, Sir George, 967, 1432
Napier, H.D., 1433
Napier, Mark, 1126
Napier, Robert, Lord, 1433-4
Napier, Sir William, 967, 972, 1429, 1432, 1435-6, 1652,
  1936
Napoleonic wars, 1902-14, 1916-20, 1922-7, 1929-2008
Nation in Arms, 552
National Army Museum, 104-5
National Book League, 45
National Defence, 551
National Library of Ireland, 106-7
National Library of Scotland, 108-10
National Library of Wales, 111
National Register of Archives, 78-9
National Service Journal, 552
Naval and Military Gazette, 553
Naval and Military Magazine, 554
Naval and Military Record, 555
Naylor, John, 2004
Neave-Hill, W.B.R., 904-5
Nevill, H.L., 2211
Nevill, Ralph, 1708
Newbolt, Sir Henry, 807
Newcastle, Henry Pelham, Duke of, 1052-3
New Jersey, 1893
Newsome, David, 650
Newton, Lord, 1040
New Zealand, 2035-9
Nightingale, Florence, 727, 1054-6

Nightingall, Miles, 1977
Nivelle, 1969
Noakes, George, 769
Nolan, E.H., 2051
Nolan, Louis Edward, 707, 1437
Norman, C.B., 1754
Norman, Sir Henry Wylie, 1438
Norris, J.A., 2030
Northumberland mss., 508
Notes and Queries, 556
Nott, Sir William, 1439
Noyes, Samuel, 1181
Nugent, Sir George, 105, 1440

Oatts, L.B., 854, 870
Observations on army administration, 596
Observations on the prevailing abuses in the British army, 220
O'Callaghan, Sir Desmond, 1441
O'Donnell, H., 775
O'Dowd, Sir J.C., 906
Officers, examinations, 443; expenses, 448, pay and
  emoluments of, 389; promotion and retirement, 393, 396,
  407, 424, 428, 452; purchase and sale of commissions,
  405, 415, 420, 427, 877-8, 894, 906, 918; retirement
  of, 413, 421, 432
Oglander, C.F.A., 1400
Oglethorpe, James Edward, 1182
Olle, J.G., 137
Olson, A.G., 1064
Oman, Carola, 1423
Oman, Sir C.W.C., 46, 459, 1940
Omond, J.S., 597
O'Neill, T.P., 138
Operations of the allied army, 1831
Operations of the British and the allied armies, 1811
Ordnance, 745, 748
Orford, Sir Robert Walpole, Earl of, 101, 1057-9
Orkney, first Earl of, 1781
Orme, Robert, 2198
Ormonde, Duke of, 1775
Ormonde mss., 509
Otley, C.B., 651, 907
Ouchterlony, John, 2032
Oudenarde, battle of, 1778, 1800
Outram, Sir James, 975, 1442-3

Pack, R., 2055
Packe, E., 764
Paget, Hon. Sir Edward, 958, 1444, 1909

Paget, George A.F., Lord, 2056
Paget, H.M., 1444
Paine, J., 47-52, 1196, 1202, 1245
Paine, Lauren, 1098
Pakenham, Sir Edward, 958, 967, 1445
Palit, D.K., 2190
Palk mss., 510
Palmerston, Henry John Temple, Viscount, 1060-2
Pargellis, Stanley, 1094, 1845, 1848
Pargellis, Stanley, and Medley, D.J., 53
Parker, Robert, 1762
Parker, William, 2068
Parker, W.M., 1821
Parkes, E.A., 728
Parkman, Francis, 1780, 1835
Parkyn, H.G., 1709-13
Parliamentary debates, 140; journals, 136; papers,
  indexes to, 123-34, 139
Parnell, Hon. Arthur, 1779
Parr, Sir Hallam, 1446
Parry, D.H., 1714
Parsons, K.A.C., 139
Parsons, R.B., 1447
Partridge, Bellamy, 1146
Pasley, Sir Charles William, 188, 1448-9
Patent Office Library, 73
Paul, W.P., 682-4
Pay and allowances, 948
Payne, A.A., 1715
Peacocke, Sir W. Marmaduke, 1450
Peard, G.S., 2044
Pearman, John, 1451
Pearn, B.R., 2015
Pearsall, R.J., 2016
Pearse, H.W., 809, 980, 1386, 2062
Peckham, H.H., 118, 1766, 1887
Peddie, R.A., 54
Pelly, L., 1374
Pemberton, W. Baring, 1001, 2076, 2165
Pericoli, Ugo, 2008
Perry, O.L., 1716
Peterborough, Charles Mordaunt, Earl of, 969, 986, 992,
  1183-8, 1797-8
Petre, F.L., 821, 824
Petrie, Sir Charles, 1526, 1824
Phayre, Sir Robert, 2100
Philippart, John, 189, 908-9
Picton, Sir Thomas, 958, 984, 1452-3
Piggott, F.S.G., 910
Pitt, William, 1008-9
Plassey, battle of, 2200
Plumb, J.H., 1058
Pohler, Johann, 55

Somerset mss., 516
South Africa, 449, 1915, 2020, 2111, 2118-29, 2138,
 2153-69
Southey, Robert, 1934
Spain and Portugal, British army in during Napoleonic wars,
 1931-79; war of Spanish Succession in, 1777, 1779, 1790,
 1793-8
Spanish Succession, war of, 1735, 1769, 1773-1802
Spaulding, Thomas M., and Karpinski, Louis C., 59
Spender, J.A., 1002
Sperling, John, 1987
Sperman, J.M., 653
Spilsbury, John, 1899
Spurrier, M.C., 1287, 1973
Stacey, C.P., 1854, 2040
Stacke, H.F., 1879
Staff College, Camberley, 636, 642, 659
Stair, John Dalrymple, second Earl of, 1191
Stanhope, Edward, 1072
Stanhope, Philip, Earl, 1517, 1777
Stanley, G.F.G., 1983
Stanley, H.M., 2103
Stanmore, Lord, 1037
Staveley, William, 1487
Stebbing, W., 1186
Stedman, Charles, 1864
Steevens, Charles, 1488
Steevens, G.W., 2149
Steevens, Nathaniel, 1488
Stephenson, Sir Frederick, 1489
Stevens, B.F., 1861, 1869
Stevens, F.J., 1680
Stevenson, John, 1490
Stewart, Charles, 1913
Stewart, Charles H., 689
Stewart, David, 731
Stewart, Sir Donald, 1491
Stewart, P.T, 849
Stirling-Home-Drummond-Moray mss., 517
Stocqueler, J.H., 194-5, 600, 1439, 1617
Story, H.H., 858
Strachen, Hew, 1724
Strathnairn, Sir Hugh Rose, Lord, 975, 1492
Stuart, H.B., 718
Stuart, James, 2175
Stuart-Smith, James, 628
Stubbs, F.W., 2193
Sturgis, J., 1231
Sudan, 2020, 2140-7, 2149-52
Sullivan, A.E., 173, 918, 951, 1136, 1260
Sullivan, R.G., 629
Summer, Dudley, 1029
Sumner, Percy, 1725-6, 1793

Verner, Sir William, 1506
Verner, W.W.C., 799, 1258, 1479
Verney, Sir Harry, 1255
Vetch, R.H., 1269, 1334
Vibart, H.M., 1458
Victorian Studies, 565
Vieth, F.H.D., 1507
Vigman, F.K., 756
Vittoria, battle of, 1963
Vivian, Hon. Claud, 1508
Vivian, Frances St. Clair, 219, 1893
Vivian, Richard Hussey, Lord, 1508
Volunteer and reserve forces, 411, 430, 434, 750-62
Voyle, G.E., 1629
Vulliamy, C.E., 2067

Waddell, L.M., 1767, 1771
Waddington, Richard, 1836
Wade, George, 109, 1821
Waine, H., 2230
Wake, Joan, 1265
Wakeham, C.E., 1312-3
Walcheren expedition, 1930, 1958
Walford, A.J., 7
Walker, Sir C.P.B., 1630
Walker, H.M., 810
Walker, T.M., 1509
Walker, W.J., 1306
Wallis, Charles, 1640
Walters, John, 199
Walton, Clifford, 205
Warburton, G.D., 1184
Ward, B.R., 656
Ward, S.P.G., 868, 1328, 1528, 1955, 1959, 1964, 2135
Wardell, J., 1474
Warner, Philip, 2086
Warner, Sir William Lee, 1438
War Office, library 76-7; lists of records, 76-7; organization
  392, 491, 441, 444-5, 450
Warre, Edmund, 1943
Warre, Sir William, 1943
Waterfield, Robert, 1510
Waterloo, battle of, 1992-2008
Watson, Sir Charles, 1541
Watson, W.A., 2194
Wauchope, A.G., 1511
Waugh, W.T., 1198
Webb, E.A.H., 797, 804
Webb, S.S., 1768
Webb-Carter, B.W., 1228

Webster, J.C., 1085
Weller, Jac, 1533, 1967, 2007
Wellesley, Muriel, 1523
Wellington, Arthur Richard, Duke of, 1515
Wellington, Arthur Wellesley, Duke of, 953, 964, 968, 973,
    979. 993, 1512-34, 1970-1, 1967, 1974
Wellington College, 650
Welsh, James, 1535
Western, J.R., 759, 922
West Indies, 1832
Westphalia, 1850
Wheatley, Edmund, 1536
Wheatley, William, 1949
Wheaton, J., 237
Wheeler, Owen, 200, 603
Wheeler, William, 1537
Whigham, Sir Robert, 243
White, A.C.T., 657
White, A.S., 61-3, 691
White, Sir George, 976, 1538, 2157
Whitehead, Alan, 747
Whitehouse, A.C., 837
Whitton, F.E., 831
Whitworth, R.H., 989, 1155
Whyte, Frederic, and Atteridge, A.H.A., 834
Wickins, Charles, 2234
Wilcocks, Sir James, 1539-40
Wilkin, W.H., 990, 1223
Wilkins, P.A., 1730
Wilkinson, F.J., 1731
Wilkinson, H.S., 992, 1073-4, 1652, 2155
Wilkinson, M.L., 228
Wilkinson, Osborn, and Johnson, W., 991
Wilkinson, R.J., 1681
Willcox, W.B., 1102, 1889
William III, 959; wars of, 1762, 1764-5, 1767, 1769-72
William L. Clements Library, 118-21
Williams, B., 1008
Williams, D. Elwyn, 214
Williams, G., 762
Williams, John, 2195
Williams, N.T. St. John, 658
Williams, Trevelyan, 789
Williamson, John, 604
Willson, Beckles, 1195
Wilson, Sir A.T., and McEwen, J.H.F., 1732
Wilson, Sir Charles William, 1541, 2141
Wilson, H.H., 2013
Wilson, H.S., 233
Wilson, Sir Henry, 1542
Wilson, John, 1003
Wilson, Sir Robert, 201, 1543-5
Wilson, W.J., 2196